Publications of the

Carnegie Endowment for International Peace

Division of Economics and History

John Bates Clark, Director

ECONOMIC AND SOCIAL HISTORY OF THE WORLD WAR

British Series

JAMES T. SHOTWELL, Ph.D., LL.D.
GENERAL EDITOR

With the Collaboration of the

For List of other Editors and the plan of the Series see end of this volume

LABOUR IN THE COAL-MINING INDUSTRY

(1914—1921)

BY

G. D. H. COLE

(AUTHOR OF 'TRADE UNIONISM AND MUNITIONS', 'WORKSHOP ORGANIZATION', ETC.)

OXFORD : AT THE CLARENDON PRESS

London, Edinburgh, New York, Toronto, Melbourne, Cape Town, Bombay

HUMPHREY MILFORD

1923

PRINTED IN ENGLAND
AT THE OXFORD UNIVERSITY PRESS

EDITOR'S PREFACE

In the autumn of 1914 when the scientific study of the effects of war upon modern life passed suddenly from theory to history, the Division of Economics and History of the Carnegie Endowment for International Peace proposed to adjust the programme of its researches to the new and altered problems which the War presented. The existing programme, which had been prepared as the result of a conference of economists held at Berne in 1911, and which dealt with the facts then at hand, had just begun to show the quality of its contributions; but for many reasons it could no longer be followed out. A plan was therefore drawn up at the request of the Director of the Division, in which it was proposed, by means of an historical survey, to attempt to measure the economic cost of the War and the displacement which it was causing in the processes of civilization. Such an 'Economic and Social History of the World War', it was felt, if undertaken by men of judicial temper and adequate training, might ultimately, by reason of its scientific obligations to truth, furnish data for the forming of sound public opinion, and thus contribute fundamentally towards the aims of an institution dedicated to the cause of international peace.

The need for such an analysis, conceived and executed in the spirit of historical research, was increasingly obvious as the War developed, releasing complex forces of national life not only for the vast processes of destruction but also for the stimulation of new capacities for production. This new economic activity, which under normal conditions of peace might have been a gain to society, and the surprising capacity exhibited by the belligerent nations for enduring long and increasing loss—often while presenting the outward semblance of new prosperity—made necessary a reconsideration of the whole field of war economics. A double obligation was therefore placed upon the Division of Economics and History. It was obliged to concentrate its work upon the problem thus presented, and to study it as a whole; in other words, to apply to it the tests and disciplines of history. Just as the War itself was a single event, though penetrating by seemingly unconnected ways to the remotest parts of the world, so the analysis of it must be developed according to a plan at once all-embracing and yet adjustable to the practical limits of the available data.

During the actual progress of the War, however, the execution of this plan for a scientific and objective study of war economics proved impossible in any large and authoritative way. Incidental studies and surveys of portions of the field could be made and were made under the direction of the Division, but it was impossible to undertake a general history for obvious reasons. In the first place, an authoritative statement of the resources of belligerents bore directly on the conduct of armies in the field. The result was to remove as far as possible from scrutiny those data of the economic life of the countries at war which would ordinarily, in time of peace, be readily available for investigation. In addition to this difficulty of consulting documents, collaborators competent to deal with them were for the most part called into national service in the belligerent countries and so were unavailable for research. The plan for a war history was therefore postponed until conditions should arise which would make possible not only access to essential documents but also the co-operation of economists, historians, and men of affairs in the nations chiefly concerned, whose joint work would not be misunderstood either in purpose or in content.

Upon the termination of the War the Endowment once more took up the original plan, and it was found with but slight modification to be applicable to the situation. Work was begun in the summer and autumn of 1919. In the first place a final conference of the Advisory Board of Economists of the Division of Economics and History was held in Paris, which limited itself to planning a series of short preliminary surveys of special fields. Since, however, the purely preliminary character of such studies was further emphasized by the fact that they were directed more especially towards those problems which were then fronting Europe as questions of urgency, it was considered best not to treat them as part of the general survey but rather as of contemporary value in the period of war settlement. It was clear that not only could no general programme be laid down *a priori* by this conference as a whole, but that a new and more highly specialized research organization than that already existing would be needed to undertake the Economic and Social History of the War, one based more upon national grounds in the first instance and less upon purely international co-operation. Until the facts of national history could be ascertained, it would be impossible to proceed with comparative analysis; and the different national histories were themselves of almost baffling intricacy and variety. Consequently the former European Committee of Research was dissolved, and in its place it was decided to erect an Editorial Board in each of the larger countries and to nominate special editors in the smaller ones, who should concentrate, for the present at least, upon their own economic and social war history.

The nomination of these boards by the General Editor was the first step taken in every country where the work has begun. And if any justification was needed for the plan of the Endowment, it at once may be found in the lists of those, distinguished in scholarship or in public affairs, who have accepted the responsibility of editorship. This responsibility is by no means light, involving, as it does, the adaptation of the general editorial plan to the varying demands of national circumstances or methods of work; and the measure of success attained is due to the generous and earnest co-operation of those in charge in each country.

Once the editorial organization was established there could be little doubt as to the first step which should be taken in each instance towards the actual preparation of the history. Without documents there can be no history. The essential records of the War, local as well as central, have therefore to be preserved and to be made available for research in so far as is compatible with public interest. But this archival task is a very great one, belonging of right to the governments and other owners of historical sources and not to the historian or economist who proposes to use them. It is an obligation of ownership; for all such documents are public trust. The collaborators on this section of the war history, therefore, working within their own field as researchers, could only survey the situation as they found it and report their findings in the form of guides or manuals; and perhaps, by stimulating a comparison of methods, help to further the adoption of those found to be most practical. In every country, therefore, this was the point of departure for actual work; although special monographs have not been written in every instance.

This first stage of the work upon the war history, dealing with little more than the externals of archives, seemed for a while to exhaust the possibilities of research. And had the plan of the history been limited to research based upon official documents, little more could have been done, for once documents have been labelled 'secret' few Government officials can be found with sufficient courage or initiative to break open the seal. Thus vast masses of source material essential for the historian were effectively placed beyond his reach, although much of it was quite harmless from any point of view. While war conditions thus continued to hamper research, and were likely to do so for many years to come, some alternative had to be found.

Fortunately such an alternative was at hand in the narrative, amply supported by documentary evidence, of those who had played some part in the conduct of affairs during the War, or who, as close observers in privileged positions, were able to record from first or at least second-hand knowledge the economic history of different phases of the Great War, and of its effect upon society. Thus a series of monographs was planned consisting for the most part of unofficial yet authoritative statements, descriptive or historical, which may best be described as about half-way between memoirs and blue-books. These monographs make up the main body of the work assigned so far. They are not limited to contemporary, war-time studies; for the economic history of the War must deal with a longer period than that of the actual fighting. It must cover the years of 'deflation' as well, at least sufficiently to secure some fairer measure of the economic displacement than is possible in purely contemporary judgements.

With this phase of the work, the editorial problems assumed a new aspect. The series of monographs had to be planned primarily with regard to the availability of contributors, rather than of source material as in the case of most histories; for the contributors themselves controlled the sources. This in turn involved a new attitude towards those two ideals which historians have sought to emphasize, consistency and objectivity. In order to bring out the chief contribution of each writer it was impossible to keep within narrowly logical outlines; facts would have to be repeated in different settings and seen from different angles, and sections included which do not lie within the strict limits of history; and absolute objectivity could not be obtained in every part. Under the stress of controversy or apology, partial views would here and there find their expression. But these views are in some instances an intrinsic part of the history itself, contemporary measurements of facts as significant as the facts with which they deal. Moreover, the work as a whole is planned to furnish its own corrective; and where it does not, others will.

In addition to this monographic treatment of source material, a number of studies by specialists is already in preparation, dealing with technical or limited subjects, historical or statistical. These monographs also partake to some extent of the nature of first-hand material, registering as they do the data of history close enough to the source to permit verification in ways impossible later. But they also belong to that constructive process by which history passes from analysis to synthesis. The process is a long and difficult one, however, and work upon it has only just begun. To quote an apt characterization, in the first stages of a history like this one is only 'picking cotton'. The tangled threads of events have still to be woven into the pattern of history; and for this creative and constructive work different plans and organizations may be needed.

In a work which is the product of so complex and varied co-operation as this, it is impossible to indicate in any but a most general way the apportionment of responsibility of editors and authors for the contents of the different monographs. For the plan of the History as a whole and its effective execution the General Editor is responsible; but the arrangement of the detailed programmes of study has been largely the work of the different Editorial Boards and divisional Editors, who have also read the manuscripts prepared under their direction. The acceptance of a monograph in this series, however, does not commit the editors to the opinions or conclusions of the authors. Like other editors, they are asked to vouch for the scientific merit, the appropriateness and usefulness of the volumes admitted to the series; but the authors are naturally free to make their individual contributions in their own way. In like manner the publication of the monographs does not commit the Endowment to agreement with any specific conclusions which may be expressed therein. The responsibility of the Endowment is to History itself—an obligation not to avoid but to secure and preserve variant narratives and points of view, in so far as they are essential for the understanding of the War as a whole.

J. T. S.

PREFACE

Nowhere is the difficulty of defining the 'war period' better illustrated than in the coal-mining industry of Great Britain; for the whole history of the mines, from the outbreak of war up to and including the calamitous dispute of 1921, forms essentially a continuous and a single story. The State did not assume full control of the mining industry until the beginning of 1917; but having done so it retained its hold until March 1921, when its decision to enforce decontrol at a date earlier than that fixed by law in the previous year was the direct cause of the great dispute which kept the pits idle until July. To attempt, in the telling of this story, to stop short at any point before the termination of this dispute would be to leave the record, not merely incomplete, but largely meaningless. To a peculiar extent, the problems raised by State control came to a head, in the case of the mines, only after the termination of hostilities in November 1918; and the campaigns and disasters of 1920 and 1921 arose directly out of, and were intimately bound up with, the control of mining operations and mining labour originally imposed as a war measure. With the exception of the railways, the mines were the last industry remaining under this system of State control, and even in 1921 control was terminated only to the accompaniment of a great industrial upheaval, and of serious loss and utter dislocation to the industry itself.

I have tried in this study to show, first, what were the specific problems and difficulties which led to the assumption of control by the State; secondly, how this control affected the workers both before and after the Armistice; and thirdly how, and with what consequences, State control was removed. Throughout I have studied these developments only from a particular angle

—for my subject has been the history, not of the mining industry, but of labour in the mining industry, during these critical years. I have therefore left unsaid much that has to do with the position of the mine owners, their relations with the Government, and the problems of the industry as a whole under war conditions. These matters, I understand, are the subject of a companion volume in this series.

No one can say that the story which I have to tell is pleasant or encouraging. It begins with the remarkable achievements of the war period, when, despite the very heavy enlistment of miners during the first year of the war, output was maintained at a high level at home. Follow the period of State control, the struggles and disillusionments of the later war period. Next comes the season of high hopes, of plans for the re-organization of the industry, of expectations of good things to follow the coming of peace. But soon the ugly ulterior consequences of war reveal themselves, and the story ends on a note of complete disillusionment, if not of positive despair. Admittedly, the end of it leaves both the mining industry and the workers employed in it—or unemployed—in a condition far worse than they have suffered for generations past; and things are made no better by calling this condition a return to an 'economic basis'. My task, however, is to recount the facts, and not to moralize over them. All I need say is that I have done my best to tell the story with the least possible intrusion of my personal opinions and beliefs. The facts explain themselves, although the explanations which they convey may appear to different readers in very different lights.

G. D. H. COLE

CONTENTS

APPENDICES

CHAPTER I

MINING TRADE UNIONISM BEFORE THE WAR

Mining was, before the War, by far the most highly organized of the industries of Great Britain. On the side of the coal-owners, the vast majority of the important collieries were linked up, through the district Associations of Colliery Owners, with the national body, the Mining Association of Great Britain. There was a number of small pits whose owners were not connected with these Associations; but the proportion of the total output which they represented was almost negligible. Within each district, practically the whole of the owners spoke with one voice in their dealings with Labour; and, while the Mining Association of Great Britain did not engage directly in negotiations with the Trade Unions, or profess to regulate labour conditions on a national scale, actually its effect in co-ordinating the action of the owners in all the coal-fields was considerable and constant. It was particularly active in stating the owners' case in connexion with any proposals to amend the laws relating to the mining industry.

The workers, on their side, were hardly less organized. In each coal-field, the great majority of the workers employed, including almost all who were employed underground, were members of the county or district Miners' Association or Federation. These bodies were separate, and usually separately registered, Trade Unions, and each of them possessed its own district rules, funds, scales of contributions and benefits, forms of administration, and local customs and traditions. Practically the whole of these district Miners' Associations were federated in the Miners' Federation of Great Britain, the most powerful industrial organization in the British Labour Movement, and perhaps in the Labour Movement of the world.

The Miners' Federation of Great Britain was not, however, the only organization representing workers employed in the mining industry. There were also, in many of the coal-fields, district

Associations representing some, if not all, of the workers engaged in some particular craft or branch of mining work. Thus the enginemen had usually their separate Associations, and a number of these were linked up in a national body, the National Federation of Colliery Enginemen. The colliery deputies, firemen, and examiners, and other subordinate officials had also their local Associations and a national Federation of their own; and in a few coal-fields there were also distinct Associations of colliery mechanics, again with a national Federation. There were also two Unions of Cokemen and By-Product Workers closely associated with the mining industry.

Generally speaking, the Trade Unions organizing mine-workers, whether they attempted to embrace all grades, or confined their scope to men of a particular craft, consisted wholly of mine-workers. There were, however, also cases in which Trade Unions organizing over a wider field had enrolled mine-workers within their ranks. Thus, some of the enginemen in certain coal-fields belonged to the National Union of Enginemen, which also enrolled enginemen, stokers, and kindred workers in many other industries, such as iron and steel production, textile manufacture, and water-side transport. A small number of mechanics and electricians working in collieries were members of such Unions as the Amalgamated Society of Engineers and the Electrical Trades Union. And, in a few coal-fields, a proportion of the surface labourers were organized in the general labour Unions of less skilled workers, such as the National Union of General Workers and the National Amalgamated Union of Labour in South Yorkshire, and the Navvies' Union in North Staffordshire.

Despite all these exceptions, however, the vast majority of the workers in and about the mines were enrolled in the district Miners' Associations, and, through them, in the Miners' Federation of Great Britain. The following table indicates, as far as figures are available, the strength of organization at the end of 1913, and the relative position of the Miners' Federation and the other Trade Unions in the industry.

MINING TRADE UNIONISM IN 1913

(Figures are given in thousands)

Name of coal-field	*Number employed under coal mines Acts*	*Membership*					*Total trade unionists in purely mining associations*
		Miners' associations	*Enginemen's associations*	*Deputies' associations*	*Other associations*		
Scotland	142	86	3·7 / 0·4	1·3	Shale Miners	1·5	93
Cumberland	11	9	0·4	0·2	Iron Ore Miners	5	15
Northumberland	59	43	1·2	1·5	Coll. Mechanics	1·6	47
Durham	160	140	3·8	2	Cokemen / Mechanics	4 / 6·1	156
Cleveland	—	9	—	—	—		9
Yorkshire	162	126	1 / 1	1·5	Cokemen	2·5	132
Leicestershire	49	7	—	—	—		7
Nottinghamshire, Derbyshire, South Derbyshire	59	34 / 41 / 5	1·7	1	—		83
Midland Federation.							
North Staffordshire	59	27	—	0·8 [a]	—		28
South Staffordshire and East Worcestershire		4	—	—	—		4
Cannock Chase		9	—	—	—		9
Pelsall District		7	—	—	—		7
Old Hill and District		2	—	—	—		2
Shropshire	23	2	0·1	—	—		2
Warwickshire		11	—	—	—		11
North Warwickshire		1	—	—	—		1
Lancashire and Cheshire	106	81	2·4	0·8	—		84
North Wales	16	13	0·4	0·1	Surfacemen	1·8	15
South Wales	226	154	7 / 1	3	—		165
Forest of Dean	15	3	—	—	—		3
Bristol		2	—	—	—		2
Somersetshire		4	0·2	—	—		4
Kent	—	0·2	—	—	—		0·2
	1,087	820	24	12·5		22·5	879

[a] Enginemen in the Midland coal-fields belonged largely to the National Union of Enginemen.

Of the Miners' Associations shown in the foregoing table (column 2), all except one, the small North Warwickshire Miners' Association, which was formed as the outcome of a local quarrel, were members of the Miners' Federation of Great Britain. This body thus represented well over 90 per cent. of the Trade Unionists organized in purely mining Trade Unions before the War. The inclusion of the colliery membership of the Societies organizing workers both in and outside the mining industry would probably bring down the proportion to slightly under 90 per cent.; but accurate figures in this case are not available. It should be mentioned that the figures given in the table are in all cases figures of gross membership as returned by the various Associations to the Chief Registrar of Friendly Societies or to the Board of Trade. They do not tally with the figures quoted by the Miners' Federation itself, for two reasons. In the first place, the local Miners' Association did not in many cases pay dues to the Federation on their full membership, and were therefore credited with a smaller number of members in its books. In the second place, under the constitutions of many of the Societies, a non-adult counted, for financial purposes, as only half a member, and two youths therefore appear as only one member in the Miners' Federation returns. For these reasons, the figures given in this table are not comparable with those quoted later (see p. 65) as showing the growth of the Miners' Federation during the war period. The Federation figure stood, at the end of 1913, at only 561,000, as against the total of 820,000 given in the table. The latter figure undoubtedly shows more accurately the actual membership of the bodies affiliated to the Federation.

While, however, the Miners' Federation represented, at the beginning of the War, not far short of 90 per cent. of the total number of Trade Unionists in the industry, the relatively tiny craft Associations were not negligible; for they represented a high proportion of the 'key' workers in the industry, and especially of the 'safety men' concerned with pumping, winding-engine work, underground shot-firing, and responsibility for the safety of the mines, and so on. Their separateness from the Federation was therefore felt as a source of weakness, and it was a part of the declared national policy of the Federation to bring all mine-workers within its ranks. In practice, however, there were wide differences from district to district in the policy adopted. In some coal-fields, as in South Wales, the Miners' Federation or Association was making a determined attempt to destroy 'sectional unionism' and to bring the enginemen and mechanics within its ranks. In other areas, as in Northumberland and Durham, the Miners' Associations and the sectional bodies worked amicably together, and local Mining Federations were formed in which the enginemen and mechanics were linked up with the Miners' Association. The position was not quite the same in respect of deputies, foremen, and examiners, who occupy positions analogous to those of foremen and supervisors in other industries, as in the case of crafts such as enginemen and mechanics. In Durham, for example, the Miners' Association had considerably more deputies in its ranks than the Deputies' Association, and the latter was not included in the district Mining Federation. In North Staffordshire, on the other hand, the district Colliery Firemen, Shotlighters, and Overmen's Association was affiliated to the local Mining Federation. In Scotland, some of the deputies had broken away and formed a separate Association, which was not recognized by the National Union of Scottish Mine Workers. In South Wales, the most 'advanced' coal-field in general policy, there was considerable opposition to the inclusion of the deputies in the miners' Union, on the ground that, as officials, they were 'employers' men'. No clearly defined or generally accepted policy in dealing with these problems of organization had been worked out nationally, and in practice each district was left to its own devices in handling them.

There was, however, a very strong opinion in almost all areas that all mine-workers should at any rate be organized in Unions composed solely of mine-workers, and there were only two instances in which any federal relations had been established between the Miners' Associations and Unions whose membership was not confined to mine-workers. One of these was Cumberland, where the close connexion between the mining and iron and steel industries had led to federal relations, not only between the Cumberland (Coal) Miners' Association and the Cumberland Iron-Ore Miners' Association, but also between these bodies and the local organizations or workers in the blast furnaces and other sections of the iron and steel industry. The other was North Staffordshire, where the district Federation included the local mining branches of the National Amalgamated Union of Enginemen and of the Navvies' Union (organizing certain classes of surface workers). These were, however, very exceptional cases, and in Yorkshire particularly there had been fierce disputes before the War between the Miners' Association and the general labour Unions which had organized some thousands of surface workers in the Yorkshire coal-field. Smaller disputes had also arisen with such Unions as the Amalgamated Society of Engineers.

Trade Unionism in the mining industry has had a chequered career of at least a century; but stable organization began only in 1863, and the present forms of organization have only been developed gradually since the founding of the Miners' Federation of Great Britain in 1888. In 1900, the numbers of Trade Unionists in the industry exceeded half a million: in 1911 it was three quarters of a million; and immediately before the outbreak of war it stood at about 900,000. This membership was scattered over the whole of the British coal-fields; but, owing to the conditions of the mining industry, it was for the most part concentrated in areas in which the mining population was predominant. There were, indeed, areas such as Lancashire, where a substantial proportion of miners lived in the industrial towns, mingled with workers employed in other industries. But most of the villages were devoid of all attempts at beauty or amenity. Where, as in South Wales, a huge population was concentrated in narrow valleys most unsuitable for the housing of any large numbers of people, deplorable social conditions were inevitably the result.

To some extent these conditions, when the initial difficulties had once been overcome, facilitated the task of Trade Union organization. In the early days, the work was difficult enough; and half a century of effort, during which one Union after another was formed only to disappear, was needed before Trade Unionism began to be firmly established. But, when once the old semi-servile conditions had been broken down, and a measure of legal protection for the miners secured by the efforts of men like Alexander MacDonald, the density of population in the mining areas, and the industrial marshalling of the mine-workers into large groups living a common social life apart from other sections of the people, made organization natural, and provided, in the various pits and pit villages, nuclei round which Trade Union branches of ' lodges ' could readily form.

It is therefore natural that, through the greater part of the mining industry, the ' pit lodge ' has become the nucleus of Trade Union organization. Sometimes small pits situated close together are grouped in a single lodge, and occasionally large pits are divided ; but normally the workers in a particular pit, or those of them who are members of the Miners' Association, form the pit lodge, which is the smallest unit of Trade Union administration and forms the basis of the whole Trade Union system in the mining industry. From the pit lodge are drawn the delegates to the Councils of the district Miners' Associations ; and the readiness with which a fully representative meeting can be called at the pit-head or in the pit village enables these delegates to be far more conversant with the views of their constituents than is usually the case with elected delegates or representatives. There is hardly another industry in which the actual conditions of production so readily provide the basis for a democratic Trade Union machine. The miner not only works in the pit : he lives in the pit village, and all his immediate interests are thus concentrated at one point. The town factory worker, on the other hand, lives often far from his place of work and mingled with workers of other callings. The townsman's experience produces perhaps a broader outlook, and a quicker response to social stimuli coming from without ; but the miners' intense solidarity and loyalty to their Unions is undoubtedly the result of the conditions under which they work and live. They are isolated from the rest of the world—even the rest of the Trade Union world ; but their isolation ministers to their own self-sufficiency and loyalty one to another. They are narrow, and slow to understand others or to feel the influence of outside public opinion. They have little skill in arguing their case before others ; but they stick together. This psychology of the miner largely explains the history of the mining industry during the war years : it throws light both on the attitude of the Miners' Federation to the rest of the Trade Unions and to the general public ; and on the attitude of other Trade Unionists and of the public towards the miners. Perhaps it helps to explain the failure of the 'Mines for the Nation' campaign and the breakdown of the Triple Alliance in 1920 and 1921.

The 'pit lodge' is the basis of mining Trade Unionism, and from it the larger units are built up. The pit lodges are usually grouped in districts, and each district has a full-time Miners' agent, a permanent official with duties corresponding to those of a district organizer in other Trade Unions. The agent is responsible both for organization and for most of the local work of negotiation in his district. In some cases he works with a representative District Council or Conference; but more often the district has no separate representative machinery of its own, and matters are dealt with either in the lodges or by mass meetings or ballot vote. There is no uniformity of practice in this respect from coal-field to coal-field, and the size of the agent's district, and the amount of autonomy accorded to it, vary widely from case to case. In South Wales there has always been a large measure of district autonomy, so that the South Wales Miners' Federation is in many respects rather a federation of district Unions than itself a Union. In Durham, Yorkshire, and other large areas, there is much less autonomy, and no representative machinery exists between the lodge (or sometimes grouped lodge) organization and the Miners' Association for the area. In the smaller coal-fields, such as Leicestershire, South Derbyshire, and Shropshire, where there are separate small Miners' Associations, the agent's district sometimes coincides with the area of the Miners' Association.

The Miners' Associations, as a glance at the table already given will show, vary greatly in size, ranging from the South Wales Federation (154,000 in 1913) and the Durham Association (140,000 in 1913) to tiny Associations such as Kent, Bristol, and the Forest of Dean. In some cases these Associations have formed area Federations of their own. Thus, in Staffordshire and the neighbouring counties of the West Midlands, seven Associations are united in the Midland Miners' Federation, and are affiliated to the Miners' Federation of Great Britain only through the Midland Federation, to which they have surrendered a part of their autonomy. In Scotland, there was until 1913 a number of distinct County Unions (Lanarkshire, Fifeshire, Midlothian, &c.) loosely federated in the Scottish Miners' Federation. In 1913 these Unions joined to form the National Union of Scottish Mine Workers, to which they made a further large surrender of autonomy. The County Unions, however, still possess their separate organization within the National Union, which is affiliated as a single body to the Miners' Federation of Great Britain. There existed a much looser combination, including the majority of the

English coal-fields except those on the North-East Coast, for purposes of common wage-negotiation with the mine-owners. This centred round the Conciliation Board for the 'Federated Area', embracing the Associations and Federations in Yorkshire, Lancashire and Cheshire, North Wales, the West Midlands, Nottinghamshire, Derbyshire, South Derbyshire, and Leicestershire. This machinery, however, existed solely for the purpose of collective wage-negotiation, and did not, save in this one respect, infringe the autonomy of the separate Associations connected with it.

Each Miners' Association possessed its own constitution and form of government and administration, its own scales of contributions and benefits, and, save on matters regulated over a wider area, its own agreements with the corresponding Association of Colliery Owners. Rates of contributions and benefits differed from area to area, the Durham and Derbyshire Associations, for example, having higher scales than most others, and the South Wales Federation unusually low scales. A tendency towards uniformity, already present in 1914, has since then been accentuated by the growing central activity of the Miners' Federation. Forms of government have throughout been very similar in all the coal-fields; but the South Wales Federation has depended more than others on eliciting the opinion of its members by means of large representative Conferences, attended by numerous delegates from all parts of the coal-field.

Negotiations with the coal-owners on wages questions were, before the War, usually carried out through Joint Boards of Conciliation, established between the Miners' and Colliery Owners' Associations. There were separate Boards for South Wales, Scotland, Durham, Northumberland, and some small districts in the West of England. The whole of the 'Federated Area', mentioned above, was covered by a single Conciliation Board, for Lancashire, Yorkshire, the Midlands, and North Wales; but the County Associations within this area had also their separate Joint Committees for the adjustment of questions other than the general variation of wage-rates over the whole area. There were also separate Joint Committees, largely the same in personnel, for the administration of the Coal Mines (Minimum Wage) Act of 1912, which was mainly on a County basis. Usually the Conciliation Boards and Joint Committees had an impartial chairman, appointed by agreement, or, failing agreement, by some agreed authority. The Chairman was called in to adjudicate on disputes which the two sides failed to settle by mutual arrangement. There was usually no automatic method of determining wage changes ; for the once-prevalent automatic sliding scale, based on the selling-price of coal, had been almost completely abandoned. The selling-price, however, remained in most cases the principal factor in the adjustment of wages, although other factors, such as the cost of living or production costs, could be taken into account.

There was thus no national or uniform system for the regulation of wages or working conditions over the whole of the coal-fields. Certain minimum conditions, such as the eight hour day for underground workers, the legal minimum wage, the right to appoint checkweighmen, the provision of minimum safety conditions, and so on, were prescribed by Act of Parliament, and the strengthening of legislative safeguards had always been the chief method adopted by the Miners' Federation for the betterment of working conditions. But even the Minimum Wage Act only provided the machinery for the establishment of district minimum rates, and the wage system in the mines thus remained wholly on a local or area basis.

The Miners' Federation, for some time before the War, included in its programme the demand for a National Wages Board, and for the national regulation of wages by direct negotiation between itself and the Mining Association of Great Britain. A plan for such a National Board was placed before the official Industrial Council in the course of its inquiry into Industrial Agreements in 1912. This was virtually a suggestion that the separate Conciliation Boards dealing with wages should be amalgamated, the local joint committees remaining for the adjustment of questions other than the general variation of wage-rates. This proposal, however, was not accepted by the coal-owners, and was not, for the time, followed up, the Mining Association refusing to accept the rôle of a negotiating body, on the ground that no authority to act in this way had been accorded to it by the district Associations of Colliery Owners.

The forms and methods of payment in the coal industry were, even before the War, extraordinarily complicated. In each coal-field there existed what was known as a 'standard' or basis rate of wages. These 'standards' represented the actual level of wages in a particular year in the past, three years, 1877, 1879 (the low-water mark of colliery wages), and 1888 being used in different areas as the basis for calculating the rate of wages. The actual rates to be paid were determined by percentage advances on the standard. Thus in 1912 wages in the Federated Area stood at 55 per cent. above the standard of 1888. The Conciliation Board agreements, which were renewed at regular intervals, usually provided that, during the currency of a particular agreement, the variation of wages should be limited within fixed points. Thus, in the Federated Area, the minimum was 50 per cent. above the standard of 1888, and the maximum 65 per cent. In South Wales the minimum was 35 per cent. above the standard of 1879, and the maximum 60 per cent. In Scotland the 1879 standard was used, and the limits of variation were 50 and 100 per cent.

This, however, does not mean that the miners of Scotland were likely to receive higher wages than those of South Wales, for the original standards were local, and the 1879 standard stood for one amount in South Wales and for others in the various parts of Scotland. Any table, such as those given in the Abstract of Labour Statistics, which expresses wages purely in terms of standards and percentages, is therefore quite unintelligible to any one who has not a direct knowledge of the industry.

The continuance of these obsolete wage-standards had, even before the War, long been recognized as an anomaly, and attempts were being made to substitute for them a new standard based on the existing condition of the industry. But for the War, this would probably have been done in most areas in 1914 and 1915; it was not, however, altogether a simple matter, because many calculations of special payments and allowances were dependent on the standard, and would have to be revised together with it.

The varying wage-standards, and the varying percentages with their *minima* and *maxima* based upon the standards, were, however, only the beginning of the complexity of the wage-system in the coal-fields. Mining, although it employs many workers who are paid by time, is predominantly a piece-work industry. Successive Conferences of the Miners' Federation have passed resolutions in favour of the abolition of piece-work; but no positive steps have been taken to get rid of it, and coal-getting in practically all districts, and in many a substantial proportion of the auxiliary work, continues to be carried on under the piece-work system. Each colliery, therefore, normally has its price-list, or sometimes several lists for different seams. These lists, which vary greatly in elaborateness according to the working methods adopted, set out the prices for hewing coal and for other forms of work carried out by the piece. In South Wales the lists are usually elaborate; for the division of labour has not been carried far in the pits, and the greater part of the work is done on the piece-work system, the piece-work hewer also executing much of the auxiliary work at specially fixed piece-work prices. In South Wales the price-list, once fixed for a particular seam or colliery, is very seldom changed even when the working conditions alter. This results in substantial differences in earnings from colliery to colliery, quite apart from any general variation in the rates of wages. In Durham, on the other hand, piece-work prices are regularly adjusted under the 'county average' system. If average actual earnings in a particular pit or seam diverge by more than 5 per cent. in either direction from the 'county average', a figure ascertained long ago and fixed, either party can, and does usually, apply for an adjustment of the price-list. The percentage variations in the general rates of wages are added to the prices, which are thus not affected by changes in the rate. In Scotland, however, where a system somewhat resembling the 'county average' prevails in some areas, percentage variations are usually added to or subtracted from the piece-work prices. In South Wales especially, it is generally admitted that many of the existing price-lists quite fail to correspond to the actual working conditions. Plans for the complete reconstruction of the methods of piece-work payment in the mining industry have been repeatedly discussed; but so far nothing has come of them, although the South Wales Miners' Federation, from 1913 onwards, has been securing that new lists shall be put into force only with the sanction of the Federation itself, and has thus been introducing some degree of uniformity.

In addition to the standard rates and percentages and to the piece-work lists in the collieries, there existed for the regulation of wages the Coal Mines (Minimum Wage) Act of 1912, passed by Parliament as a means of settling the national mining strike of that year. This Act applied only to underground workers, and provided for the fixing, by a Joint District Board with an impartial Chairman, of legal minimum rates of wages in each district of the Federation. The Boards were instructed, in fixing rates, to 'have regard to the average daily rate of wages paid to workmen of the class for which the minimum rate is to be settled'. Obligatory minimum rates were in force before the War in each coal-field under this Act; but it was expressly provided that these rates were not to interfere with the operation of any higher rates secured by agreement or by other methods. The actual rates fixed by collective bargaining might, therefore, be higher than the legal minimum wage.

The principal importance of the minimum wage came from the solution which it attempted of the vexed question of the 'abnormal place-men'. Naturally, it is not equally easy to hew coal at all places in the pit or seam; and, under piece-work conditions, the miner who finds himself allocated to a place in which coal-getting is difficult is often unable to earn a reasonable wage. This may also affect the earnings of other workers dependent on the hewer. It was mainly out of these conditions that the demand for a guaranteed minimum rate, which was the principal issue in the national miners' strike of 1912, arose. The Minimum Wage Act conceded this principle, although not in the form in which the miners had demanded it. This had one important effect on the operation of the piece-work system. Where coal-getting conditions were difficult, or price lists unduly low, the miners, unable to earn more than the minimum wage, which was now guaranteed to them by law, became in effect time-workers, although they were still nominally paid at piece-work rates. The official figures purporting to show the numbers of piece-workers and time-workers in the industry thus ceased to give a true account of the position, and the disparity between the nominal and the actual proportion of piece-workers increased with the greater working of poor and thin seams during the period of control. This increase in the proportion of actual time-workers in the industry, and the accompanying decay of the piece-work system, doubtless helped to further the movement for the abolition of 'payment by results', which found expression at successive Annual Conferences of the Miners' Federation.

The hours of labour of mine-workers were regulated before the War under the Coal Mines Regulation Act of 1908, which conceded the long-demanded principle of the eight hour day for underground workers. The concession was not extended to surface-workers, and even for those working underground the method of reckoning the hours of labour, by which 'winding time' was not included in the eight hours, increased the actual average length of the working day to over eight and a half hours, and in some cases involved a day of more than ten hours from 'bank to bank'. Surfacemen in many cases worked considerably longer hours than these. The demand for a general and effective application of the eight hour day 'from bank to bank' already figured prominently in the programme of the Miners' Federation before the War.

In addition to the Acts regulating wages and hours, and guaranteeing the right to appoint checkweighmen, there was a large body of legislation regulating the conditions of operation and employment in the mining industry. The most important of these Acts, embodying a great many earlier statutes obtained by agitation during the last century, are the Coal Mines Regulation Act of 1887 and the Coal Mines Act of 1911. These Acts prohibit the employment underground of women and of boys under fourteen, and restrict their employment on the surface to ten hours a day or fifty-four hours a week. They make special provisions for safety and inspection, including the right of miners to appoint representatives of their own to inspect the mines on their behalf; and they define the duties and responsibilities of coal-owners and mine-managers and officials in respect of safety provisions. Under these Acts, numerous official inquiries have been held into colliery accidents, especially explosions, and it has been an important part of the work of the Miners' Federation to represent the workers at such inquiries, and to reinforce the Coal Mines Department in securing the strict observance of the law relating to coal-mines.

The nationalization of the mining industry had figured for many years before the War in the policy of the Miners' Federation; and in 1912 a Bill for the Nationalization of Mines and Minerals, approved by the Annual Conference of the Federation, was introduced into Parliament on its behalf by the Labour Party. The character of this Bill, and the differences between it and the Bill drafted by the Federation and presented to the Coal Commission in 1919, will be described in a later chapter. Here it is only necessary to observe that the demand for national ownership of the mines was of long standing, and had won general acceptance among the miners' organizations for a considerable time before the War.

The object of this chapter has been merely to sketch, in very general outline, the pre-war position and strength of the Trade Union movement in the mining industry. The miners had tried their strength in the great national strike of 1912 ; but this dispute, although it ended in the concession of the legal minimum wage in a modified form, had by no means disposed of the outstanding issues, and in 1914 the miners were actively engaged in preparations for a further forward movement. As a means to more effective national action, the Miners' Federation was taking steps to secure a simultaneous termination of district agreements over all the coal-fields, with a view to the formulation of national demands and the pressing of the claim, mentioned above, for a uniform national system of wage-negotiation. Moreover, actual experience of the railway, transport, and mining strikes of 1911–12 had proved to the Trade Unions in the three industries that the outbreak of a dispute in any one of them necessarily dislocated the others, and had led to the preliminary conversations which paved the way for the Triple Alliance of Miners, Railwaymen, and Transport Workers. This Alliance, however, was only in the preliminary stages of formation on the outbreak of war, and the War for a time interrupted its formation, as it also caused the threatened strikes and forward movements which were developing in the three industries in the summer of 1914 to be indefinitely postponed.

CHAPTER II

FROM THE OUTBREAK OF WAR TO THE ASSUMPTION OF STATE CONTROL

Section 1. Enlistment, Output, and Absenteeism.
,, 2. Strikes, Conciliation, and Agreements.
,, 3. The Triple Industrial Alliance.
,, 4. Absenteeism (1916) and Pit Committees.
,, 5. Labour Troubles in South Wales.

SECTION 1. ENLISTMENT, OUTPUT, AND ABSENTEEISM

THE outbreak of war in August 1914 was immediately followed by a widespread dislocation of trade and industry, both at home and abroad. The demand for industrial coal fell off sharply, and the export markets were thrown largely out of gear. Consequently, many miners were thrown out of work, or found their opportunities for employment restricted to considerably less than a full working week. As in many other industries in which shortage of labour was soon to become a pressing problem, the War at first seemed likely to create widespread unemployment; and little attention was directed to the necessity of maintaining output.

From the first days of the War, the rate of enlistment among mine-workers was exceptionally heavy. When the first figures were compiled in the spring of 1915, it was found that, out of 1,116,648 workers employed in the mines at the outbreak of war, 191,170, or over 17 per cent., had enlisted by the end of February 1915. As the total figure of workers employed includes youths and boys as well as adults, the percentage quoted gives an under-impression of the extent of enlistment. In April 1915 it was estimated that a further 30,000 miners had joined the Forces, and by August the total number was well over 250,000.

For some time before this figure was reached, the urgency of maintaining the production of coal had been realized. The Admiralty was making large demands for steam coal; shipping and railways were largely engaged on war services; and the demand for industrial coal had been swollen by the increased production of munitions and other war requisites. The reduction in the export trade was balanced by expansion in the home demand. Meanwhile, in consequence of the heavy enlistments of miners, output had inevitably fallen, and in February it was estimated that the decrease in production for 1915 would be fully 36 million tons, whereas only 24 millions would be liberated through the restriction of the export markets.

Early in 1915 an agitation was set on foot by certain of the coal-owners for a suspension, during the war period, of the Coal Mines Eight Hours Act, which contained a clause under which suspension could take place in time of national emergency. To this, however, the Miners' Federation objected, on the ground that suspension was both unnecessary and inexpedient. Nor were the coal-owners united in pressing the demand in face of opposition. It was clear, however, that the whole question of mining organization under war-time conditions would have to be considered; and on the 23rd February 1915 the Government appointed a Committee, on which both the coal-owners and the miners, as well as the Mines Department of the Board of Trade, were represented, to go into the whole question and bring up a report at the earliest possible moment. There was some preliminary difficulty about the terms of reference for this Committee, the Miners' Federation objecting to the inclusion among them of a direction to 'facilitate enlistments among mine-workers'. Only when this direction was deleted did the Miners' Federation agree that its nominees, Messrs. Robert Smillie, Vernon Hartshorn, and Stephen Walsh, should serve upon the Committee.

This difficulty having been surmounted, the Coal Mining Organization Committee got rapidly to work, and produced its first Report on the 7th May 1915. Although before this date there had been an important crisis in the industry on the question of wages, it will be well, before discussing that crisis, to deal with the salient points in the Committee's Report. The following is the text of the 'Summary of Conclusions' embodied in the Report itself:

1. The number of persons from coal-mines who have joined H.M. Forces up to the end of February 1915 is 191,170.

2. We find from returns representing 89 per cent. of the total labour

employed in coal-mines that the net decrease in mine labour at the end of February amounted to 134,186 persons, or 13½ per cent. of the persons employed in July 1914, and that there has been, over the seven months August 1914 to (and inclusive of) February 1915, as compared with the corresponding months twelve months earlier, an average fall in output of 3,044,329 tons (or a total loss in output of 13½ per cent.), which loss will continue unless means are taken to prevent it.

3. We find also that absence from work over all classes of mine-workers, on the days on which the mines were open to work, was, for seven months succeeding the outbreak of war, an average of 9·8 per cent., and we have arrived at the conclusion that fully 4·8 per cent. of this is avoidable absence. The absenteeism, taking the coal-getters only, is very much higher, and, were there no avoidable absenteeism, the output would be increased to the extent of between 13 and 14 million tons ; but perfection in this respect is not to be expected. We believe, however, that the case has only to be put before the miners in order to secure a great response on their part, and we suggest that the body best fitted in all respects to put forward the case is the Executive of the Miners' Federation of Great Britain.

We suggest also, that the question of the curtailment of holidays and 'stop-days' during the War might receive the attention of the same body.

4. It is not possible to determine the exact extent of the home demand without very far-reaching inquiry, and, indeed, it is very doubtful whether it is determinable ; but from the evidence before us and the inquiries we have instituted, we incline to the belief that it is not far from what it is in normal times.

5. The loss in production for the year commencing from the outbreak of war will, unless means are taken to reduce the loss, probably amount to 36 million tons, against which must be put a probable reduction in the quantity of coal exported of 24 million tons, leaving a net shortage of 12 million tons ; but if the miners continue to be recruited for the Forces the deficiency will be increased.

The evidence before us is conclusive that if labour is further withdrawn from the collieries (notwithstanding the adoption of all possible ameliorative measures) the output will be so reduced as to seriously affect the industrial position of the country, and the time appears to the Committee to have arrived when very full consideration should be given to the question as to whether further recruiting among the miners should be encouraged.

6. With reference to the Eight Hours Act, we suggest that the owners and workmen should confer together and determine to what extent, if at all, the Act should be suspended in individual districts, i. e. to what class of labour the suspension should apply, and the amount in point of time the suspension should cover.

7. We do not advise that women should be employed to a greater extent than at present on the surface of the mines.

8. We do not suggest that the age limit at which boys can be employed below ground or on the surface should be reduced.

9. We have indicated certain directions in which, possibly, internal reorganization in the mines might be further carried out.

10. If the restriction of the export of coal to neutral countries is found to be advisable, we have pointed out that special consideration should be given to those mining districts which, to a large extent, depend on export for the existence of the collieries.

11. We think that the importance of economy in the use of coal should be brought before the public. Savings which at once occur to the mind are economies in public and private lighting, whether by gas or electricity, and the manufacture of luxuries which require coal. The rise in the price of coal will no doubt create a tendency towards economy, but we believe that a considerable further saving could be effected if it were brought home to the public that it is a patriotic duty to economize coal during the period of war.

12. The basis of all the proposals and suggestions made by the Committee is harmonious co-operation between employers and employed through the medium of the organizations on both sides thoroughly representative of the parties.

Unless the organizations possess this power, and are able to act with authority for both owners and workmen, friction may arise and stoppages of work take place which ought to be avoided at the present time to the utmost extent possible.

In the highest interests of the nation it is especially desirable that during the period of the War the employers should co-operate with the representatives of the workmen on such questions as non-unionism, or other questions likely to lead to any friction or stoppage during the present unprecedented circumstances.

It will be seen that this Report, which was signed by the representatives of owners and miners alike, gave little encouragement to those who had been urging such drastic measures as the entire suspension of the Eight Hours Act, or the employment of women and young boys. It was realized that the effect of lengthening the hours of work might be more than offset by an increase of absenteeism, and that the labour of women and young boys would, under the special conditions of mining production, be no real substitute for adult male labour. It was also agreed that, if the skilled labour force of the industry were much further depleted, no measures of substitution or reorganization could possibly prevent a heavy decline in output.

Accordingly, the principal effort was concentrated, at this

stage, on a national attempt to reduce absenteeism at the mines. The miner, especially the coal-hewer, whose work is arduous in the extreme, does not normally work, week in and week out, a full week of six days. The working customs vary from district to district. In some cases, a five days' week is the rule ; in others, eleven days a fortnight. In yet others, the pits are regularly open six days a week ; but miners take days off irregularly from time to time. It will be seen, from clause 3 of the above summary, that the Coal Mining Organization Committee found the total absenteeism to be just under 10 per cent., of which it estimated that rather less than half was 'avoidable absenteeism', i. e. was due, not to the inability, but to the unwillingness, of the miner to work. The Miners' Federation was accordingly asked, in the national interest, to make every possible effort to diminish this 'avoidable absenteeism' among its members, with a view to increased production despite the reduced numbers of skilled men available. The curtailment of holidays, and the suspension of the practice of closing the pits on one day in each week or fortnight, were also recommended.

The Miners' Federation at once took these matters in hand. Holidays were largely curtailed or given up ; and the miners' leaders did their best to induce more regular time-keeping. On the 8th June the Executive of the Federation agreed to the suggestion of the Home Secretary (Sir John Simon), that a National Mining Conference, representative of the whole industry, owners as well as miners, should be called to discuss the Report of the Coal Mining Organization Committee, and to give the Government an opportunity of placing before the delegates an account of the gravity of the situation. This Conference, presided over by the Home Secretary and addressed by Mr. Lloyd George, was held in London on the 29th July, only a few days after the settlement of the second great war-time industrial crisis in the industry. A national joint meeting between the Miners' Federation and the Mining Association of Great Britain, at which joint measures were concerted for carrying the proposals of the Coal Mining Organization Committee into effect, followed on the 2nd September, the Home Secretary again presiding. No very definite results, however, followed this meeting, except that further efforts were made by the miners to reduce absenteeism, and measures were concerted for preventing disputes over the question of non-unionism from leading to stoppages during the War. Before this, action had been taken on others of the Coal Mining Organization Committee's suggestions. A special Coal Exports Committee was set up at the end of May to regulate the export trade; and in July the Coal Prices Limitation Act, limiting the increase permitted in the pit-head price of coal, was passed into law. The 'standard increase' above pre-war pit-head prices was limited to 4*s*. a ton, and this amount could be exceeded only in cases where special permission was secured from the Board of Trade. The Act did not deal with retail prices, which remained unregulated by the law and subject only to voluntary arrangements made among the merchants with the cognizance of the Board of Trade.

Section 2. Strikes, Conciliation, and Agreements

At the time of the outbreak of war the outlook in the mining industry, as we have seen, was threatening. Claims for advances in wages, and counter-claims for reductions by the employers' associations, were being brought forward in a number of coal-fields. For the most part these difficulties were temporarily adjusted in August 1914, and the only changes in wage rates which took place during the last five months of the year were certain reductions in Northumberland and Durham—districts in which coal prices were largely affected by the dislocation of the export trade. A serious situation was, however, also developing in the West Yorkshire coal-field. In July 1914 an award had been given by Judge Amphlett under the Coal Mines Minimum Wage Act, raising the minimum wage rate. A dispute had then arisen between the coal-owners and the Yorkshire Miners' Association concerning the effect of this award upon the wages to be paid. The question at issue was whether the three advances of 5 per cent. previously awarded by the Conciliation Board would now be payable over and above the advanced minimum rate, or whether they would be merged in this new rate. The owners contended that they should be merged; the miners, that the revised minimum would be payable plus the 15 per cent. Conciliation Board advance.

Reference to the section in the previous chapter describing methods of wage negotiation in the coal-fields will readily explain why such a situation could arise.

The dispute dragged on for the last five months of 1914 and into the new year. On the 7th January 1915 the matter came before a National Conference of the Miners' Federation, and sanction was given to the Yorkshire Miners' Association to take a strike ballot. This meant that in the event of the Yorkshire miners deciding to strike they would have behind them the support of the Miners' Federation as a whole. The strike ballot resulted in a large majority in favour of a strike, 26,676 voting for, and 7,211 against, strike action. This decision led to the resumption of negotiations, and on the 9th February a settlement was reached, the owners agreeing to concede the miners' demands for the war period without prejudice to their action subsequently.

Meanwhile the rapid rise in the cost of living was already leading to a new cause of difficulty. We have seen that the movements for increased wages which were in progress during 1914 had been stopped by the outbreak of war, and that the only wage changes during the winter had been decreases in certain of the exporting districts. In face of the rise in prices, it became necessary early in the new year for the miners in all the coal-fields to seek advances in wages, and on the 17th March, on the recommendation of the Executive, a National Conference of the Miners' Federation decided to put forward a demand for a national advance of 20 per cent. on current earnings, and to ask for a national joint meeting with the coal-owners for the purpose of discussing this demand. This, of course, raised the question, already discussed in the first chapter, of national versus district negotiations, and the Mining Association of Great Britain at once replied to the miners' request that it was not the competent body for the discussion of wage questions, and that the miners should take up the matter through the Conciliation Boards in the various coal-fields. On the 6th and 7th April the refusal of the owners to agree to a national meeting was reported to the Executive of the Miners' Federation; and this refusal was persisted in, although the Miners' Federation expressed its willingness to agree that a national meeting under the existing conditions should not be treated as a precedent in the pushing of the demand for a National Wages Board and for permanent national methods of wage variation. No progress, however, was made, and on the 21st April a full Conference of the Miners' Federation decided to ask the Government to intervene for the purpose of securing that a national meeting should take place between the Federation and the whole of the coal-owners. On the same day the Executive of the Federation met Mr. Runciman and discussed the whole situation with him, and on the 23rd April the Executive met the Prime Minister, Mr. Asquith, and placed before him their demand for a national joint meeting under Government auspices.

This application was successful, and on the 29th April the national joint meeting was held under the presidency of the Prime Minister, the coal-owners having agreed, under protest, to attend. The owners were asked if they would not concede the full demands of the miners or make an alternative offer, and on the 30th April, despite their previous refusal to make any proposal on a national basis, they offered to recommend that an advance of 10 per cent. on the existing piece rates should be made through each Conciliation Board. Any local advance previously given during the War was to be deducted from this 10 per cent., and any future advance under the Conciliation Board was to be merged in it up to the amount of 10 per cent. The miners put forward an alternative suggestion that an advance of 12½ per cent. on total earnings should be conceded on a national basis; but to this the owners refused to agree, and a deadlock was reached. On the 1st May the Miners' Conference considered the situation and agreed, on the suggestion of the Prime Minister, to refer the whole dispute to him with powers to settle it. He had, at this stage, given no indication of his attitude, apart from the fact that he had helped to bring a national meeting about; but hopes were undoubtedly entertained strongly among the miners that he would award a national advance.

Mr. Asquith's award, however, issued on the 5th May, while it recognized the necessity for advances in all districts, was based on the view that the difference in circumstances from one district to another was such as to make a uniform national award impossible. He therefore ruled that the claim for an advance should be referred to the separate districts with instructions to deal with the matter as a special question untrammelled by any provisions, in the Conciliation Board Agreements, as to the maximum advance to be awarded. Any advances given were, however, to be merged in future percentage advances awarded by the Conciliation Boards under their regular rules.

The miners accepted this decision under protest, although it did not realize their desire for a settlement on a national basis. Indeed, the district awards issued under the Prime Minister's scheme showed very big differences between one district and another. The Federated Area of Lancashire, Yorkshire, the Midlands, and North Wales secured an advance of 15½ per cent. on earnings; South Wales 17½ per cent. on the old basis of 1879; Northumberland and Durham 15 per cent. on the old basis of 1879; and Scotland 18¾ per cent. on the basis of 1888.

This national dispute, although the Miners' Federation endeavoured to keep it clearly distinct, became to some extent confused in certain areas with other negotiations which were proceeding at the same time. As we have seen, the Miners' Federation at its Annual Conference in 1914 had carried a resolution providing that all agreements entered into by the district Miners' Associations must terminate at the same time, subject to a uniform notice of three months; that the obsolete wage standards of 1877, 1879, and 1888 must be swept away, and a new standard established incorporating all the actual advances in operation over and above the various standards at the time of the termination of the existing agreements; that a minimum wage of not less than 5*s.* a day should be fixed for all adult surface workers; and that three months' notice to terminate all existing agreements should be given on the 1st April 1915.

After the outbreak of war the question arose whether the attempt to secure new wage standards and agreements should be allowed to lapse for the time being, or whether the Federation should proceed with its efforts to secure a new uniform basis for wages throughout the industry. On the 4th February the Executive passed a resolution that any new agreement drafted in any coal-field must be submitted to the Federation itself before being ratified. This provision was, of course, intended to facilitate the carrying out of the recommendations of the Scarborough Conference in securing uniformity of agreements over all the districts. Accordingly, on the 1st April notice was duly given in all the coal-fields, and the district Miners' Associations endeavoured to enter into negotiations for new agreements based on the principles laid down at the Scarborough Conference of 1914. Difficulties, however, at once arose in many of the areas. The owners put forward the contention that it was impossible and undesirable to conclude new agreements during the emergency, and that the existing agreements ought to be allowed to run on until after the conclusion of the War. This course was manifestly disadvantageous from the miners' point of view, as most of the agreements included provisions which, if they had been observed, would have prevented the concession of the advances necessary to compensate for the increased cost of living. The agreements and the wage standards established under them were, moreover, entirely obsolete, and it was a serious matter to contemplate their further continuance for an indefinite period.

Actually, difficulties were not experienced in all areas. In the Federated Area, for example, a new agreement, establishing a new wage standard, was concluded, more or less in harmony with the Scarborough decisions. This agreement was to run for three years. New agreements were also made in Cumberland and Durham, and in Scotland a working arrangement to continue without a new agreement was arrived at. In Northumberland the notice to terminate the existing sliding scale agreement was withdrawn and the old agreement continued in force. The most serious difficulties arose in the South Wales area, and led to an important dispute in June and July 1915, which will have to be discussed separately. In face of the difficulties encountered, the Miners' Federation did not find it possible to establish a new and uniform wage basis over the whole of the coal-fields, but some advance towards a more up-to-date wage standard and a more uniform system was made.

Before dealing with the South Wales dispute, it will be convenient to describe certain other events which had an important bearing upon it. In March 1915 the Government, acting on the advice of the Committee on Production appointed during the previous month, summoned at the Treasury [1] an important Labour Conference, before which it placed proposals for the acceptance of arbitration and prevention of disputes during the war period, and for the dilution of labour by the admission of less skilled workers to skilled jobs. The miners were hardly affected by the latter of these proposals; but the question of compulsory arbitration in industrial disputes did affect them very seriously. Their delegates attended the Treasury Conference on the first day, 17th March, but withdrew as soon as they found that a committal decision, for which they had no mandate, was likely to be taken on the question of compulsory arbitration by the majority of the Unions represented. At the same time they intended to affirm their willingness to discuss directly any proposal for the prevention of disputes in the mining industry during the war period. Some slight discussion on this point followed, and strong recommendations for the peaceful adjustment of all disputes, and for the extended use of arbitration on a voluntary basis, were made. Further difficulties, however, arose when Mr. Lloyd George, on the 23rd June, introduced the Munitions of War Bill, which would have had the effect of giving legal sanction to the conclusions reached at the Treasury Conference and of applying compulsory arbitration, or at least making it applicable by Royal Proclamation, to all industries concerned with war production. The Miners' Federation immediately resolved to insist on the exclusion of the mining industry from the Munitions of War Act, and on the 25th June they met Mr. Lloyd George and placed this demand before him. Mr. Lloyd George, in his reply, refused to agree to exclusion. When, however, two days later, the Miners' Executive made a voluntary offer that all war-time disputes should be referred to the independent chairman of the Coal Conciliation Boards in the various areas, finally Mr. Lloyd George agreed to insert, in the section which enabled the compulsory arbitration clause of the Munitions of War Bill to be applied by Proclamation to disputes in any industry, a provision in the following words: 'If, in the case of any industry, the Minister of Munitions is

[1] For a fuller description of the Treasury Conference, and of the recommendations agreed to by it, and also for the full text of the Munitions of War Act mentioned below, see the companion study in this series, *Trade Unionism and Munitions.*

satisfied that effective means exist to secure a settlement without a stoppage, of any difference arising on work other than munition work, no proclamation shall be made under this section with respect to such difference.' It was soon to become clear that the insertion of this provision was far from assuring the exclusion of the mining industry from the terms of the Munitions of War Bill, which became an Act on the 2nd July 1915.

While these negotiations were proceeding a serious situation had been developing in the South Wales coal-field. On the 3rd March the South Wales Miners' Federation put forward its proposals for a new agreement to replace the existing Conciliation Board Agreement of 1910. These proposals were based on the Scarborough Conference decisions of 1914. The most important demand was for the abolition of the obsolete wage standard of 1879 and the establishment of a new standard 50 per cent. above the 1879 standard (i.e. merging the pre-war percentage advances actually in force). In addition, a minimum daily wage of 5*s.* for surface workers was demanded, and a claim was put forward that workers on afternoon and night shifts should be paid at the rate of 'turn and a fifth' for each shift worked. It was also claimed that the new agreement should apply to all members of the South Wales Miners' Federation, to whatever craft or grade they might belong, and that it should not apply to non-members. These last demands raised in an accentuated form both the non-unionist question, and the relation of the South Wales Miners' Federation, which was aiming at the organization of all grades of workers in the coal-field, to the sectional Unions organizing particular crafts.

The South Wales owners met these demands with a blank refusal to negotiate, urging the South Wales Miners' Federation to accept the continuance of the old agreement for the war period, and to postpone until after the War all negotiations for a new basis. Thereafter matters dragged on until almost the end of June, the owners still refusing to negotiate, and the full seriousness of the situation apparently not being realized by the Government until within a few days of the expiration of the three months' notice to terminate the old agreement, which had been handed in by the miners on the 1st April. At last, almost at the end of June, Mr. Runciman, the President of the Board of Trade, intervened in the dispute, and a series of Conferences were held between him and the miners and the owners. On the 30th June the efforts of Mr. Runciman to secure a settlement were reinforced by the three Labour members of the Government, Messrs. Arthur Henderson and G. H. Roberts, and Mr. William Brace, who had, until he became a member of the Government, been President of the South Wales Miners' Federation. In consequence of this intervention, the South Wales Miners' Executive agreed to recommend that the amended proposals put forward by Mr. Runciman should be accepted as a basis for discussion, and that meanwhile the miners should continue to work on day-to-day contracts for a period of a fortnight. This recommendation was accepted by the delegate meeting of the South Wales Miners' Federation by a very narrow majority, and a strike was thus for the moment averted. The proposals put forward by Mr. Runciman and thus accepted as a basis for discussion were as follows:

1. The rates of surfacemen which are below 3*s*. 4*d*. per day to be advanced to 3*s*. 4*d*. per day.
2. Night men to receive six turns for five.
3. Hauliers employed on afternoon and night shifts to be paid the same rate of wages as those employed on the day shift.
4. A new standard of 50 per cent. on the 1879 standard to be established. Any standards in operation other than the 1879 standard to be correspondingly adjusted. (It is not intended that the alteration of the standard shall in itself effect an immediate change in wages.)
5. The maximum and minimum provided for in the 1910 agreement not to be operative.
6. Any question of interpretation of these terms to be submitted in writing.

Difficulties immediately arose as to the interpretation to be placed upon these proposals, and both owners and miners asked Mr. Runciman to explain very carefully what they meant. He explained that, if his suggestions were accepted, the question of the rates to be paid to surface workers would be remitted to the Conciliation Board for settlement, and that the question of the grades of workers to be covered by the award would also be remitted to the decision of the independent Chairman of the Conciliation Board. The ground for leaving these questions unsettled was that they required 'more investigation and inquiry into local circumstances than Mr. Runciman can at present undertake '.

This interpretation, as well as some of the terms of Mr. Runciman's original proposals, were regarded as unsatisfactory by the miners, and, although the South Wales Miners' Executive endeavoured to secure further continuance of work on a day-to-day basis, the Delegate Conference rejected its recommendation and carried the following resolution on the 12th July :

> That we do not accept anything less than our original proposals and that we stop the collieries on Thursday next unless these terms are conceded.

This decision was arrived at by a majority of 850 votes on a total vote of 2,900 delegates. On the following day two important events took place. First, the Executive of the Miners' Federation of Great Britain issued an unavailing appeal to the South Wales miners to remain at work. Secondly, the Government proclaimed the dispute under the Munitions of War Act, and thus made any stoppage illegal, and any member who stopped work in defiance of the proclamation liable to punishment. Nevertheless the strike began on the 15th July. Work in the coal-field was completely suspended, and, although the Government had found it easy enough to issue a proclamation of the South Wales dispute under the Munitions Act, it was quite another matter to carry the proclamation into effect or to take proceedings for infringement of it against two hundred thousand mine-workers on strike. Accordingly, after the strike had been in progress for four days, Mr. Lloyd George, Mr. Runciman, and Mr. Arthur Henderson, again intervened and came to South Wales for the purpose of securing a settlement. After six days' negotiation a settlement was arrived at. The Government conceded the greater part of the miners' demands and undertook that effect should be given to these demands by the coal-owners. A new wage standard in accordance with the recommendations of the Scarborough Conference was accordingly established, and the principle of payment for afternoon and night shifts, for which the miners had contended, and the minimum rate for surface workers were also conceded.

This, however, was not the end of the dispute. A return to work took place immediately after the settlement of the 20th July :

but a month later further differences arose as to the interpretation of the agreement arrived at. Mr. Runciman was asked to give an interpretation on the disputed point, whether the agreement covered craftsmen, enginemen, &c., who were members of the South Wales Miners' Federation. He ruled on the 20th August that the agreement did not apply to these sections, in spite of a clause in it which stated that it would apply to 'all the workers who may be members of the Miners' Federation'. Upon this a further stoppage was immediately threatened, and was only averted by Mr. Runciman's act in revising his decision, and by the conclusion of a supplementary agreement including the craft workers who were members of the South Wales Miners' Federation. This supplementary agreement was duly signed on September 2nd 1915, and the unrest which had been prevalent throughout the summer thereupon subsided.

Section 3. The Triple Industrial Alliance

I mentioned in my opening chapter that at the time of the outbreak of war negotiations were proceeding between the Miners' Federation and the great Trade Unions of Railwaymen and Transport Workers for the conclusion of an Alliance between the three groups. These negotiations were interrupted by the outbreak of war; but in 1915 it was decided to resume them and to bring the Alliance fully into being without further delay. Accordingly, on the 9th December 1915, a Joint Conference of miners, railwaymen, and transport workers definitely ratified the constitution of the Triple Industrial Alliance, and brought into being what was, on paper at least, the most formidable industrial organization in the world.

Some account must be given of the origin and purposes of this body. In October 1913 the Conference of the Miners' Federation at Scarborough passed a resolution in which it requested its Executive 'to approach the Executive Committees of other big Trade Unions with a view to co-operative action, and the support of each others' demands'. This resolution was the result of a considerable amount of previous discussion, which had its origin mainly in the experience of the miners and of the other sections concerned in the great disputes of 1911 and 1912. When the transport workers and railwaymen came out on strike during the summer and autumn of 1911, the immediate effect of their action was to throw many thousands of miners out of work, because the facilities for transporting coal from the pit-head were no longer available. Similarly, when the miners struck on a national scale in 1912, many railwaymen and transport workers were thrown out of employment because there was no coal to transport over the railways or to ship at the ports. In both cases these strikes cost large sums of money in unemployment and similar benefits to workers who were not directly concerned in them. The National Union of Railwaymen, for example, spent nearly a hundred thousand pounds as a result of the miners' strike in 1912. It was, therefore, natural that the idea should arise in the minds of members of all three organizations that it was bad economy to strike separately, and that it would be far better policy to arrange for united action. This, as will be seen, would involve not merely the conclusion of a working alliance between the three bodies, but arrangements mutually made by which working agreements in the three industries would terminate simultaneously, and fresh demands be simultaneously advanced on behalf of all sections. Only if this were done would it be possible for the three groups to act as a united whole and to obviate the expenses and disadvantages involved in separate action. Moreover, it was believed that united action would add greatly to the strength of the three organizations, and that the united power of the Triple Alliance would be great enough in most cases to remove the necessity for strike action, and to secure the concession of any reasonable demands which might be put forward.

It will be seen that the resolution from which I have quoted empowered the Executive of the Miners' Federation to approach the Executive Committees of *other big Trade Unions*, and did not refer specifically to the railwaymen and the transport workers. It was, however, generally anticipated that the initiative would be taken in the first instance by these three bodies alone; and the Miners' Federation decided, in the words used by Mr. Smillie, its President, at the joint meeting on the 23rd April 1914, 'to content themselves in the first place, with endeavouring to get a joint meeting of these three bodies, at least in the initial stage'. From the first, however, the possibility of a subsequent extension of the Alliance to other big Trade Unions was contemplated, although in fact no such extension took place.

In April 1914 the Executives of the Miners' Federation, the National Union of Railwaymen, and the Transport Workers' Federation met several times in Joint Conference, and as a result of these meetings a sub-committee was appointed to draw up a scheme of joint action. This sub-committee reported to a further Joint Conference held in June 1914; but difficulties arose as to the detailed terms of the Alliance and further negotiations between the three bodies were found to be necessary. These negotiations were still proceeding when the War broke out. Nothing was done therefore until the summer of 1915, when the railwaymen, at their Annual Conference, passed a resolution urging that the Alliance should be ratified immediately upon the conclusion of the War. The miners, in their turn, urged that action should be taken at once, and, as we have seen, the constitution was finally ratified and the Alliance brought into being in December 1915. The following scheme was then unanimously adopted:

1. That matters submitted to this joint body, and upon which action may be taken, should be those of a national character or vitally affecting a principle which in the opinion of the Executive making the request necessitates combined action.

2. The co-operation of the joint organization shall not be called upon nor expected unless and until the matter in dispute has been considered by and received the endorsement of the National Executive of the organization primarily concerned, and each organization instituting a movement which is likely to involve the other affiliated organizations shall, before any definite steps are taken, submit the whole matter to the joint body for consideration.

3. For the purposes of increasing the efficiency of the movement for combined action, periodical meetings of the three full Executives shall be held at least half-yearly.

4. There shall be appointed a Consultative Committee of six, composed of two members chosen from the Executive Committee of each of the three bodies, whose duty it shall be to meet from time to time, and who shall be empowered to call at any time a special conference of the Executives of the three bodies if in their opinion such conference be necessary. That a meeting be called on application made by any one of the three bodies.

5. With a view to meeting all management expenses incurred, each affiliated body shall contribute a sum of 10*s*. per 1,000 members per annum, or such sum as may be decided upon from time to time.

6. Simultaneously with these arrangements for united action between the three organizations in question every effort shall proceed among the three sections to create effective and complete control of their respective bodies.

7. Complete autonomy shall be reserved to any one of the three bodies affiliated to take action on their own behalf.

8. That joint action can only be taken when the question at issue has been before the members of the three organizations and decided by such methods as the constitution of each organization provides, and the conference shall then be called without delay to consider and decide the question of taking action.

9. No obligation shall devolve upon any of the three bodies to take joint action unless the foregoing conditions have been complied with.

This scheme was to some extent the result of a compromise. The Miners' Federation has always worked very strictly upon the rule that no committal action shall be taken except as the result of a ballot vote of all the members affected. The miners' procedure, when an important issue arises, is to call a full national Delegate Conference for its discussion, and at this Conference to formulate proposals, or perhaps alternative proposals, for submission to a ballot vote of the whole of the members. In the National Union of Railwaymen, on the other hand, the Executive Committee possessed the power to declare a strike without reference either to the members or even to a Delegate Meeting. A Delegate Meeting has been in practice often called to deal with important issues ; but the ballot has practically never been employed. The Transport Workers' Federation was not a single Trade Union, but a federation of a large number of distinct Societies organizing different sections of transport workers or competing for members among the same sections. These Unions had many different rules and methods of procedure in dealing with important questions, and the taking of a ballot vote, which would commit the members to a final course of action, was not within the competence of the Transport Workers' Federation Executive, unless power to take this course was specifically conceded to it by the various affiliated Unions in accordance with their own constitutions.

When, therefore, the miners wished to incorporate in the

rules of the Triple Alliance a regulation that joint action should only be taken as a result of a ballot vote of the members of the three organizations, both the railwaymen and the transport workers objected that such methods of procedure would not suit their case. Clause 8 of the above Constitution represents the compromise arrived at. Each organization was placed under the obligation, before united action could be taken, of consulting its members ‘ by such methods as the constitution of each organization provides ’. In other words, the miners would have to call a Conference and take a ballot, whereas the railwaymen would not; and the transport workers would have to adopt procedure that would satisfy the different constitutions of their various component Unions.

It was clear from the first that the great industrial machine thus created would be exceedingly difficult to operate. The railwaymen urged the importance of rapid action because they realized that in such an industry as the railways a strike must be sudden, and sympathetic action by other sections must also be sudden if it is to be of use. In the mining industry rapidity of action matters far less; for the effects of a mining strike, while they may be as great in the long run as those of a railway strike, are far slower in making themselves felt. Moreover, it was realized that it would not be easy to provide for the simultaneous termination of agreements in the case of all three organizations. The miners had already found it difficult enough to secure anything like uniformity in the termination of the various district agreements in the coal-fields; and the co-ordination of railway and transport with mining agreements promised to be a far more difficult business. In fact, simultaneous action by each of the three bodies composing the Triple Alliance *on its own grievances* has never been realized, although eight years have passed since the Alliance was formed, and all the sections have been involved in numerous negotiations and important disputes since that date. Nor, despite frequent threats, has there been, at any time, a united strike of the Triple Alliance. At the time, however, when the Alliance was concluded, hopes of its effect in strengthening the organization of Labour ran high. The Miners' Federation was recognized to be by far the strongest Trade Union body in Great

Britain, and the National Union of Railwaymen, which had more than three hundred thousand members at the time when the Alliance was ratified, and rose subsequently to more than twice this membership, was also a very powerful unified organization, speaking for the great majority of the organized workers on the whole of the railways. So far as organization was concerned, the main weakness lay in the loose structure of the Transport Workers' Federation, and the small powers which the Federation possessed to bind the constituent Unions of which it was composed. This weakness, however, did not reveal itself clearly until the attempt was made to bring the machinery of the Alliance into action.

The basis of the Triple Alliance was from the first definitely industrial. By this is meant that each of the organizations composing it aimed at including within its ranks the whole of the workers employed in the industry with which it was concerned. In no case was this aim completely realized. Outside the ranks of the Miners' Federation, as we have seen, were numerous small associations of craftsmen, deputies, enginemen, &c., sometimes loosely federated on a district basis with the Miners' Associations, but as a rule wholly independent and competing for membership with the associations affiliated to the Miners' Federation. Outside the National Union of Railwaymen were the important Associated Society of Locomotive Engineers and Firemen, which embraced rather more than half the organized workers in the three locomotive grades of drivers, firemen, and cleaners, the remainder being in the National Union of Railwaymen; and the Railway Clerks' Association, which organized the clerical workers and certain of the supervisory grades. The workers in the locomotive and other workshops owned by the railways were also largely outside the National Union of Railwaymen, and the engineers and skilled men in these establishments were organized in such Unions as the Amalgamated Society of Engineers. The Transport Workers' Federation included the great majority of the Unions organizing transport workers other than railwaymen; but there was a number of small Associations outside it, and the degree of unity within the Federation itself was inadequate. Accordingly, it was from the first one of the instructions of the Alliance that each of the organizations within it should aim definitely at an effective control over the whole labour force of the industry in which it was concerned. Certain of the craft associations mentioned above, which found themselves excluded by the constitution of the Alliance from participation in it, made an effort early in its career to secure admission. The National Federation of Enginemen, which included both the Associated Society of Locomotive Engineers and Firemen and certain of the Unions of colliery enginemen, claimed admission to the Alliance as a separate body. Admission was, however, refused, the bodies connected with the Alliance taking the view that the basis of representation must be industrial, and that the right course for outside sections which desired admission was that of amalgamation with the appropriate constituent body of the Alliance itself.

It is interesting to note that the Miners' Federation made during the war period an effort to broaden its ranks by the inclusion of the grades of workers who were organized in separate Associations. In October 1916 the Federation Conference at Southport passed a resolution stating that all mine-workers must belong to the Miners' Federation. In view of the federal structure of the miners' organization, there was more than one possible method of achieving this object. One was to endeavour to break up the sectional Societies, and to transfer their members to the Miners' Associations. The other, which was actually adopted, was to admit these Societies, or certain of them, as constituent units of the Miners' Federation. Accordingly, negotiations were opened up with certain of the separate Societies of craftsmen, and in December 1916 the Executive of the Miners' Federation agreed in principle to the admission of the National Union of Cokemen and By-Product Workers, and of the National Federation of Colliery Enginemen as constituent units of the Federation, on the same basis as the district Miners' Associations. Admission was, however, refused to any Society the whole of whose members were not employed in the mines, and such Unions as the National Union of Enginemen, which enrolled members both in the mines and other industries such as the iron and steel industry, were therefore not regarded as eligible for affiliation.

The National Federation of Colliery Enginemen and the National Union of Cokemen both joined the Miners' Federation as ' districts ' during the war period. In 1921, after the unsuccessful mining strike of that year, the colliery enginemen decided to withdraw, having found their policy to be frequently in opposition to that of the Federation as a whole. At the same time, however, they determined to approach the Miners' Federation with a view to the conclusion of a working agreement between the two bodies.

No similar steps were taken by the National Union of Railwaymen to broaden its ranks, and the Associated Society of Locomotive Enginemen and Firemen and the Railway Clerks' Association alike remained, and remain up to the present moment, wholly independent. The former Society, however, when it had voted in favour of the principle of ' sympathetic ' strike action in support of the miners in 1921, was admitted to the Conferences of the Triple Alliance at which sympathetic action was first decided upon, and thereafter revoked on ' Black Friday '.

This account of the subsequent development of the Triple Alliance in respect of membership has involved a digression. We must now return to the time at which the Alliance was definitely formed at the end of 1915. The first full meeting of the newly constituted body was held in April 1916, for the purpose of formulating the general policy of the Alliance on after-war problems. A comprehensive plan was drawn up, and it was decided to submit this plan to the Government with a view to its official adoption. The deputation from the Alliance was not received by the Prime Minister, Mr. Asquith, until the 3rd August, when the scheme, which included a plan for demobilization not by military units, but by industries, and demands for the restoration of Trade Union conditions, and for full maintenance by the State of discharged soldiers, munition workers, and workers employed as substitutes during the War, was put forward in detail. The reply received was on the whole non-committal; but there is no doubt that the action taken by the Alliance had a considerable effect in influencing the Government plans in respect of demobilization.

I do not propose to discuss in detail the various measures which were taken by the Triple Alliance during the war period. From time to time Conferences were held and demands put forward, usually by the method of deputation to the Government.

For example, the Triple Alliance pressed throughout the war period for the increase of old age pensions to a more reasonable sum. It also took an active part in the successful opposition offered to the Government plan for the introduction of foreign, especially Chinese, labour in order to deal with the shortage of workers due to enlistment. It was active in pressing the Labour demands in respect of after-war policy upon the Government, and was recognized as one of the most influential organizations in the Labour world. The opportunity, however, for industrial action, or for the pressing forward of demands unitedly by the three bodies on questions relating directly to their own industrial concerns, did not arise until after the conclusion of the War. In June 1917 a full representative meeting of the three bodies forming the Alliance, representing over a million and a quarter of organized workers, formally ratified the provisional constitution of the Alliance, which thereafter remained unchanged.

Section 4. Absenteeism (1916) and Pit Committees

Reference has been made in the first section of this chapter to the serious problem created by the heavy enlistment of mine-workers. As the year advanced, this position became increasingly difficult; for, although fresh labour was being brought into the mines to fill up some at least of the gaps created by enlistment, it was impossible to fill adequately the places of the numerous skilled men who had joined the Forces. When the Derby Recruiting Scheme, the precursor of military conscription, was introduced in October 1915, and a general invitation to 'attest' was extended to all men of military age, whether they were engaged on indispensable work or not, the Miners' Federation at once took up with the Government the question of the civil rights of men who enrolled under the scheme. For at this stage, the fear that under cover of military conscription some form of industrial conscription, involving the carrying on of industry under a semi-military discipline, might be introduced, was widespread, and the miners were determined to make clear at the outset that they would not tolerate any attempt to interfere with the civil rights of men employed in the mining industry. On the 19th November 1915 an undertaking was secured from the Home Secretary, Sir John

Simon, that miners attesting under the Derby Scheme would retain their full civil rights. At the same time the necessity arose for preventing the enlistment of men whose work was indispensable to the maintenance of the output of coal, and Colliery Recruiting Courts, on a voluntary basis, were established.

On the 27th January 1916 the first Military Service Act became law, and conscription became applicable to all single men of the prescribed ages. The Colliery Recruiting Courts instituted under the Derby Scheme were then adapted to serve as special tribunals for the purpose of granting or withholding exemption on occupational grounds to men engaged in the mining industry, and this special procedure for dealing with colliery cases was maintained throughout the war period. Despite the restrictions imposed on enlistment, the figures compiled by the Coal Mining Organization Committee showed that, in March 1916, 282,000 miners had already enlisted.

The imposition of compulsory military service inevitably affected the situation in the mines, as in all other industries. The question of absenteeism was still leading to a good deal of friction; for, although the measures taken by the Miners' Federation had resulted in a decrease in the amount of absenteeism, they were still held to be insufficient, and, as soon as compulsory service came into force, the demand began to be made that men who were 'persistent absentees' should lose the protection offered to them by their occupation as miners. To this, for a long time, the Miners' Federation refused to agree. Further measures were, however, devised for the purpose of dealing with absenteeism. On the 16th May 1916 the Miners' Federation and the coal-owners agreed in principle to the establishment of Joint Absenteeism Committees on the lines recommended by the Coal Mining Organization Committee, and in June these Committees were established in a number of coal-fields, although not universally. In October 1916 the Lancashire and Cheshire Joint Absenteeism Committee decided to agree that exemption certificates should be withdrawn from persistent absentees; but this example was not generally followed, and the question continued to give rise to difficulties. The whole question of absenteeism was fully discussed at a second National Mining Conference, similar to the Conference of 1915, which has already been mentioned, convened by the Government at the end of October. The necessity for further measures to deal with absenteeism was strongly pressed upon the workers by the Government spokesmen, and the establishment in all areas of Pit Committees was strongly urged.

Partly as a means of preventing the extension of the practice of demanding the withdrawal of certificates of exemption in cases of absenteeism, the Miners' Federation, on the 22nd November 1916, agreed to accept the principle of fines for absenteeism, and on the 6th December endorsed a general scheme for the establishment of Pit Committees on lines suggested by the Coal Mining Organization Committee, and subsequently worked out in detail with representatives of the Government and the owners. The following is the scheme placed before and accepted by the National Conference of the Miners' Federation on the 6th December :

SUGGESTED RULES FOR THE GUIDANCE OF OUTPUT COMMITTEES

(Approved at Conference of Miners' Federation, 6 December 1916)

In order to increase the output of coal the following rules are recommended for adoption in each district of the Federation :

1. Where workmen are unable to work in their own working places such persons shall work in other places where there are vacancies, but they shall only be sent into places where men are regularly earning satisfactory wages. If no such places are available and the man in consequence has to go home, he shall not be returned to the Authorities as an Absentee on that day.

2. Men prevented from getting to their work at the proper time due to the workmen's train or car, or other conveyance, being late, shall on its arrival be allowed to go to work.

3. All deputations shall be held at such hours, whenever possible, as will cause no loss of time to the members of such deputations, or the men who appear before them.

4. All persons shall attend every day on which the pit is working unless prevented by illness or other reasonable cause.

5. That a District Committee be set up, consisting of an equal number of coal-owners and workmen's representatives.

If all members are not present, only an equal number shall vote on each side.

6. That the District Committee shall meet as agreed upon for the purpose of dealing with disputes which have arisen under the Local

Committee, and any other business, except in the event of urgent business, in which case a meeting may be called on the representation of either side to specially deal with the matter.

7. That a Local Committee shall be established at each colliery, consisting of an equal number of coal-owners and workmen's representatives to carry out these rules. If all members are not present, only an equal number shall vote on each side.

8. The Local Committee shall meet at least once a week, and the Management shall supply a 'Time List Sheet' showing the names of the men against whom there is a complaint, and the Local Committee shall decide upon whom they shall summon to the next meeting.

9. The men who are called upon to appear before the Committee shall have at least two days' notice given to appear. Failing to attend they will be dealt with in their absence, and the method of giving notice to attend shall be left to the Committee at each colliery.

Meetings are to take place so that men may attend without losing time.

10. The Local Committee shall be empowered to impose fines, and the persons so fined shall have the option of signing a book for such fine to be deducted or to be dealt with by the management, or appear before the magistrates.

(*a*) If the first method is selected by the workman and he attends and works full time for one month after the fine is inflicted, the fine to be returned to him.

(*b*) All fines not so redeemed to be paid over to some charitable institution to be selected by the Local Committee.

11. The Local Committee shall report all cases in dispute and all cases of men continuing to absent themselves to the District Committee.

12. Excuses for absence must be bona fide, and where an absentee claims he was away owing to illness, a doctor's note must be produced if demanded.

13. Any official responsible for the men losing work, or failing to do his best to get work for them, shall be reported to the Local Committee, who shall deal with him in a manner similar to the way in which a workman who regularly absents himself is dealt with, it being understood that so far as possible the men shall be found work when they present themselves at the pit.

Meanwhile another difficulty had arisen and been settled. In order to meet the shortage of labour and enable more men to be released for military service, especially in the tunnelling sections in the Army, which had to undertake dangerous work such as only skilled mine-workers could efficiently perform, disabled men, and men unfit for further military service, were being returned from the Army to the industry. At first, the certificates of release from active military service and transfer to the Reserve issued to these men were conditional on their working in one particular mine, and the men were not free like other workers to move from place to place or to choose their employers within the industry. The Miners' Federation regarded this action of the military authorities as a violation of the pledges by the Government that no form of industrial conscription would be introduced, and a declaration was finally secured from the Home Office that 'a miner returned from the Army and placed in Army Reserve Class B, is, in all respects of employment, in the same position as a miner in civil life, and is at liberty to move from one particular colliery to any other colliery in the United Kingdom, provided he notifies the military of the change. He is also in the same position as the civilian miner as regards lost time' (i.e. he cannot be recalled to the Forces on account of absenteeism unless his recall is specifically authorized by the Colliery Recruiting Court).

Section 5. Labour Troubles in South Wales

The year 1916 was one of calm in most of the coal-fields of Great Britain; but in South Wales it was a time of constant unrest, and on several occasions serious industrial conflicts, extending over the whole of the South Wales coal-field, appeared to be imminent. This was a matter of grave national concern; for the South Wales coal-field was the main source of supplies both for the Navy and for the British Mercantile Marine, and it was of course indispensable, from the standpoint of the Government, that both these services should be maintained during the War without even a brief interruption of regular supplies.

On the 1st February 1916 an adjustment of wages fell due under the Conciliation Board Agreement arrived at during the previous year at the end of the serious dispute which has already been described in this study. The South Wales Miners' Federation applied to the Board for a wage advance of 5 per cent., while the coal-owners counterclaimed for a wage reduction of 3¾ per cent. Both these claims were professedly based on the economic circumstances which the Board, according to its constitution, was directed to take into account; but, whereas the miners held that the advance which they claimed was due to them on account of the rise in the selling-price of coal, the owners maintained that a reduction was due because, although coal prices had increased, costs of production had risen more than proportionately to the increase. According to the constitution of the Conciliation Board, attention was directed to the selling-price of coal as the main, but not necessarily the exclusive, factor determining wage rates; but in previous ascertainments wages had been based as a rule, practically without question, on the ascertained selling-price. On the 7th February Lord Muir Mackenzie assumed office as impartial Chairman to the South Wales Coal Conciliation Board, in succession to Viscount St. Aldwyn, who had resigned, and on the failure of the two sides of the Board to agree on the question of wages, the task fell to him to adjudicate between the claims put forward. His decision, given on the 21st February, was a rejection both of the owners' and of the miners' claims. The effect of this decision was that wages would remain at the existing level for a further period of three months.

Meanwhile other causes of dispute were accumulating in the coal-field. One of the most serious of these was the difficulty arising over the position of 'non-unionists', a term which was used to embrace both men who refused to join the Federation and those who, while they had been members of the Federation, were seriously in arrears with their contributions, and refused to make themselves clear on the books. On the 27th February 1916 the miners in the Merthyr and Dowlais areas threatened a strike unless the non-Unionists were removed or joined the Federation, and by the 8th March the trouble had spread to a number of other districts within the South Wales coal-field. On this day Sir George Askwith undertook the task of mediation between the owners and the miners, and on the 16th March a settlement was arrived at under his auspices by which the owners agreed, without prejudice to their action after the War, to make membership of one of the recognized Unions of colliery workers a condition of employment for the war period. The agreement in which this concession was embodied was not finally signed until the 18th April 1916, but the provisional agreement of the 16th March settled the difficulty.

Certain other questions in dispute were not so easily dealt with. The settlement arrived at under the auspices of Mr. Lloyd George in 1915 was by no means free from ambiguities, and over several matters arising out of it a complete deadlock was reached between the owners and the South Wales Miners' Federation. The chief question at issue was the rate at which payment should be made for the Sunday night shift. This, it was held by the men, was an optional shift, and should, where it was worked, consist of six hours only, and any time worked beyond six hours should be paid for as overtime. The owners, on the other hand, insisted that the shift was compulsory, and that the full hours must be worked without overtime payment. A crisis developed when the workmen at the Albion Colliery refused to work the shift unless they received overtime payment for more than six hours. The coal-owners took the case into court, and the stipendiary magistrate found against the workmen, who were therefore compelled to work the full eight hours without overtime payment. The miners contended that under the agreement of 1915 they had a right to the basis of payment which they had put forward. Less vital but still important points of difference as to the interpretation of the 1915 agreement referred to the bonus to be paid to ostlers and the rate of pay for the craft workers on the surface of the pits. By the 21st March these grievances had assumed serious proportions, and a strike was threatened. The South Wales Miners' Federation approached Mr. Runciman, the draftsman of the 1915 agreement, and asked him to interpret the meaning of the agreement on the disputed points. Mr. Runciman at first refused to intervene; but on the 23rd March he agreed to nominate a conciliator, and on the following day Judge O'Connor was appointed to act in this capacity. But, before his decision could be given, a far more serious crisis had developed over the question of wages.

On the 1st May a further readjustment of wages became due, and once more both parties made applications to the Conciliation Board. The miners this time demanded a wage advance of 15 per cent., while the owners counterclaimed for a reduction of 7½ per cent. Once more the parties on the Conciliation Board failed to agree, and Lord Muir Mackenzie had to be called in. But, before any meeting of the Board with Lord Muir Mackenzie could be held, he made the fatal mistake of addressing to both owners and miners a letter, setting forth his view as to the proper basis for calculating the disputed wage. The South Wales Miners' Federation immediately issued a protest against this action of the impartial Chairman in pre-judging the issue before the two sides had had the opportunity of stating their cases before him. This protest was followed on the 25th May by Lord Muir Mackenzie's resignation from the chairmanship of the Board, and at the same date the South Wales Miners' Executive met Mr. Runciman and informed him that unless the wage advance of 15 per cent. were granted a strike of the whole coal-field would take place. Government intervention was thus rendered inevitable, and on the 27th May Sir George Askwith was entrusted with the task of settling the dispute. He at once proceeded to South Wales, and there held prolonged meetings with both sides. He then made his report to the Government, which on the 2nd June granted to the miners the increase of 15 per cent. which they had demanded. The owners immediately issued strong protests against this action, and at first declared their intention of refusing to pay the advance; but on the 5th June they withdrew from this attitude and agreed to pay the revised wages under protest. On the 19th June Judge O'Connor issued his award on the matters which had been referred to him on the 24th March. His conclusions were, on the whole, favourable to the miners, whose contention concerning the payment to be made for the Sunday night shift was granted, although the rates awarded for surface craftsmen were lower than those demanded by the South Wales Miners' Federation.

One of the grounds alleged by the coal-owners in their protest against the concession of the wages demanded by the miners was that the latter had broken the Conciliation Board Agreement by refusing to agree to the appointment of an impartial Chairman in succession to Lord Muir Mackenzie until their wage demand had been complied with, or to refer the question of wages to the Chairman in accordance with the constitution of the Board. The miners' reply to this had been that it was useless to agree to arbitrate in view of the difference which existed as to the interpretation of the Conciliation Board Agreement itself; but, after the concession of the 15 per cent. advance, they agreed that a new

Chairman should be appointed, and after the two sides had failed to find a nomination by mutual consent, Lord Justice Pickford was appointed impartial Chairman on the nomination of the Lord Chief Justice in accordance with the rules of the Conciliation Board.

On the 1st August a further revision of wages became due. Once more, both owners and miners submitted competing claims. The miners demanded an increase of 12½ per cent. and the owners a reduction of 15 per cent., that is to say, the removal of the actual advance which had just, a short time before, been granted. Lord Justice Pickford, on the 31st August, followed the ill-starred example of his predecessor and rejected both claims. This led to a considerable turmoil in the coal-field, and on the 16th October the South Wales Miners' Federation definitely decided to put forward a demand that the books of the owners should be jointly audited on behalf of both parties, with a view to the ascertainment of selling prices and costs of production. This demand the South Wales coal-owners rejected on the 16th October.

On the 1st November rival claims for a wage revision from both owners and miners were once more submitted to the Conciliation Board. This time the miners demanded an increase of 15 per cent., and the owners a decrease of 10 per cent. The miners, moreover, coupled with their demand a claim for a joint audit of the owners' books, to which the latter refused to agree. On the 10th November the Conciliation Board made an effort to arrive at a settlement. The miners this time refused to allow the matter to go to the impartial Chairman and decided to approach the Government directly with their double claim. Strike action was threatened in the event of a failure to concede the advance demanded, and for the next three weeks the coal-field was in a ferment, although no stoppage actually took place.

Meanwhile a great controversy raged in the press. The refusal of the owners to agree to a joint audit of their books had set public opinion largely against them, and *The Times* in particular was vehement in its denunciation of their attitude. On the 23rd November the South Wales Coal-Owners' Association issued an announcement that it would be prepared to allow the owners' books to be audited by an independent auditor, but that it still refused the claim for a joint audit. The right of the miners to a direct participation in an ascertainment of the selling-prices on which their wages depended was thus still repudiated, and on the 24th November the miners met the Government and informed them that, failing an immediate settlement, a general stoppage in the coal-field was inevitable. Negotiations were protracted for some days longer; but on the 29th November, on the eve of the threatened stoppage, the Government issued an order, under the Defence of the Realm Act, taking over the South Wales coal-field and establishing a system of State control. At the same time a telegram, which became celebrated in the subsequent controversy, was sent by the Government to the South Wales coal-owners instructing them to 'carry on as usual'. This was almost the last act of the Asquith Government, which fell from power a few days later.

The South Wales miners at first protested against the Government's action in controlling the coal-field, not on the ground of any objection to State control, but on the ground that such a measure ought to be national and ought not to be applied to one particular coal-field while it was not applied to others. Soon, however, it became known that the new Lloyd George Government intended to apply control to the whole of the coal-fields of Great Britain, and in these circumstances the position was accepted. The negotiations concerning the new situation thus created became a matter for the Miners' Federation of Great Britain as a whole rather than for the South Wales Federation. Almost the first action of the Government on assuming control in South Wales was to grant the advance of 15 per cent. claimed by the miners and thus restore industrial peace.

The whole story of the South Wales troubles up to 1916 is inevitably perplexing to the outsider; for clearly everything turns on the question whether the miners were or were not justified in claiming the advances which they ultimately secured. The fact that on both the occasions on which matters came to a head these advances were granted by the Government after a full investigation of the position seems to indicate that the miners were in the right, although, of course, the necessity for maintaining an uninterrupted supply of steam coal for war purposes must have influenced the Government and made it anxious above all else to avert a stoppage. There is, moreover, no doubt at all that during the period under review the South Wales coal-owners were making very high profits, and it will hardly be claimed that their attempts to reduce wages in face both of rising coal prices and of the steadily increasing cost of living could be justified. To some extent these claims for reductions were of course intended mainly to prevent the concession of the miners' claims for wage advances; but this can hardly be held to justify the attitude adopted by the owners, which almost the whole of the press was united, in November 1916, in regarding as unreasonable. The South Wales miners are admittedly not easy people to deal with, and it is probable that the trouble was accentuated by a good deal of pig-headedness on both sides. This seems to be evidenced by the fact that in the other coal-fields of the country adjustments of wages were made with comparatively little difficulty during the very period when the South Wales coal-field was in a state of permanent unrest. Thus, during the year 1916, wages in the Durham coal-field rose from 75 per cent. to 107½ per cent. on the standard of 1879. In the Federated Area they rose from 27 per cent. in December 1915 to 40 per cent. in October 1916 on the standard of 1911. In Scotland they rose from 118 per cent. to 150 per cent. on the standard of 1888. All these changes were made without any stoppage of work, or serious threat of stoppage. These facts seem to indicate that there was a marked difference in the attitude of the owners in South Wales and in the other coal-fields, and that the advance from 88 per cent. to 133 per cent. on the South Wales standard of 1915 was not unjustified.

CHAPTER III

THE MINES UNDER STATE CONTROL IN WAR TIME

Section 1. State Control.
,, 2. Military Service.
,, 3. Wages and Hours.

SECTION 1. STATE CONTROL

THE Government assumed control of the railway service immediately upon the outbreak of war, and this control inevitably gave it a considerable measure of authority over coal distribution, and thereby, indirectly, over the coal industry. This intervention tended to increase during the year 1915, when it was at first exercised through the Railway Department of the Board of Trade. In the summer of 1915, as we have seen, further steps towards control became necessary. In May the Coal Exports Committee was formed to exercise authority over the export trade, and was given powers for the prevention of export of coal required at home, and for the securing of supplies to Allied countries. Its work soon came to include the regulation of export prices for the various classes of coal. In July 1915, as we have seen, the pit-head price of coal was regulated by the Price of Coal (Limitation) Act. Out of this Act arose the voluntary arrangements made in the autumn of 1915 with the various sections of the coal distributors, under which the merchants agreed to voluntary limitations of profits. In the London area these arrangements were made directly by the Government, while in the provinces they were, in many cases, carried through by the local authorities. No compulsory regulation of retail coal prices was, however, introduced. In December 1915 a further step towards control was taken by the formation of the Central Coal and Coke Supplies Committee, and of a number of district Committees nominated by the various Coal-owners' Associations. These bodies, which undertook important duties in ensuring the supply of coal in accordance with national requirements, were at first voluntary; but before long compulsory powers were found to be necessary, and in June 1916 Defence of the Realm Regulation 2 D empowered the Government to issue orders as to priority of coal supplies. About this time the Cabinet set up a special Committee, under the chairmanship of Lord Milner, for the purpose of co-ordinating the various official bodies dealing with the coal industry on its productive and distributive sides. This was the position when the troubles in South Wales, which have already been dealt with, precipitated the assumption of direct State control over the South Wales coal-field on the 29th November 1916. Control in South Wales was assumed by the Asquith Government; but a few days later, on the 5th December, the political crisis culminated in Mr. Asquith's resignation, and on the 7th December Mr. Lloyd George became Prime Minister. In the course of his negotiations with the Labour bodies on his assumption of office, Mr. Lloyd George undertook that the State should immediately assume control of the whole of the coal-fields, couching his undertaking in terms which many of the Labour representatives interpreted as an assurance that actual nationalization of the industry would take place.

It was clear that, both in South Wales and in other coal-fields, the position of the workmen might be considerably affected by the assumption of control by the Government. The Miners' Federation accordingly lost no time in asking for a meeting with the new Prime Minister for the purpose of discussing the situation with him, and of ascertaining what was likely to be the effect of control on the position of the operatives. The points on which the miners specially desired enlightenment were, first, the question whether the civil rights and freedom of labour would be interfered with by the State's assumption of control in the same way as they had been interfered with in the engineering and kindred industries by the Munitions of War Acts; and, in the second place, what would be the effect of control on the future course of wages. Would the method of varying wages under the existing agreements through the Conciliation Boards in the different coal-fields still continue in force, or would the State itself assume control of wage regulation?

On the 21st December the Executive of the Miners' Federation met Mr. Lloyd George and discussed these matters with him. He made it clear that the form of control contemplated in the coal-mines was based rather on that which was already in operation on the railways than on the system in the munitions industries, and that the aim was rather to control the output of coal than to make any alteration in the methods of colliery management as they affected labour. The miners, he said, could therefore be assured that no interference with their civil rights, and no machinery similar to the Tribunals set up under the Munitions Acts, was contemplated. On the question of wages the Prime Minister gave an assurance that wages would not be reduced unless the cost of living fell, even if Government regulation of the trade resulted in a fall of coal prices, which under normal procedure of the Conciliation Board would carry with it a reduction in wage rates. He further gave a pledge that in any case no reduction of wages would take place without previous consultation with the miners' representatives.

From the 29th November 1916 until February 1917 the South Wales coal-field, which was alone under control, was supervised by an inter-departmental Committee consisting of representatives from the Home Office, the Admiralty, and the Board of Trade. On the 14th February, however, it was announced that a new Department, to be called the Mines Department, would be established under the Board of Trade, and that a Coal Controller would be appointed to take charge of it. The duties of the various bodies dealing with the coal industry were for the most part to be transferred to the new Department; but the Mines Inspection Department was to remain under the Home Office. On the 22nd February the preliminary arrangements were completed. The whole of the coal-fields were taken over under the Defence of the Realm Act, and Sir Guy Calthrop officially entered upon his duties as Coal Controller at the Mines Department.

On the 27th of the same month the Miners' Federation Executive met Sir Albert Stanley, President of the Board of Trade, and Sir Guy Calthrop, in order to discuss with them the position in which the miners would be placed by the imposition of control. Security of miners' civil rights was again affirmed, and on the question of wages the reassuring answer previously given by the

Prime Minister was repeated, and the details were left to be decided subsequently.

It was also made clear at this meeting that the Coal Controller desired to work with an Advisory Committee, representing the coal-owners and the miners, and that this body would take over the functions previously exercised by the Coal Mining Organization Committee, to which reference has already been made. Early in March this Advisory Committee was appointed, and it was thereafter consulted from time to time by the Coal Controller on matters of policy. It never attained, however, to great importance; for the majority of questions were raised with the Controller separately, either by the Miners' Federation of Great Britain or by the Mining Association on behalf of the coal-owners.

Up to this time, although the State had definitely assumed control of the mines, the terms of control, so far as they affected the owners, had not been defined, and in particular, the financial basis of the new arrangement and its effects on coal profits remained to be settled. The war years had been years of extraordinary prosperity for the coal-owners, and exceedingly high dividends had been realized. This was the more significant in that the years immediately preceding the War had been the most prosperous in the whole history of the coal trade; but the profits of these pre-war years were largely surpassed by those of 1915 and 1916.

Early in March 1917 the Mining Association of Great Britain, acting on behalf of the coal-owners, appointed a special Consultative Committee to negotiate with the Coal Controller and the Government concerning the financial terms under which control was to be exercised. Meanwhile, a provisional arrangement was instituted whereby the Colliery Companies should continue to pay dividends to their shareholders, but that these dividends should be paid only subject to the sanction of the Controller. The negotiations between the coal-owners and the Mines Department were protracted, and it was not until the 12th June that a provisional agreement was arrived at between the Consultative Committee of the coal-owners and the Department. This agreement was then sent out confidentially to all chairmen of Colliery Companies, with a recommendation from the coal-owners' Committee that it should be accepted without amendment. Considerable opposition, however, was offered to some of the terms by the Colliery Companies; and, in face of this opposition, modifications in the interests of the coal-owners were made in the scheme, which was then signed on the 20th July by the Government representatives and the Chairman and Secretary of the coal-owners' Consultative Committee. It was intended at this stage that this agreement, similar in form to the agreement under which the railways were controlled, should be allowed to stand by itself without further legislation, the Controller and the Law Officers taking the view that the powers under the Defence of the Realm Act were adequate to give force to the agreement without direct legislative sanction; but despite the fact that the agreement had been made and ratified by a fully representative Committee of the coal-owners, a number of the leading owners refused to accept it, and took legal opinion as to its validity. They were assured by their legal advisers that it could not be valid without direct legislative sanction, and that they would therefore be within their rights in resisting the attempts of the Government to limit profits under it. In these circumstances the Government thought it best to secure legal sanction for the agreement, and in October 1917 it was announced that a Bill, based upon the agreement, would be introduced into Parliament at once. The recalcitrant coal-owners rapidly mobilized their forces in opposition to this Bill, and on the 8th November the Second Reading was talked out in the House. Further discussions then took place, and on the 12th November the Second Reading was carried without a division being challenged by the recalcitrants. On the Committee stage, however, an important amendment was introduced, limiting the operation of the agreement to coal-mines, and thereby excluding subsidiary undertakings, such as coke-ovens and blast-furnaces carried on in conjunction with coal-mines. This had an important effect on the financial results of the measure; for very high profits were made during the remainder of the control period on the working of these subsidiary enterprises, and these profits were retained by the coal-owners in addition to the standard profits under the Act.

With this and other amendments, the Coal Mines Agreement

Confirmation Act was finally passed into law on the 6th February 1918. It contained a provision under which it was to come automatically to an end six months after the 'conclusion of the War', a phrase which was interpreted, in this as in many other cases, to mean not the conclusion of hostilities, but a date, to be fixed by Order in Council, subsequent to the actual signing of the treaties of peace. Broadly speaking, the agreement between the coal-owners and the Government embodied in the Coal Mines Agreement Confirmation Act was based on the following principles. For the purpose of the Excess Profits Tax, arrangements had already been made for the calculation of excess profits on the basis of the standard pre-war profits of the various colliery concerns. This standard was based on the best two out of three or the best four out of six pre-war years—an arrangement which, owing to the abnormal prosperity of the coal trade before the War, worked out very favourably to the coal-owners. Of excess profits upon this standard the Government took 80 per cent. in Excess Profits Duty and the owners retained the balance of 20 per cent. Under the Coal Mines Agreement this system was retained as a basis, but adapted to the changed conditions. The standard profits remained the same, except that a relation was established between the standard and the tonnage output of each concern, and, if the output fell below the average pre-war output, a deduction less than proportionate to the fall in output was made from the standard profits. This reduced standard was, however, not merely allowed to be retained by the coal-owners, but actually guaranteed to them. In return for this concession, and in order that the cost might fall not upon the Treasury but upon the industry itself, 15 per cent. out of the 20 per cent. of excess profits retainable under the Finance Act was to be paid into a special fund, which was to be used in making up the guaranteed profits of the concerns which failed to reach the standard and in meeting the administrative expenses of the Coal Controller's Department. The profits retained by any concern were not in any case to exceed six-fifths of the standard profit. Provision was also made for special allocations to the colliery concerns to meet arrears of maintenance and development accumulated during the war period. Reference to the table contained in Appendix A will show the actual effect of these measures on profits in the coal industry during the period of control.

It is not intended in this study to deal with the effects of control on the coal trade as a whole or to give an account of the various measures for the control of distribution and prices which were developed under the auspices of the Mines Department. A new scheme of coal distribution was introduced on the 20th July with the object of shortening railway mileage and promoting the use of coal as near as possible to the place at which it was mined. In September 1917 a direct system of fixed retail prices was introduced under the Coal Prices Order of that month. Thereafter the system was gradually developed during the latter part of the War, more rigid control becoming necessary as, with the enlistment of miners in 1917 and 1918, the problem of coal output became more serious.

Section 2. Military Service

Up to the end of 1916, although there had been occasional friction between the miners and the military authorities arising out of such matters as the civil rights of soldiers returned to the pits, the wrongful calling up of some exempted man, and so on, the imposition of compulsory military service had exercised, on the whole, very little effect on the mining industry. Indeed, the official policy had been that of preventing the enlistment of miners, and of maintaining the depleted labour forces of the industry in order to secure a greater output of coal.

From the beginning of 1917 the position was gradually changing. The increasingly urgent demands of the military authorities were compelling the Government to make further inroads on the man-power even of essential industries, and the process of 'combing-out' these industries was being taken seriously in hand. The places of the miners who had enlisted had been taken, to some extent, by substitutes who had entered the mining industry for the first time; and undoubtedly some of these substitutes had come to the mines as a refuge from military service. It was partly against these men, and partly against men accused of persistent absenteeism, that the attack was at first directed. Attempts had already been made to get the Colliery

Recruiting Courts to agree to the withdrawal of exemption certificates from men who had a bad record of absenteeism, and in October 1916 the Lancashire and Cheshire Miners' Federation had agreed to this course.

At the beginning of 1917 the Government announced the immediate taking of further measures. On the 24th January a statement was issued that all unskilled surface workers and men who had entered the mines since August 1915 were to be medically examined, and those fit for general service released for the Army. Military representatives were also instructed to bring up cases of persistent absenteeism before the Colliery Recruiting Courts. Action was immediately taken on this order. Travelling Medical Boards began their work, and calling-up papers began to be issued.

These measures at once led to trouble, especially in South Wales. The Miners' Federation lost no time in taking the whole question up with the Government. On the 2nd February the Home Office agreed that the Order relating to military appeals against the absentees should not be retrospective in its operation, and that only future absenteeism should be taken into account. This concession was regarded as inadequate in a number of districts; and, especially in South Wales, the agitation against the Government scheme continued unabated.

In these circumstances further negotiations were held between the Miners' Federation and the Home Office and the military authorities. At length, on the 8th March, the War Office agreed to suspend all the calling-up notices which had been issued to miners, but had not taken effect, as at this time a period of two months' grace was allowed under the Military Service Acts. Instead of the compulsory operation of these Acts, an appeal for volunteers was to be made, with the support of those miners' leaders who were prepared to co-operate in recruiting; and by this means an attempt was to be made to secure the 20,000 recruits from the mining industry demanded by the Man-Power Distribution Board. Two months were to be allowed for the securing of these recruits; but, if they had not been secured at the end of this period, it was understood that the calling-up notices suspended for the duration of the arrangement would come into force.

Unfortunately, before the two months were up, the Government considered it necessary to make a further demand upon the man-power of the mining industry. On the 4th April the Miners' Executive met the Coal Controller and General Sir William Robertson, and had placed before them a demand for a further 20,000 men. On the 16th April the South Wales Miners' Federation announced its intention of resisting this comb-out; but on the 20th April the Executive of the M.F.G.B. agreed to support the combing-out of men who had entered the industry during the war period. Finally, on the 20th June, this attitude was endorsed by a National Miners' Conference, and for the time the crisis ended.

It was not long before the trouble was renewed. Failing to secure the numbers anticipated for the Army by the methods adopted in the spring, the Government in August came forward with a proposal that the exemptions of men between 18 and 25 years of age should be withdrawn in sufficient numbers to make up the quota of recruits demanded from the industry. This proposal met with very strong opposition; and, on the 7th September, a National Miners' Conference demanded that before any regular miners were recruited, a clean sweep should be made of all the men who had entered the industry since the outbreak of war.

Matters thus reached a deadlock between the Government and the miners' representatives. Early in October the Government brought forward a National Service Scheme designed to secure an easier transference of labour in the mining industry. This led to further trouble, and, on its definite rejection by the Miners' Federation at the beginning of November, it was dropped. Meanwhile the attempted comb-out of the miners had been resulting in further friction in the South Wales coal-field. Sporadic strike action against the taking of men for the Army occurred in various districts, and a general strike of the South Wales coal-field was threatened. Strong pressure was, however, brought to bear against a strike both by the South Wales officials and by the Miners' Federation of Great Britain, and on the 11th November the strike policy was finally rejected. The situation, however, was still very threatening; and it was clear that, if the Government attempted to put its policy of combing-out the younger miners into force, without previously removing more completely the men who had entered the industry during the war period, serious stoppages would become inevitable. Accordingly, on the 22nd November, the Government agreed to accept the miners' terms, and, before taking the younger pre-war miners for the Army, to remove all possible men who had entered the industry since the outbreak of war.

For the moment this put an end to the crisis. But the military situation was already compelling the recruiting authorities to make further demands upon the industry. On the 8th January 1918 Sir Auckland Geddes met the Miners' Federation with a further and far more drastic demand for the release of men for the Army. This time the demand was that 50,000 men should be immediately released for the Army, and that a further 50,000 should be held in reserve, to be released as the occasion arose. These demands at once created an acute situation. The Miners' National Conference, which met to consider them on the 31st January, reached no decision, and was adjourned until the 27th February in order to enable further consultation to take place both between the Miners' Federation and the Government and between the delegates and the rank and file of the miners in the various coal-fields. When the Conference reassembled on the 27th February, a solution seemed to be no nearer ; but at this meeting it was agreed to take a national ballot of the whole membership of the Federation, on the questions whether the proposed comb-out should be accepted, and whether the machinery of the Miners' Federation should be employed in order to secure the necessary men. The Government, however, was already tired of waiting, and on the 8th March it was announced that the Ministry of National Service proposed to proceed with the comb-out without waiting for the result of the ballot which the miners were then taking. This decision was followed by widespread threats of strike action, in the midst of which the ballot proceeded. The National Conference met again on the 20th March, and had before it the figures of the ballot vote, which had resulted in the rejection of the proposed comb-out by a small majority (219,000 in favour of acceptance, and 248,000 against). Faced with this acute division of opinion, the Conference decided to approach the Government and to endeavour to secure some modifications in the demand for men. Representatives of the miners accordingly met the Prime Minister and Sir Auckland Geddes on the following day; but no modifications of the terms could be secured, and the Conference, when it reassembled on the 22nd March, had accordingly before it only two alternatives—strike action, or the acceptance of the comb-out. In view of the smallness of the majority against acceptance of the terms, the Conference decided not to resist the comb-out, which was therefore put into effect so far as the first 50,000 men demanded for the Army were concerned.

In May a further demand was brought forward, and the National Service Department asked for the release of the second 50,000 men, who had been held in reserve under the demand originally put forward in January. Negotiations followed; and, as a result of these, it became clear even to the military authorities that it was impossible to take from the industry anything like the number of men contemplated in the scheme. In June, therefore, the additional number to be taken was limited to 25,000, and it was explicitly laid down that 25,000 miners already with the Forces should be returned to the industry at the earliest possible moment. These would, of course, be men who, by reason of wounds or physique, were not of first-class military value, and it was certain that these disabilities would also to some extent affect their value to the industry.

In the negotiations of May 1918 it had already become clear that the limit of military recruiting in the mining industry had been reached, and that further men could not be taken from the industry without fatally impairing its productive power and disabling it for the production of the quantities of coal which were essential for the minimum national requirements. During the remaining months of 1918 the emphasis rapidly shifted from the recruitment of miners to efforts to bring back to the industry as many men as the military authorities could be induced to spare. The menace of declining production had become so serious as to outweigh the military demand, which had become less urgent with the appearance of larger American forces in Europe. There was, therefore, no further crisis over the question of military service. Many complaints were made of the slowness with which the military authorities carried out their promise to release men for work in the mines, and towards the end of the year the process of release was noticeably speeded up as a result of these protests. Immediately after the declaration of the Armistice, special steps were taken to release, in advance of general demobilization, as many as possible of the experienced miners who were with the Forces, in order that no time might be lost in improving output with a view to the re-establishment of the export trade in coal.

Section 3. Wages and Hours

The imposition of Government control on the mining industry gave to the miners what they had previously failed to secure—the regulation of wages on a uniform national basis. From 1917 until the removal of control in 1921 the variations in mining wage rates were made nationally, and the normal machinery of wage regulation, already seriously strained by the events of 1915 and 1916, was in abeyance. It was not, indeed, at once perceived that this would be the effect of State control; and, when the miners' representatives met Mr. Lloyd George in December 1916 in order to discuss this question, their chief concern was lest control should prevent the concession of further district advances by the Conciliation Boards, in face of the rising cost of living and other factors making for higher wages.

Before long, however, it was realized that the imposition of Government control over the whole of the coal-fields had removed, for the time being, the strongest argument against the granting of advances on a national basis. The owners had maintained that this was out of the question—and Mr. Asquith had supported them in 1915—because of the varying financial circumstances of the different districts. But Government control, carrying with it the institution of a profits pool and a unified financial supervision, swept this argument aside, and left the way clear for the opposite contention, accepted almost at the same time for the regulation of wages in the munitions industries, that claims based practically on a uniform ground—the cost of living—in all parts of the country would be most reasonably met by uniform advances on a national basis.

It was not until July 1917 that the question was forced to the front. From the 24th to the 28th July the Miners' Federation was holding its Annual Conference. Besides passing a unanimous vote in favour of State ownership and control of the mining industry, and carrying once more a resolution in favour of the abolition of piece-work, the delegates, acting on instructions from the district Miners' Associations, formulated a demand for a national war bonus of 25 per cent. on earnings at the date of the application.

This demand was the result of strong pressure from certain of the districts, and was held by many of the miners to be long overdue. Already in July there was widespread impatience; for the cost of living, although it had been held temporarily in check by the new measures adopted early in 1917, was still rising sharply. Unfortunately, the negotiations arising out of the miners' demand were protracted, and it was not until about the end of August that the first full meeting was held between the Miners' Federation and the President of the Board of Trade. Further meetings took place early in September; but for some time the Government refused to agree to an advance on a national basis. However, on the 11th September, the Coal Controller was at last empowered to offer an advance of 1*s*. per day to adult miners and of 6*d*. to juniors; and, on the 23rd September, the offer was increased to one of 1*s*. 3*d*. per shift, subject to the condition that it should be liable to reduction in conjunction with any decrease in coal prices or in the cost of living.

This offer was rejected by the Miners' National Conference on the 26th September; but already the miners had agreed to substantial modifications of their original claims. On the 18th September their Conference had agreed that any advance conceded should be on a 'flat rate' basis, instead of the percentage basis which they had at first proposed. This principle of 'flat rate' advances, already accepted in the munitions trades and in other instances, meant, of course, that the grades of workers whose rates were lowest benefited more than they would have done under a percentage system, and that the real difference between their earnings and those of the more highly skilled grades was lessened. The acceptance of the principle by the miners, in place of the system of percentage advances which was firmly established in the industry by custom, was therefore a change of considerable importance.

On the 18th September, moreover, the miners offered to accept an advance of 1*s*. 8*d*. per day, in place of the 1*s*. then being offered by the Government. At last, on the 28th September, the dispute was settled by the acceptance of an offer of 1*s*. 6*d*. per day for adults and 9*d*. per day for juniors. This was the first 'war wage' advance conceded by the Government during the period of control. It was negotiated without any serious stoppage of work; for, although unrest was widespread and the negotiations extended over a long period and passed through several critical phases, the only district in which there was any general suspension of work was the tiny coal-field of South Staffordshire, where the men struck without official sanction, but returned to work on the 23rd September on the advice of the Miners' Federation.

No further wage claim was put forward by the miners until the middle of 1918. A National Conference then met on the 5th June, and decided to place before the Government immediately a demand for a further advance. This time the 'flat rate' principle accepted in 1917 was made the basis of the application, and the demand was for an increase of 1*s*. 6*d*. per day in the amount of the war wage. Negotiations with the Coal Controller resulted in an offer of 6*d*. per day, made on the 27th July; but on the following day, in face of a serious crisis, the Government conceded the full demand of 1*s*. 6*d*., making the concession conditional on agreement to extend the system of Pit Committees throughout the coal-fields, with a view to the greatest possible output and the elimination of local friction. To this condition the Miners' Conference agreed.

Wages remained at the point thus reached until after the conclusion of hostilities. The 'war wage' of 3*s*. a day was payable throughout the whole of the coal-fields over and above the varying district advances conceded up to 1917. Moreover, under special conditions agreed to by the Government, this war wage was paid for a full week even where, owing to circumstances outside his control, such as a breakdown of transport from the pit-head, or a shortage of tubs, a miner was not actually able to work the full customary number of shifts. It was also payable when work was suspended owing to the operation of any Order or regulation of the Coal Controller. The 'war wage' thus served the additional purpose of providing a sort of under-employment pay, and of giving to the miner a small assured income not dependent on day-to-day industrial uncertainties. As we shall see, the miners, on the termination of control, were keenly desirous of retaining in some form this assured minimum payment, which was nevertheless swept away, with the rest of the gains of the war period, after the calamitous struggle of 1921.

It is significant that, from the beginning of 1917 to the end of 1918, that is, during the whole period of actual war-time State control, there was no really considerable stoppage of work in the coal-mines. There were inevitably a number of small disputes; and several times there were 'crises', in the newspaper sense of the word, involving the whole industry. All these larger issues, however, were dealt with without serious interruptions of work. The most serious, apart from the two 'war wage' crises of 1917 and 1918, was the trouble about the hours and conditions of surface workers, which arose in South Wales during the autumn of 1918. This dispute entered upon an acute stage in October, when a deadlock was reached between the South Wales owners and miners. The latter desired to establish a uniform maximum working day of eight and a half hours for surface workers, who were excluded from the provisions of the Eight Hours Act; but to this the owners would not agree. The Government was forced to step in: it offered the concession of a working day of eight and a half hours, to be made six months after the conclusion of peace. On the 7th November, a Miners' Conference rejected this offer, and decided to take a ballot on the question whether surface workers should be instructed to stop work after eight and a half hours, without waiting for the consent of the coal-owners. This threat, however, did not have to be carried into effect; for on the 27th November, the Government and the miners came to an agreement, under which 49 hours were agreed upon as the normal working week for colliery surface workmen. On the day on which this settlement was approved, the Miners' Executive also decided upon the further demand for an increase in wages. It was this demand, with others put forward in conjunction with it at the end of 1918, that precipitated the appointment of the Sankey Commission in February 1919.

CHAPTER IV

THE MINERS' PROGRAMME

Section 1. The Miners' Federation After the War

Superficially the structure of the Miners' Federation of Great Britain underwent little change during the war period. The membership, it is true, rose from 673,000 in 1914 to 768,000 in 1918, but these figures are to a considerable extent misleading, because the various Miners' Associations adopted different practices in either retaining on, or removing from, their membership lists those who were serving with the Forces. The actual increase in membership, if miners serving with the Forces were in all cases included in the total, would therefore be greater than the rate of increase suggested. The table on p. 65 shows in detail the changes in membership of the various Associations affiliated to the Miners' Federation of Great Britain both for the war period and for the three post-war years 1919–21.

While the structure of the Miners' Federation changed comparatively little during the years under review, certain important developments did take place. In 1916 the Miners' Conference at Southport passed a resolution urging that every possible effort should be made to enrol all mine-workers within the ranks of the Miners' Federation of Great Britain, and from this time forward a definite attempt was made to widen the scope of the Federation and to bring within it those classes of workers who had hitherto been for the most part outside. Already in March 1916 an agreement had been arrived at in the South Wales coal-field under which the coal-owners agreed, for the period of the War, to require all their employees to be Trade Unionists. The South Wales Miners' Federation had attempted to secure an agreement under which all mine-workers should be compelled to join the South Wales Miners' Federation, but they were not successful in securing this concession, and certain grades of workers continued, in South Wales as in other coal-fields, to belong to sectional Associations, not connected with the Miners' Federation of Great Britain. The South Wales agreement, however, and similar less formal arrangements concluded subsequently in other coal-fields, helped to increase the membership of the Federation without making it an all-embracing body.

MINERS' FEDERATION, 1914–21. MEMBERSHIP (*in thousands*)

	1914	*1915*	*1916*	*1917*	*1918*	*1919*	*1920*	*1921*
Yorkshire . .	90	90	100	100	100	100	142	142
Lancs. and Cheshire.	72	70	75	75	75	80	80	90
Midlands . .	54	54	54	54	54	54	64	64
Derbyshire . .	33	35	35	35	39	39	49	49
Notts . . .	28	30	30	30	30	30	35	35
Leicester . .	6	6	6	6	7	7	7	8
South Derbyshire .	4	4	4	4	5	5	6	6
North Wales . .	12	10	12	12	13	13	15	16
Somerset . .	4	4	4	4	5	5	6	6
Bristol . . .	2	1	1	1	1	1	1	2
Scotland . . .	75	90	90	90	90	90	90	110
South Wales . .	116	134	127	147	158	160	180	200
Northumberland .	38	38	37	36	40	40	41	41
Durham . . .	120	120	120	120	120	126	126	126
Cleveland . .	9	8	9	9	9	9	9	9
Cumberland . .	8	8	8	8	8	13	13	13
Forest of Dean .	2	2	2	2	5	5	6	6
Kent . . .	—	·3	·6	·5	1	1	1	2
Cokemen . .	—	—	—	—	8	9	9	10
Enginemen . .	—	—	—	—	—	14	19	20
	673	704	714	733	768	801	899	955

Note.—It should be noted that according to the rules of the Miners' Associations two boys are usually counted as equivalent to one adult. These figures, therefore, represent in all cases a larger number of individuals.

As we saw in the introductory chapter of this study, the principal groups of workers outside the Miners' Federation in 1913 were to be found among the colliery deputies and officials, the enginemen, the cokemen and by-product workers, and, in certain districts, the mechanics. In none of these cases were the whole of the grades concerned organized in the sectional Associations, and a considerable number in all of them belonged to the

Miners' Associations. But the division was serious enough to be regarded as important, particularly because some of the workmen who were outside the Federation occupied important strategic positions in the industry. During the later years of the War the Executive of the Miners' Federation was almost continuously in negotiation with various other Unions organizing particular grades of mine-workers. In so far as these negotiations were conducted with Societies such as the Electrical Trades Union, the Amalgamated Society of Engineers, and the National Amalgamated Union of Enginemen, which organized mining craftsmen together with craftsmen belonging to other industries, no progress was made; for the Miners' Federation still clung firmly to the principle that no recognition should be extended to any Trade Union not consisting wholly of mine-workers. But the case was different with the craft Associations confined to particular grades of mine-workers; and in October 1917 the National Union of Cokemen and By-Product Workers, and in May 1919, the National Federation of Colliery Enginemen, were admitted to direct affiliation to the Miners' Federation of Great Britain. Furthermore, local arrangements were made in certain cases, in addition to those mentioned in the first chapter of this book, by which certain local craft Associations of mine-workers became affiliated to the district Miners' Associations, and thus established an indirect connexion with the Miners' Federation. The Deputies' Associations and those Associations of Enginemen which were not connected with the National Federation of Colliery Enginemen, however, still remained outside the Miners' Federation, and for the most part connected themselves with a new organization, the National Council of Colliery Workers other than Miners, which was formed at the beginning of 1917. This body included also certain general labour Unions which had members employed on the surface of the pits.

The tendency towards 'industrial unionism', strongly marked in the Miners' Federation before the War, had thus achieved certain advances by the end of the war period; but the process of transformation of the Miners' Federation into an industrial Union was still very far from complete, and the local autonomy of the separate district Miners' Associations still remained almost complete, each Association retaining its separate funds and rules, together with the right of independent action in the declaration of local strikes, even against the wish of the Miners' Federation as a whole. The financial separateness of the district Associations had, of course, an important bearing on the strike power of the Federation as a whole; for it meant that, as there were large inequalities in financial resources between one district and another, the strength of the whole Federation might well turn out to be only that of its weakest link. Realizing this, the leaders of the Federation were already attempting, during the war period, both to strengthen the financial position of the Federation itself, and to secure a levelling up of the contributions levied by the district Associations to an amount which would ensure the possession of adequate finances. The steps taken shortly before the War to secure simultaneous termination of agreements, and to bring all agreements under the scrutiny of the Federation as a whole, were intended to strengthen the power of the central body, and the national negotiations which, especially under State control, largely replaced the previous local methods of settlement, also inevitably tended towards an increasing measure of centralization. A strong central power was also clearly aimed at by the important step, taken in 1918, of transferring the central office from Manchester, where it had been conducted in conjunction with the Lancashire and Cheshire Miners' Federation, to London, and in the election of two full-time officials to take charge of the work of the Federation. Mr. Smillie, who had previously been part-time President of the Federation, was elected in 1918 as full-time President; and Mr. Frank Hodges became the first full-time Secretary.

Side by side with these official developments of Federation machinery, there had been a strengthening of semi-official and unofficial organization among the rank and file. Before the War, the rank and file 'left-wing' movement among the miners was strong in the South Wales coal-field, where it had already resulted, in 1912, in the issue by the 'Unofficial Reform Committee' of the famous pamphlet, 'The Miners' Next Step', in which proposals were laid down for the reorganization of the machinery of the Federation with the definite object of overthrowing capitalist control and replacing it by a system of workers' control in the industry. Other organizations, such as the Industrial Democracy League, had also been vigorously following up the work of the Unofficial Reform Committee.

This movement, however, had hardly extended before the War beyond the South Wales coal-field, and it was not until 1917 that similar rank and file movements made their appearance with any strength in other coal-fields. By this time, however, both on the north-east coast and in Yorkshire, and in the west of Scotland, important unofficial movements influenced to some extent by the 'shop-stewards' movement' in the munitions industries, were beginning to appear. 'Reform Movements' were founded in a number of coal-fields, and left-wing groups among the miners began to get in touch one with another. It was not until the beginning of 1920 that a definite national unofficial organization, the Mining Section of the Workers' Committee Movement, came into being. Considerably before this, however, the increasing left-wing pressure in the various coal-fields was beginning to exert an important influence on the policy of the various Miners' Associations, and even on the official programme of the Miners' Federation of Great Britain.

We have seen that, during the early years of the War, Pit Committees were set up in a number of areas to deal with questions of output and absenteeism. We saw also that, when the second national war wage advance was conceded by the Government in July 1918, it was made a condition of the granting of the advance that the Miners' Federation should do all it could to secure the general adoption of the pit-committee system. A memorandum of agreement was drawn up at this time between the Coal Controller and the Federation, and was accepted by the Annual Conference of the Federation in July 1918. This memorandum, defining in general terms the constitution and duties of Pit Committees, was worded as follows :

1. That Joint Pit Committees shall be established at all the collieries throughout Great Britain and charged with the duty of decreasing voluntary absenteeism and increasing output.

2. Each district shall be at liberty to adopt its own rules for, or revise the existing rules of, the Joint Pit Committees, provided they carry out the principles of this memorandum.

3. The Joint Pit Committees shall comprise representatives of the

management and the workmen, and the details of their composition shall be left to be settled by the local Associations of Coal Owners and Miners, or, in the event of their being unable to agree, by the Controller of Coal Mines.

4. Each week the Joint Pit Committee shall be supplied by the management with particulars of absenteeism, stating (as far as may be known to the management) whether the absenteeism is voluntary or involuntary, together with the names of the absentees. The Committee will then investigate the cases of alleged voluntary absenteeism, and, by interviewing absentees and in other ways, endeavour to exert their personal influence to prevent its recurrence. In the case of persistent absenteeism the Committee shall post each week the names of the offenders at the pit head.

5. The management shall supply the Committee weekly with particulars showing the average output per man in the case of coal-getters, and also the average output per person employed in or about the mine, commencing with the week comprising the last pay day before Sunday, June 30th. The Committee will investigate cases of declining output and consider to what extent the cause is due to more difficult physical conditions in the seam or altered physical or mechanical conditions in the haulage roads, or to any other cause whether personal to the getter or other workers, or the management, or not. Where the output is less than could be reasonably expected, having regard to all the circumstances, the Committee will interview the management, or workmen, or both, with a view to an improvement.

6. Generally, all members of the Joint Pit Committee will combine to secure harmony at the pit, and to carry out the pledge given by the Executive Committee of the Miners' Federation to the Government that they would do what they could to improve output and decrease voluntary absenteeism.

The establishment of Pit Committees never became absolutely general; but by the end of 1918 the method had been adopted in the great majority of districts, and most of the important collieries had Committees of this type at work. The owners as a rule desired to confine the activities of the Committees within narrow limits and to keep them as far as possible to the one question of absenteeism. The miners' representatives, on the other hand, claimed the right to raise any question affecting the output of coal at the colliery, and under this heading it was clearly possible to bring in a great many questions of management and control. This was done with varying degrees of success and persistency. The Pit Committee movement did not as a whole produce any great results; but, so far as it went, it was undoubtedly a factor tending to stimulate among the miners the desire for a greater measure of control over the conditions of their industry. This was especially the case where the left-wing movement was present in any considerable strength.

Section 2. The Miners' Post-War Demands

Year after year up to 1918 the Miners' Annual Conference passed in one form or another resolutions demanding the nationalization of the coal industry. A year before the War a Bill providing for nationalization was prepared and issued on behalf of the Federation by Mr. H. H. Slesser. This was a straightforward nationalization proposal, dealing almost entirely with the transference of ownership and making no special provision for workers' representation in the management of the nationalized industry. For the first three years of the war period the Miners' Conference contended itself with reaffirming, in general terms, its desire for nationalization; but in 1918 the ordinary nationalization proposal was replaced by the following extremely important resolution, moved by Mr. Winstone on behalf of the South Wales Miners' Federation, and seconded by Mr. Frank Hodges:

> That in the opinion of this Conference the time has arrived in the history of the coal-mining industry when it is clearly in the national interests to transfer the entire industry from private ownership and control to State ownership, with joint control and administration by the workmen and the State. In pursuance of this opinion the National Executive be instructed to immediately reconsider the Draft Bill for the Nationalization of the Mines (as agreed upon at the Swansea Conference, 1912, and subsequently amended by the Executive Committee and the Labour Party) in the light of the newer phases of development in the industry so as to make provision for the aforesaid joint control and administration when the measure becomes law. Further, a Conference be called at an early date to receive a report from the Executive Committee upon the draft proposals and to determine the best means of co-operating with the National Labour Party to ensure the passage of a new Bill into law.

At the same Conference two further resolutions, which have an important bearing on the earlier events of 1919, were carried. The first, which assumed the following form, was a demand for the amendment of the Coal Mines Act of 1908, so as to secure a six hours working day, which would mean, with winding and waiting time, that in practice about seven hours on the average would be spent at the colliery :

> This Conference is of opinion that the Coal Mines (Eight Hours) Act, 1908, should be amended forthwith so as to provide that on the appointed day, which shall not be more than four weeks after the declaration of peace, the hours of labour for all persons employed in and about the mines shall be in no case more than six hours per day.

The second decision was that a further wage demand should be put forward, and that in any post-war settlement provision must be made 'for the continuance in the wage rate of all advances in wages paid either in consequence of a rise in the average selling-price of coal, or in consequence of advances given to meet the increased cost of living due to the War'. No steps were taken to give effect to these demands until after the Armistice; but as soon as the Armistice was concluded the Miners' Federation proceeded to take action. On the 9th January 1919, a demand for an advance of 30 per cent. on total earnings, exclusive of the war wage, was presented to the Coal Controller. In the following week a special Conference of the Miners' Federation was held at Southport for the purpose of drawing up a comprehensive programme of demands. At this Conference the following resolutions, usually known as the 'Southport Resolutions', were carried, and together with the wage demand were made the basis of the subsequent negotiations with the Government.

Demobilization

(*a*) That this Conference demands that all demobilized mine-workers shall be fully discharged from the Army and Navy, and, as soon as they are able, and desire, to resume work, shall be reinstated in the mines they left at the time of enlistment.

(*b*) Any such mine-worker not able to perform a normal day's work shall be paid full wages appertaining to the grade to which he belonged, or would have belonged had he not enlisted.

(*c*) Demobilized men who are partly disabled and unable to follow work in the mines shall be trained for other suitable occupations, and paid during training an allowance equal to what they would have earned in and about the mines had they not been disabled. The allowance to continue after training until suitable employment is found. The cost of training and allowance to be at the expense of the State.

(*d*) Demobilized mine-workers and men who are displaced to make room for men returned from the Army or Navy shall be paid from State funds an out-of-work allowance equal to the wages they would have earned had they been employed in or about the mines.

(*e*) In no case shall wages or allowances interfere with pensions to which discharged soldiers and sailors are, or may be, entitled.

(*f*) All matters coming within the above proposals shall be first dealt with by the Joint Pit Committee of mine-owners and mine-workers, and, if necessary, submitted to the District Joint Committees.

(*g*) In order to make easier the realization of these demands we press the Government to amend the Mines Eight Hours Act, so that 'six hours' shall be substituted for 'eight hours' in that Act.

Also for this purpose, and in the interests of miners in particular, and the community in general, we urge the Government to proceed at once to the nationalization of all mines and minerals.

(*h*) That the Executive Committee interview the Prime Minister or some other Government representatives on these proposals. Failing a satisfactory answer, a further Conference be convened to determine the policy to be adopted to press these demands.

No time was lost in instituting negotiations on the basis of these demands, and on the 31st January the Miners' Federation met representatives of the Government headed by the Minister of Labour, Sir Robert Horne, who, after discussing the demands, stated that they would be placed before the Cabinet at the earliest possible moment. On the 15th February a further meeting was held, at which the Minister of Labour communicated to the miners the Government's reply. The Government was prepared to offer an additional war wage of 1*s*. per day ; the demands dealing with demobilization were for the most part rejected, and the remaining demands the Government proposed to refer to a Committee of Inquiry, with terms of reference wide enough to permit it to deal with the whole position of the coal industry. The miners submitted the Government's reply to a further special Conference of the Federation, which met at Southport on the 12th and 13th February. The Conference rejected the offer and decided to take a strike ballot of the whole Federation. At the same time it strongly urged the members to vote in favour of strike action. The following was the form of the ballot paper :

1. Application for 30 per cent. increase in wages.
2. Six-hour day.

3. Full maintenance at Trade Union rates of wages for mine-workers unemployed through demobilization.

4. Nationalization of the mines.

5. The Government having failed to grant any of the above proposals, are you in favour of a National Strike to secure them ?

Yes.................... No....................

Place an 'X' opposite 'Yes' or 'No' in the space provided for the purpose.

The decision of the Miners' Conference was followed by a considerable controversy in the press, the newspapers being plentifully supplied by the Government with contentions hostile to the miners' claims. Negotiations were renewed on the 21st December, on the invitation of the Prime Minister, who invited the Federation Executive to meet him on that day. The Prime Minister at this meeting asked the miners to postpone for a fortnight the date of the strike notices, which were dated to expire on the 15th March, and to participate in a Commission of Inquiry which would be instructed to present an interim report, at the latest, by the 31st March. The miners urged that, even if other matters were left over for the Commission, the wages claim should be dealt with immediately, and, on the Prime Minister refusing to accept this proposal, they decided to refer the offer to a further Conference. The Prime Minister, however, determined to take action at once. On the 24th February the Coal Industry Commission Bill, establishing a Royal Commission of Inquiry into the coal industry, was introduced into the House of Commons. The Labour Party made an effort to secure the elimination of the questions of wages and hours from the terms of reference, and to persuade the Government immediately to concede the demands of the miners upon those points. The only concession secured, however, was that the Interim Report of the Commission should be published by the 20th March.

Meanwhile the miners' strike ballot had been completed, and the figures, which were issued on the 25th February, showed a majority of nearly six to one in favour of a strike, 615,164 votes were cast in favour of a stoppage, and 105,082 against. With these figures before them the miners' delegates met in Conference on the 26th February. On the following day, the Conference agreed to participate in the proposed Commission and to postpone strike notices until the 22nd March, provided that a satisfactory agreement could be arrived at as to the personnel of the Commission. The object of the miners was, of course, to secure that the Commission should be one on which they would secure fair representation; and with this object in view they claimed that half the members, apart from the Chairman, should be either appointed by the Miners' Federation itself or agreed to between the Federation and the Government. After considerable further negotiations this suggestion was finally accepted by Mr. Lloyd George. The Coal Industry Commission Act was passed into law at the end of February, and on the 1st March the Commission was constituted as follows:

Hon. Mr. Justice Sankey (Chairman)

Labour side:		Employers' side:	
Mr. Robert Smillie Mr. Herbert Smith Mr. Frank Hodges Sir Leo Chiozza Money	Appointed by the Miners' Federation.	Mr. Arthur Balfour Sir Arthur Duckham Sir Thomas Royden	Government nominees.
Mr. R. H. Tawney Mr. Sidney Webb	Agreed upon between Government & Miners' Federation.	Mr. Evan Williams Mr. R. W. Cooper Mr. J. T. Forgie	Coal-owners.

The Act constituting the Coal Industry Commission was very sweeping in its provisions. Wide powers were conferred upon the Commissioners; and the terms of reference were drafted widely enough to enable any question connected with the organization of the industry to be brought under review. Its scope is clearly indicated in the first section of the Act, which is worded as follows:

1. His Majesty shall have power to appoint Commissioners, consisting of a chairman, who shall be a judge of the Supreme Court, a vice-chairman, and such other persons as His Majesty may think fit, for the purpose of inquiring into the position of, and conditions prevailing in, the coal industry, and in particular as to—

(*a*) The wages and hours of work in the various grades of colliery workers, and whether, and if so, to what extent, and by what method, such wages should be increased and hours reduced, regard being had to a reasonable standard of living amongst the colliery workers, and to the effect of such changes on the economic life of the country.

(*b*) Any inequalities between different grades of colliery workers as regards wages, hours of work, and other conditions, and whether, and, if so, to what extent any of these inequalities are unjustifiable and capable of remedy.

(*c*) The cost of production and distribution of coal and the general organization of the coal-fields and the industry as a whole;

(*d*) Selling-prices and profits in the coal industry.

(*e*) The social conditions under which colliery workers carry on their industry.

(*f*) Any scheme that may be submitted to or formulated by the Commissioners for the future organization of the coal industry, whether on the present basis, or on the basis of joint control, nationalization, or any other basis.

(*g*) The effect of the present incidence of, and practice in regard to, mining royalties and wayleaves upon the coal industry and the cost of coal, and whether any and what charges in these respects are desirable.

(*h*) The effect of proposals under the above head upon the development of the coal industry and the economic life of the country.

The appointment of the Coal Commission for the moment postponed the mining crisis. Everything now depended on the Report which the Commission was under an obligation to present by the 20th March. This, of course, was not to deal with the whole of the miners' demands, and it was expected that, if the immediate crisis was successfully tided over as a result of the first Report, the Commission would then proceed to deal in detail with the remainder of the miners' claims, and with the whole organization of the industry.

At the time when the Coal Commission was appointed the industrial position was exceedingly threatening, not only in the mining industry, but also in many others. Unofficial strikes in support of the demand for a shorter working week had been in progress during February on the Clyde and in Belfast; and, although these unofficial movements had failed for the moment, unrest was very widespread, and the workers in many industries were threatening strike action. The mining crisis was not the only one with which the Government was at this time compelled to deal; and, simultaneously with the appointment of the Coal Commission, an attempt was made to avert the threatened troubles in other industries by the summoning of a National Industrial Conference, to which all Trade Unions and Employers' Associations were invited to send delegates. The combined effect of these two steps taken by the Government was to afford a respite from serious industrial troubles at the cost, not of actual concessions, but merely of setting up the machinery which encouraged Trade Unions to believe that substantial concessions would subsequently be given. How far these hopes were realized in the case of the mining industry we shall see from the subsequent history of the Coal Commission and the reception of its Reports by the Government.

CHAPTER V

THE COAL COMMISSION

Section 1. The First Stage.
,, 2. Between the Stages.
,, 3. The Second Stage.

Section 1. The First Stage

The Coal Commission, as it was generally called, held its first meeting on the 3rd March 1919, in the King's Robing Room at the House of Lords. With one short break after the issue of its Interim Report, it continued to sit in public several times a week up to the beginning of June. During these months its proceedings were reported at length and frequently 'starred' in the press. There passed before it as witnesses an extraordinarily varied collection of personages—great landed proprietors such as the Duke of Northumberland and the Earl of Durham, great industrial leaders such as Mr. Benjamin Talbot, bankers such as Dr. Walter Leaf, Mr. Ryan, the Prime Minister of Queensland, civil servants from the Mines' Department, professors of economics professing all manner of opinions, journalists, experts, Labour and Co-operative leaders, as well as the representatives of the various associations of coal-owners and colliery workers. From the first the inquiry developed on dramatic lines, and made a good newspaper 'story'. Mr. Robert Smillie, the miners' leader, cross-examining the Duke of Northumberland concerning the origin of his claim to the land and the coal under it on which he based his right to royalties and wayleaves, Mr. Sidney Webb and Sir Leo Money seeking to convict private enterprise of inefficiency, Mr. Harold Cox conducting a vigorous counter-offensive against public ownership, Mr. William Straker of the Miners' Federation eloquently pleading the case for workers' control in the mining industry—all these and many more received an amount of publicity never before accorded in the Press to the discussion of the fundamental issues of industrial politics.

From the very beginning of the inquiry the miners were

successful in holding the initiative. They successfully kept 'private enterprise' on its trial before the Commission, and compelled the mine-owners to remain throughout on the defensive. The strongest opponents of nationalization were speedily compelled to recognize that the case presented day by day by the witnesses on the miners' side, or drawn from other witnesses in examination by their representatives, was creating a profound impression on the public mind, and was making the concession of the miners' major claims appear almost a foregone conclusion. In Labour circles, there was the greatest elation at the progress of the inquiry. Capitalism, it was said, was on its trial; and the breach which was being made in its solid front could not but lead to a withdrawal all along the line in face of the advancing forces of Labour.

The remainder of this book will be largely an account of the manner in which these Labour hopes came to shipwreck, and the effects of the Coal Commission were washed away by the rising tide of the resistance of the advocates of private enterprise and still more by force of economic depression. But of this in its turn. For the moment we are concerned with the situation which existed in March 1919, when the Coal Commission began its labours.

The Commissioners had but little time before them. The threat of a national coal strike still hung, suspended, over the country, and they were under pledge to produce at least an Interim Report on the more urgent of the questions at issue in little more than a fortnight—that is, by the 20th March 1919. The two main questions which fell to be thus rapidly decided were the questions of wages and hours included in the miners' demands. These had to be dealt with by concrete and definite proposals, to which immediate effect could be given by the Government. But, if a strike was to be averted, it was also necessary that the Interim Report should make some reference to the wider questions raised by the miners, particularly to the issue of public *versus* private ownership and control, and that some indication should be given of the further course which the Commission proposed to follow in dealing with this matter. From the standpoint of the miners' leaders, who desired to justify to their own constituents their action in entering into the Commission, as well as to influence the public and, through it, the Government in support of their claims, it was essential to make a rapid impression, and to marshal at once all the dramatic evidence that could be quickly presented in substantiation of the miners' case.

There can be no dispute that this was done with very considerable skill and effect. It is no part of the purpose of this study even to summarize the very voluminous evidence presented to the Commission, and subsequently published as a Blue Book in three bulky volumes. A part of this immense field is covered in a companion volume of this series, and I shall have to deal summarily with certain sections of the evidence which bear directly on the miners' standard of life and conditions of employment, and with their claims for a change in the industrial system. But the evidence as a whole ranged over a very wide field, including every aspect of the production, sale, and distribution of coal at home and abroad, the relations of the mining industry to other industries and to the Exchequer, the various aspects of State control, the methods of management and technical administration, the land system and its effects upon mining, and a host of other special problems. Reference must be made for the full story to the published Report of the Commission's proceedings, which will remain an indispensable document for students of the mining industry and of Labour questions in Great Britain.

During the hurried first stage of the inquiry, the net was not spread quite so widely for evidence as during the second stage. The miners' representatives concentrated mainly on driving home five points: (1) the inadequacy of the wage advances conceded during the war period; (2) the necessity, on human and social grounds, for a reduction in working hours, and the economic practicability of making the reduction; (3) the bad conditions both in the pits and in respect of housing and social amenities under which the men were compelled to live; (4) the undue increase in the profits realized by the owners during the war years; (5) the inefficiency of the existing system of production and distribution, and its inevitability under conditions of divided private ownership and control.

On the first point, that of wages, the principal witness for the miners was Mr. Vernon Hartshorn, the South Wales leader. According to his evidence the total advances in miners' wages averaged over all the coal-fields amounted to 78 per cent. This figure seems to have been based on the daywork rates payable to colliers working underground, the class of workers usually taken as central in the computation of mining wage rates. The more detailed figures which he presented for the South Wales coal-field showed advances of 78 per cent. in the case of colliers, and of 86 per cent. for all classes of adult miners, as against a rise in the cost of living of 120 per cent., according to the official computation published by the Ministry of Labour. Sir Arthur Lowes Dickinson and the Coal Controller, representing the Mines Department, presented a summary table showing a rise in the total yearly wages bill from £91,000,000 in 1913 to a rate of £157,000,000 in September 1918, since when the rates of wages had remained unchanged. The pre-war earnings per person employed were estimated by Sir Arthur Lowes Dickinson at £82 per annum, and the wages at the end of 1918 at a rate of £169 per annum, the total number of employees having fallen, in consequence of war enlistments, from 1,048,956 to 929,524. Another table, presented by the Coal Controller, showed that the wages in November 1918 were practically the same as in September.

This apparent conflict of testimony as to the advance in wages during the war period is, at least in part, accounted for by the fact that the figures presented by the Mines Department apply to all workers employed, whereas the Miners' Federation figures relate only to adults. The method of flat-rate advances adopted during the period of war-time control resulted, moreover, in the securing of larger percentage advances by the lower-paid than by the higher-paid grades, on whose earnings computations of the change in mining wages had been previously based. The flat-rate advances granted to non-adults were only half those granted to men; but even this represented a higher percentage advance to non-adults than to adult workers. Consequently, any inclusive figure relating to all grades of workers necessarily showed a higher percentage advance than figures relating only to colliers, or to underground workers, or even to all adult labour.

Whatever figure might be accepted as representing the actual war-time increase in rates of wages, it was still clear that wages had not risen in correspondence with the rise in the cost of living.

The miners, working on the basis of an actual advance of 78 per cent. to colliers, held that a further advance of 42 per cent. on pre-war rates was required in order to bring the wages of colliers up to the pre-war standard, and urged that the larger percentage increase which other grades would receive was due to them on account of the unduly low rates paid to them before the War. But, in addition to demanding that real wages should be brought up to the pre-war standard, the miners also claimed that their standard of life should be improved. Their demand for an advance of 30 per cent. on current earnings was designed to cover three points —to bring wages in all grades up to the pre-war standard, to maintain the levelling-up of the lower-paid grades which had been secured during the War, and to produce an actual improvement in the pre-war standard of life for all grades of workers in the industry.

The second matter, the urgency of which the miners' spokesmen desired at once to impress upon the Coal Commission, was the necessity for a reduction in working hours. In the first place, it was sought to make both the Commissioners and the public understand that the miners were not in enjoyment of the eight hour day. The Coal Mines (Eight Hours) Act of 1908 applied only to underground workers; and, thanks to an amendment introduced in the House of Lords and accepted by the House of Commons at the end of the session under pressure of time, the eight hours for underground workers were timed from the moment at which the *last* man of each shift entered the cage in order to descend the shaft to the moment at which the *first* man again reached the surface. Thus, the miners contended, the average working day even for underground workers was much nearer nine hours than eight hours, and in some cases where winding presented difficulties particular groups of men had to be at work for ten and a half hours.

Tables prepared for the Commission by the Mining Statistics Branch of the Home Office showed that the addition to the working day represented by ' winding time ' varied considerably from case to case. Some districts, especially Lancashire and Cheshire, showed an average winding time far above the average for the whole country; and there were big differences between one pit and another in the same coal-field. In all, it was found that in 39·8 per cent. of the 778,000 cases examined the winding time was less than half an hour. In 28·2 per cent. of the cases it was between half an hour and three quarters, and in 25·8 per cent. between three quarters of an hour and an hour. The remaining 6·2 per cent. of the underground workers had winding times longer than one hour. Thus, in more than 60 per cent. of the cases, the underground had a day, not of eight hours, but of more than eight and a half. The hours of surface-workers were, on the average, longer than those of underground workers.

In pleading for a reduction of hours, the miners laid special stress on the frequency and severity of colliery accidents. There were, it was pointed out, between 160,000 and 176,000 notified casualties every year in the mines, and these included from 1,500 to 1,700 fatal accidents. Between 1907 and 1916, 12,400 miners had been killed in the course of their employment. These accidents, it was urged, were largely preventable, and one of the most effective means of reducing their number would be a shortening of the hours of labour. In other occupations, it was urged, shortening of hours had led to a more than proportionate diminution of accidents, and, even if the diminution were only proportionate, the result would be greatly to decrease the collier's existing risk to life and limb. Stress was laid on the exceptional hazards and arduous conditions of the miners' life and work, and on the justification which these afforded for a shorter working day.

On the third point, bad housing conditions and absence of social amenities, abundant evidence was submitted to show how insanitary and unfit for decent human existence are many of the villages in which the mining population is densely congregated. In England and Wales as a whole, the percentage of persons living more than two to a room is 9. In the great mining counties of Northumberland and Durham it is nearly 29, and in some of the mining villages in these counties it is over 40. Scotland and South Wales were also shown to have abominable housing conditions in the mining areas. It was shown that tuberculosis was exceptionally common in the overcrowded colliery districts. The necessity for better houses, for pithead baths, for more adequate inspection by the State, for the fundamental alteration of conditions in the colliery villages, was pressed home with marked effect upon both the public mind and the Commission. The badness of the conditions was also advanced as a conclusive reason for the raising of wages to a point which would make possible a higher standard of living, under the exceptional conditions of the miners' calling.

The fourth point, the vastness of the sums realized as profits in the coal industry during the war years, loomed large throughout the inquiry. This demonstration was calculated to serve several objects. It was to show that the industry could afford the improved wages and conditions which the miners demanded; and it was also likely to convince the public that the miners were right in denouncing the failure of private enterprise to serve the public properly. The consumer was to be made to feel that he, like the miner, was being exploited by the coal-owners, and was thus to be persuaded to join with the miners in demanding a change in the ownership and control of the industry.

The facts about mining profits were, indeed, startling enough. For the five years before the War (1909–13), the average annual profits to all colliery undertakings, apart from mining royalties, amounted to £13,000,000. The years immediately preceding the War were exceptionally prosperous, and the total annual profits, averaged for 1912 and 1913, reached £18,600,000. In 1909, on the other hand, they had been as low as £9,000,000.[1]

During the war years, profits rose to an extraordinary height. After a fall in 1914 to £16,500,000, they rose in 1915–18 to £21,500,000 (1915), £37,800,000 (1916), £27,700,000 (1917 i.e. after the imposition of control), and £29,500,000 (estimated for 1918 on the figures for the first three quarters of the year). During the third quarter of 1918 alone, and, it is believed, also during the final quarter, profits were at the rate of £39,000,000 per annum, or more than in the record year of 1916.

Moreover as the result of an amendment introduced into the Coal Mines Agreement Confirmation Bill during its passage through Parliament,[2] coke-ovens and similar auxiliary undertakings carried on in conjunction with coal-mines were not placed under State

[1] For fuller details see Appendix A. [2] See *ante*, p. 53.

control, and the figures of colliery profits during the control period therefore do not include the profits realized from coke-ovens and by-product works, which were estimated as amounting to about a further £6,000,000 per annum. The profits on coke-ovens and by-products are included in the totals quoted for colliery profits both before the War and up to the imposition of State control. In other words, as the miners stated the case, colliery profits had risen in September 1918 to more than 4*s*. a ton, as compared with less than 1*s*. per ton—the average profit during the five pre-war years. Even excluding profits on by-products and coke-ovens, the miners published a table showing that, according to the official figures, wages had risen by 106 per cent. in comparison with the pre-war position, pithead prices by 183 per cent., and profits by 269 per cent. Excess profits, of course, took their toll; but, owing to the extraordinary prosperity of the coal industry in 1912 and 1913, the coal-owners were able to retain an exceptionally large proportion of their war-time profits. The statutory rate of interest allowed to colliery concerns under the Finance Acts was 9 per cent., and owners were allowed in the fixing of their pre-war standard profits, which were not subject to Excess Profits Duty, to take the two best out of three pre-war years. This in practice meant that the pre-war standard profits allowed to colliery concerns were based, in nearly all cases, on 1912–13 and not on 1909–13, or, in other words, on an average annual profit of £18,600,000 instead of £13,000,000.

These figures, and the virtually guaranteed profits secured to coal-owners under the Coal Mines Agreement of 1917, were used to considerable effect by the spokesmen of the miners, and received fuller press publicity than is usually secured by facts of this order. The profits actually realized in the coal industry were probably not so large as those reaped by capitalists in some other essential services during the war period; but the circumstances under which they were made known, and the semi-judicial character of the tribunal before which they were quoted, added to the impressiveness of the statement, and caused the public to take notice.

On the fifth point, that of wastefulness and inefficiency in production and distribution, stress was laid by the miners' advocates on the bad service which the consumer received under private ownership. Coal prices, it was urged, were virtually controlled by a ring, and the numerous middlemen through whose hands the coal passed on its way to the consumer exacted, it was urged, a greatly excessive charge. It was shown, for example, that in London the addition to the cost of coal allowed by the Coal Controller to the dealer, after railway, wagon, and factor's charges had all been paid, was no less than 12*s.* 6*d.* per ton. Private ownership of wagons, it was urged, also inflated the cost of transport, and a unified system of control would enable the average length which coal had to be hauled to be very largely reduced by means of a scientific plan of distribution, such as the Coal Controller's department actually enforced during the War. Sir Leo Money estimated that 3*s.* a ton at least could be saved by a better organization of coal distribution, and the example of the Co-operative Societies was quoted as showing a saving of from 2*s.* 6*d.* to 5*s.* in comparison with the private merchants.

The above, of course, is not intended to be a summary of the evidence presented to the Coal Commission during the first stage, but merely an indication of the line of argument followed by the miners and their supporters. The coal-owners were not slow to present counter-evidence, and the miners shared the limelight with the representatives of the Government, whose evidence was for the most part confined to a presentation of the facts with regard to the financial position of the industry, the conditions of labour, and the working of State control. It was not until the second stage of the inquiry that the battle over the question of ownership and management was joined by the full forces of the owners as well as of the miners.

The presentation of the evidence referred to above had all to be concentrated in a very brief space of time; for the Commission was under obligation to produce an Interim Report by the 20th March. In this it was successful; and three Reports, signed by the various members of the Commission, duly appeared on that date. The three miners' leaders, Mr. Robert Smillie, Mr. Herbert Smith, and Mr. Frank Hodges joined with Mr. Sidney Webb, Mr. R. H. Tawney, and Sir Leo Money in signing one Report: the three direct representatives of the coal-owners presented a second; and the Chairman of the Commission, Sir John Sankey, put in a third Report, which was also signed by the other three employer members of the Commission, Sir Thomas Royden, Sir Arthur Duckham, and Mr. A. Balfour of Sheffield.

The miners' Report urged the immediate concession of the wage advance of 30 per cent. on current earnings (apart from war wage) which had been demanded by the Miners' Federation. It also urged the amendment of the Coal Mines Regulation Act of 1908 by the substitution of a maximum working day of six hours for one of eight hours, i. e. on the average, with winding time, of 6½ hours for 8½ hours. In addition, it maintained that 'in the interest of the consumers as much as in that of the miners, nationalization ought to be, in principle, at once determined on'.

The coal-owners' Report confined itself solely to the question of wages and hours. A wage advance of 1*s.* 6*d.* per day for adults and 9*d.* for juveniles was recommended, and it was proposed that a maximum working day of seven (i. e. seven and a half) hours should be instituted, with eight hours for surface-workers.

Sir John Sankey and his co-signatories steered a middle course between these two Reports. The immediate substitution of 'seven' for 'eight' hours in the Coal Mines Regulation Act was recommended, and it was also urged that, 'subject to the economic position of the industry at the end of 1920', the hours should be further reduced to a legal maximum of six. For surface-workers, the proposal was for a working week of 46½ hours, exclusive of meal times. Wages, it was urged, should be at once increased by 2*s.* a day or shift in the case of adults, and by 1*s.* for non-adults. A levy of 1*d.* per ton on all coal raised was suggested, the proceeds to be applied to the improvement of miners' housing and amenities. In order that the cost of the concessions proposed might not be transferred to the consumer, the Report of Sir John Sankey further recommended that the State control of the mines should be continued, pending a full decision as to the future regulation of the industry, and that the Coal Mines Agreement should be so amended as to provide for the retention by the owners of only 1*s.* 2*d.* per ton, instead of the high rates of profit mentioned above.

On the broad issue of the ownership and control of the industry, the first Sankey Report made only tentative and provisional recommendations. These, however, were so drawn as to indicate with some clearness the Chairman's attitude, and to pave the way for definite proposals both for national ownership and for the granting to the workers of a share in the control of the industry. The salient paragraphs bearing on these points in Sir John Sankey's Report read as follows :

> IX. Even upon the evidence already given, the present system of ownership and working in the coal industry stands condemned, and some other system must be substituted for it, either nationalization or a measure of unification by national purchase and/or by joint control.
>
> XV. We are prepared . . . to report now that it is in the interests of the country that the colliery worker shall in the future have an effective voice in the direction of the mine. For a generation the colliery worker has been educated socially and technically. The result is a great national asset. Why not use it ?

Section 2. Between the Stages

During the first stage of the Coal Commission's proceedings, the threat of a national mining strike still remained in being, and the postponed strike notices were due to expire on the 22nd March, two days after the Interim Reports were presented to the Government. No time was was therefore to be lost in taking action, and, on the evening of the 20th March, the day on which the Reports were issued, Mr. Bonar Law stated in the House of Commons the Government's readiness to accept the proposals contained in the Report of Sir John Sankey. He also intimated that, if a miners' strike took place, the whole resources of the State would be used without hesitation to deal with the emergency.

This was the situation when the Miners' National Conference assembled in London on the morning of the 21st March. Mr. Bonar Law's threat was resented by the delegates, and it was also pointed out that no official intimation of the Government's intentions had been conveyed to the Miners' Federation. A letter was accordingly dispatched by hand to Mr. Bonar Law, asking for an explicit declaration of the Government's intentions, and this speedily brought the following reply :

> 11, Downing Street,
> Whitehall, S.W.
> 21st March 1919.
>
> Dear Sir,—Speaking in the House of Commons last night I made a statement with regard to the Government policy in connexion with the Report of the Coal Industry Commission. I have pleasure in confirming,

as I understand you wish me to do, my statement that the Government are prepared to carry out in the spirit and in the letter the recommendations of Mr. Justice Sankey's Report.

Yours faithfully,
A. Bonar Law.

The Secretary, Miners' Federation.

The receipt of this letter cleared the air, and, after a long discussion, it was agreed that the strike notices should be further postponed, and that the miners should continue at work on day to day contracts until the following Wednesday, when the Conference was to meet again in order further to consider the position. Meanwhile, the Executive Committee was instructed to get into touch with the Government, and to enter into negotiations with a view to clearing up ambiguities and securing modifications in the Sankey Report.

The Executive took action immediately, and on the following day, the 22nd March, a meeting was held with Mr. Bonar Law and Sir Robert Horne. At this meeting, it was made clear that the Government would not agree on any of the principal issues to go further than Sir John Sankey towards meeting the miners' claims; but modifications and adjustments were secured on a number of lesser points. These related principally to the granting of the advance retrospectively, the payments of the full weekly amount of 12*s.* for five shifts work where, under the arrangement known as the 'bonus turn', five shifts were already paid for as six at the standard rates, and the relation of the wage advance to piecework earnings.

Armed with minor concessions on these points, but faced with the refusal of the Government to go further towards meeting the full demands of the Miners' Federation, the Executive Committee met the adjourned National Conference on the 26th March. After a long discussion, it was agreed that the terms proposed by the Government should be submitted to a national ballot vote, and that, in the accompanying statement from the Federation, the miners should be recommended to accept the terms, and to allow the Coal Commission to proceed with its inquiry. Meanwhile the men were instructed to continue at work on day to day notices until the completion of the ballot, which was to be over by the 14th April.

In view of the strong recommendations in favour of acceptance made both by the Miners' Executive and by the Conference delegates, the result of the ballot was from the first a foregone conclusion, and the decision of the Conference on the 26th March virtually brought the immediate crisis to an end, although there remained for settlement the larger questions with which the Commission was pledged to deal during the later stages of its work. The figures of the ballot were announced on the 15th April. 693,684 votes had been cast in favour of accepting the Government's terms, and only 76,992 against. Every district of the Federation showed a large majority in favour of acceptance, and even South Wales, which showed the largest minority vote, had registered 142,558 votes for acceptance, and only 19,429 against. Accordingly, the Miners' National Conference, which met again on the 16th April, had no hesitation in endorsing the result of the ballot vote, ordering the withdrawal of the strike notices, and definitely accepting the Government's terms.

The crisis was thus ended, at least for the time, and, at the cost of some concessions, of which the most important was the seven hour shift,[1] the Government had successfully emerged from a very perilous industrial situation. Almost at the same time, the National Industrial Conference had presented its Report, unanimously agreed upon by the representatives of employers and employed, recommending the general adoption of the eight hour day, endorsing the principle of the legal minimum wage, and embodying other important proposals for industrial reform. The Labour troubles following the restoration of peace seemed, for the time, to have been successfully laid to rest.

From the 20th March until after the definite acceptance by the miners of the Sankey Report, the Coal Industry Commission remained in a state of suspended animation; for the continuance

[1] It should be noted that the Government refused to insert into the Bill which was necessary in order to make this change effective any definite provision for the further reduction of the length of the shift to six hours in 1921. The miners tried hard to persuade the Government to insert a provision under which the further reduction would come into force in 1921 without fresh legislation; but this the Government refused to do, stating that the question would have to be considered when the time came. In the Coal Industry Act as finally passed in August 1919, provision was made for the institution of the six hour shift only by resolution of both Houses of Parliament, passed after the end of the year 1920.

of its work was regarded as conditional on a settlement being reached between the Government and the miners, and until the strike notices had been withdrawn and the Sankey Report accepted it was not permitted to continue its work. The decision of the 16th April enabled it to resume its operations, and it met again, and entered upon its second stage on the 24th April 1919.

Section 3. The Second Stage

The second stage of the Coal Commission's proceedings began on the 24th April 1919, and continued until the 23rd June, when the Commissioners submitted their Final Reports. The evidence submitted during this period was far more voluminous, and covered a far wider field, than that which was taken during the first stage of the inquiry. For the Commission had now to deal not with the immediate issues of an industrial dispute of the ordinary kind, but with the wide questions of policy which had been raised by the Miners' Federation. As we have seen, two of the three Interim Reports submitted in March contained definite references to these wider questions. The Labour Report expressed the view that nationalization ought, in principle, at once to be conceded; and the Report signed by the Chairman and three other members explicitly condemned the existing system of ownership and control and pronounced in favour of unification, while it left the form of the future conduct of the industry undecided.

In the official Report of the Coal Commission's proceedings, the first stage fills a closely printed Blue Book of 438 pages, while the second runs to no less than 838 pages. In the separate volume of Appendices, 156 pages, mainly dealing with wages, relate to the first stage, and 84 pages only to the second. This difference serves to indicate an essential difference in the character of the two stages. Up to March the Commission was concerned mainly with statistical facts about wages, profits, costs of production and distribution, prices, and so on; after April it was concerned mainly with views concerning the future conduct of the industry. These views were, of course, supported by facts; but they did not lend themselves in the same way to statistical treatment.

From the standpoint of the miners, there were, during the

second stage of the Commission's sittings, two outstanding issues—public ownership and ' workers' control '. Their object was to ensure that the nation should be recommended to assume the ownership of the industry, including the actual colliery concerns as well as the mineral rights, and that the system of administration to be established under national ownership should be based, not on bureaucracy, but on a full participation of the organized workers, by hand and brain, in the management.

In support of this object, the Miners' Federation officially submitted to the Commission, on the 23rd May, its own detailed proposals for the institution of public ownership and workers' control. These took the form of a full draft of a Bill to be introduced into Parliament; and the terms of this measure, the first detailed scheme for the conduct of industry under public ownership ever issued by a Labour organization, are so important that I have quoted the whole measure in an Appendix to this study.[1]

In support of this Bill, evidence was offered by Mr. William Straker, the veteran Secretary of the Northumberland Miners' Association and Chairman of the Evidence Committee of the Miners' Federation of Great Britain. He was supported by other representatives of the Federation and by Mr. H. H. Slesser, who, as its Standing Counsel, was responsible for the drafting of the measure in the proper legal terms. In addition, two of the Labour members of the Commission, Mr. Sidney Webb and Sir Leo Chiozza Money, went into the witness box in order to give evidence in support of public ownership, and other witnesses, including the present writer, were called in support of the scheme of administration propounded by the Miners' Federation. The action of Mr. Webb and Sir Leo Money in giving evidence before a Commission of which they were members was subsequently used by Mr. Lloyd George and by critics of the Commission for the purpose of discrediting its findings, although precedents for their action were quoted from the Poor Law Commission and from other previous inquiries.

No attempt will be made in this study even to summarize the evidence offered on the question of nationalization. Those who desire to have before them a compendium of the arguments on this

[1] See p. 246.

matter cannot do better than study the second volume of the Coal Commission's Report, in which are set down the views of almost all the leading authorities on both sides. Here it is only necessary to emphasize a distinction which speedily appeared in the arguments on which the condemnation of the present system in Mr. Justice Sankey's Interim Report had been based. Many of the arguments used by the advocates of public ownership were based on an exposure of the waste involved in the existing system of divided ownership both of the coal measures and of the colliery undertakings. Divided ownership, it was pointed out, meant huge loss of coal used for barriers, wasteful shaft development and unnecessary underground haulage, undue expense in draining, and even the impossibility of a systematic provision for drainage, inefficiency in marketing, extra expense in railway wagonage, and so on. But it was possible to admit the force of these arguments without favouring national ownership of the coal-mines; for many of them could be met if only the ownership of the coal measures were assumed by the State, and if the mines were brought under a co-ordinated control through some system of unification under private ownership. This seems to have been the attitude of Sir R. Redmayne, H.M. Inspector of Mines, who gave very full evidence; and it was the basis of the Report submitted by Sir Arthur Duckham, one of the Commissioners, in favour of a system of unification of the industry on a district basis under private, quasi-trust, ownership.

As against this attitude, the advocates of public ownership contended that, if the case for unification was admitted, the case for nationalization must be admitted too; for the alternative would involve the placing in the hands of a trust or combine powers which would inevitably be exercisable against the public interest. It would be impossible, it was urged, effectively to control a trust such as unification would require; and the safeguards suggested by Sir Arthur Duckham would, it was held, fail to be operative in reality. In addition, the nationalizers contended that the special position of the coal industry, underlying all others and affecting the whole economic position of the nation, was such that it ought not to be allowed to remain under private ownership. Mr. Straker went further than this, and declared that the principle of public ownership ought to be applied not only to the mines, but also progressively to industry generally—a demand which was also made by the Trade Union representatives at the National Industrial Conference.[1]

The case for public ownership, as it was stated by the miners and their friends, was of course closely interrelated with the case for the democratic administration of the industry embodied in the draft Bill of the Miners' Federation. Arguing in favour of national ownership, Mr. Straker gave his view that

> Mining can be more economically carried on by the executive power of mining being in the hands of those engaged in it, and who, as a matter of course, must know most about it, instead of, as at present, by so many people, such as shareholders and directors with no practical knowledge, who so largely dominate mining policy at the present time.

The miners' proposal, then, was that the actual management of the mining industry under public ownership should be placed, both nationally and locally, as far as possible in the hands of the workers by hand and brain and of their representatives. At the same time, the necessity for the final control of policy and finance by the community as a whole was recognized, and provision was made for giving a voice in control to the representatives of the various classes of coal consumers.

The governing proposal in the miners' plan was that the administration of the coal industry should be handed over, not to a Government department of the normal type, but to a National Mining Council, over which the Minister for Mines, responsible to Parliament on behalf of the Council, would preside. To some extent this proposal was based on the actual structure of the British Army Council, although, of course, the Mining Council would differ in being primarily a representative body. Half the members of this Council, apart from the Chairman, who would be a member of the Government appointed by the Prime Minister, were, in the miners' scheme, to be nominated by the Miners' Federation of Great Britain as representing the manual workers in the industry. The other half were to be nominated by the Government, and it was specially urged that they should include

[1] See *Memorandum on the Causes of, and Remedies for, Labour Unrest*, in the Report of the National Industrial Conference, 1919.

representatives of the various classes of experts, technicians and managerial workers who are at present outside the ranks of the Miners' Federation. The National Mining Council was thus intended to be, mainly or even exclusively, representative of the various grades of workers by hand and brain whose co-operation is essential to the efficient conduct of the industry.

Under the National Council, there was to be in each coal-field or group of coal-fields a District Mining Council. Half of the members of this body would be nominated by the district Miners' Association as representing the manual workers, and the other half by the National Council mainly from the same classes as the Government nominees on the National Council. Under the District Councils in turn there were to be Pit Councils, reproducing the same essential structure as the national and district bodies. On these too the manual workers were to have half the representation. For the representation of the standpoint of the consumers, there was to be an advisory Fuel Consumers' Council, to be nominated by the Government; but no detailed scheme for the constitution of this body was submitted by the Miners' Federation, though actual proposals were made by Mr. Arthur Greenwood [1] and by other witnesses.

The need for the avoidance of undue centralization was recognized by the miners; but it was felt to be impossible to define in advance the precise scope of the respective duties of the National, District, and Pit Councils. Accordingly, the whole authority for the management of the industry was transferred to the National Mining Council; but full provision was made for the delegation of all or any of its powers to the District Councils or, through them, to the Pit Councils. The National Mining Council would thus, under the scheme, subject only to a general Treasury control of expenditure and to the ultimate financial and policy control of Parliament, have become the fully responsible managing authority for the whole of the mining industry.

It is not too much to say that the proposals submitted by the Miners' Federation stood for a new conception of nationalization. They were the first attempt to embody in an immediately practical

[1] Formerly assistant secretary to the Ministry of Reconstruction, and subsequently the present writer's successor as officer for Advisory Committees to the Labour Party.

form the double aspiration of organized Labour for public ownership combined with democratic control of industry. They aroused, naturally, a storm of comment. Opponents denounced them as 'Syndicalism'—something far worse than the 'State Socialism' of the old nationalization policy. On the other hand, the extreme left within the Miners' Federation was also dissatisfied with them, and a section of the South Wales Miners produced, under the title 'A Plan for the Democratic Control of the Mining Industry' a rival scheme based on a complete system of workers' control to be won by militant action through a reorganized Miners' Federation. According to the authors of the pamphlet, 'a joint control with the State, with all its necessarily bureaucratic administration, would force us into the illogical position of fighting against our own control. While for obvious reasons control with the State offers an alluring prospect to "leaders", to the working miner it is simply a change of masters.' The pamphlet therefore urged the entire transference of the industry to the Miners' Federation of Great Britain, the State retaining a 'control through demand', exercised by a Coal Controller appointed by the Government who would negotiate with the Miners' Federation as the representative of 'supply'.

This plan did not come before the Coal Industry Commission: but the official plan submitted by the Miners' Federation was very fully discussed, and produced an undeniable impression. The miners, however, failed to secure its endorsement by the Commission as a whole; and, when the Final Reports were issued on the 23rd June, there were no less than four separate sets of proposals. The personnel of the Commission was by this time slightly different from that with which it began its work. Sir Thomas Royden, one of the members originally appointed by the Government to represent employers not connected with the coal industry, resigned after the first stage, and was succeeded by Sir Allan Smith, the Chairman of the Engineering Employers' Federation and of the National Confederation of Employers' Organizations. Sir Allan Smith had also been the Chairman of the employers' representatives at the National Industrial Conference. A little later, Mr. J. T. Forgie, one of the coal-owners' representatives, also resigned from the Commission, and was succeeded by

Sir Adam Nimmo, well known as one of the ablest of the coal-owners, and their principal leader in Scotland. These changes materially strengthened the employers' side of the Commission, and foreshadowed a stiffening resistance to demands for public ownership or workers' control.

Of the four Reports submitted at the end of the second and final stage of the Commission's proceedings, one was signed by the six Labour members, one by the three coal-owners and also by two of the other representatives of employers, Sir Allan Smith and Mr. Arthur Balfour, one by Sir Arthur Duckham alone, and one by the Chairman alone. There was, however, agreement on many points between the Chairman and the six Labour representatives, and, on these points, their Reports could practically be read together as a Majority Report.

On one matter of substance all four Reports were in agreement. The Commissioners were unanimous in recommending the acquisition by the State of complete ownership of the coal measures, and therefore the transference to the State of all mineral rights, royalties, and wayleaves affecting the production of coal. The Government Committee on the Acquisition of Land had recently, in its Report, pointed out the difficulties, anomalies, and waste arising from the divided ownership of mineral rights, and abundant evidence of this had also been submitted to the Commission. Most of the Commissioners proposed that the present owners should be compensated for the loss of their mineral rights ; but the three miners' representatives, while agreeing that the colliery owners should be compensated, since their property consisted of improvements, objected to compensation being given to the landowners, on the ground that minerals are, of right, not a private but a public possession.

On one other point there was general agreement. All the Reports recommended that the machinery of local authorities and co-operative societies should be further utilized for the distribution of coal.

It is interesting to observe that neither of these recommendations, on which the Commission reached unanimity, has been carried into effect.

In considering the controversial part of the four Reports, it is most convenient to take first the Report signed by five employer members of the Commission, including the three representatives of the coal-owners. The signatories, following in the main the line of the proposals submitted by the coal-owners' national organization, the Mining Association of Great Britain, rejected the demand for national ownership, and recommended only minor modifications in the conduct of the coal industry. Nationalization, they held, would not prevent unrest or conduce to efficiency, whether it followed lines of bureaucratic administration or the lines proposed by the Miners' Federation. Nor did they favour any scheme of compulsory unification under private ownership. They recommended the establishment of a permanent Mines Department, but not the conferring upon it of any wide control over the industry. Apart from details, and the public ownership of the coal measures, the only important change which they proposed was the institution of a system of joint councils throughout the industry. In each colliery they proposed the establishment of a joint Pit Committee equally representative of the management and of the mine-workers. In each coal-field they proposed a joint District Council for the common discussion of problems of a district character 'which, in the opinion of the Council, it is in the mutual interest of the parties to discuss'. This proposal, in fact, would have involved no change; for already in each coal-field the miners and owners were in the habit of meeting regularly, through a Conciliation Board or Joint Conference, for the discussion of precisely the same range of questions. The owners also proposed the setting up of a joint National Council, to be appointed by the district bodies of owners and miners, 'for the purpose of dealing with any question of national interest which may be referred to it'. This would have been an innovation; but the absence of any definition of the functions of the proposed National Council robbed the suggestion of value from the standpoint of the miners. The owners, it was clear, were not prepared to concede the principle of a National Wages Board and national determination of wages and conditions for which the Miners' Federation had long been pressing.[1]

Far more drastic were the proposals submitted by Sir Arthur Duckham, a professional engineer who had directed important

[1] See *ante*, p. 10, and *post*, Chapter IX.

munitions factories during the War on behalf of the Ministry of Munitions. His proposal, which, as we shall see, formed at a later stage the basis of a scheme propounded by Mr. Lloyd George, was for unification of the mining industry on a district basis, and under private ownership. Under Sir Arthur Duckham's plan the whole of the coal-fields were to be assigned to certain ' areas ', and in each area a Statutory Company (or District Coal Board) was to be established by the complete unification of all colliery concerns within the area. Dividends at the rate of 4 per cent. were to be guaranteed by the Government on the stock of the unified companies, provision being made against the further watering of capital. Profits above the amount necessary to pay interest at 4 per cent. were to go (*a*) to form such reserve funds as might be approved by the Minister of Mines, (*b*) to pay a further dividend of 2 per cent. Of any remaining surplus one-third might go to pay further dividends ; but the remainder must be used so as to reduce the price of coal. For the workers, a system of minimum rates plus a bonus on output was proposed. Each company was to have not less than seven directors, of whom one would be elected by the managerial staffs and two by the rest of the workers, the majority being chosen by the shareholders. A system of Pit Committees was also suggested.

This, it will be seen, was virtually a proposal for trustification of the coal industry on a district basis, with workers' representatives, in a minority, on the Boards of Directors. It bears a close resemblance to the scheme propounded a little later by Sir Eric Geddes, as spokesman of the Government, for the railways. This scheme contained a similar proposal for workers' representation on Boards of Directors ; but this provision was dropped in face of the opposition of the companies and the doubtful attitude of the Trade Unions when the Act providing for railway amalgamation was finally passed in 1921.

The Report submitted by Sir John Sankey recommended that not only the coal measures, but also the colliery undertakings throughout the country, should be acquired by the nation, and that, until this had been done, the system of administration suggested should be enforced by the continuance of Government control. Sir John Sankey's proposal thus met one of the two main demands of the miners. On the question of administration, however, the plan which he put forward differed materially from theirs. He proposed that at every mine there should be a Local Mining Council (equivalent to the Pit Council proposed by the miners); but he urged that this Council should be purely advisory, and that only four of its ten members should be appointed by the working miners. The manager, under-manager, and commercial manager of the mine were to be *ex-officio* members, and three members were to be appointed by the District Mining Council. This District Council, in its turn, was to consist of fourteen members, of whom only four were to be chosen by the workers. The Minister of Mines was to appoint a Chairman and a Vice-Chairman; and the remaining members were to be appointed by the National Mining Council. Of these, four were to represent consumers, two mining technicians, and two commercial experts connected with the industry. The National Mining Council was to be drawn from the District Councils, each district appointing one member for every 5,000,000 tons of output.

An important difference between the miners' scheme and that of Sir John Sankey was that, whereas the miners proposed that authority should be vested in the National Mining Council, with power to delegate functions to the District Councils, Sir John Sankey made the District Councils the operative bodies entrusted with the conduct of the industry, and the National Council a deliberative body meeting normally only three times a year. The Minister of Mines was, however, to be assisted by a Standing Committee drawn from the National Council.

Sir John Sankey also differed from the miners in that he proposed that the contracts of all workmen should embody an undertaking not to strike on any question until the matter in dispute had been before the Local and District Mining Councils, and these bodies had failed to settle the difficulty. This proposal was strongly opposed by the Labour representatives in their separate Report.

This Report, signed by the six Labour members of the Commission, was very brief. The signatories contented themselves with affirming that, while they were in substantial agreement with the Chairman's Report, in their view fuller provision should be made for the representation of the workers on the various Mining Councils, on the lines of the Miners' Federation plan already discussed, and with making certain other reservations to which reference has already been made.

These four Reports were issued on the 23rd June. Strictly speaking, there was no Majority Report; for none of the four was signed by a majority of the whole Commission. But, on most of the issues involved, the Reports of the Chairman and of the six Labour members virtually formed a single Report; and the question that at once arose was whether or not the Government would make the agreed conclusions of the majority of the Commissioners the basis of its policy. The actual history of the Reports after their issue, and the subsequent struggle over the question of public ownership, are dealt with in the next chapter of this study.

CHAPTER VI

THE NATIONALIZATION STRUGGLE

SECTION 1. THE RECEPTION OF THE COMMISSION'S REPORTS

THE Final Reports of the Coal Industry Commission were ready on the 23rd June 1919. During the weeks immediately following the situation developed rapidly, and it became clear to the miners that national ownership and democratic control of their industry would be won, if at all, only after a severe struggle. Already, during the second stage of the Commission's proceedings, the opposition had been mobilizing its forces ; and the employers' organizations of every sort and kind had been holding meetings, and passing resolutions, against any extension of the principle of public ownership in industry. This opposition was influentially represented in the House of Commons, and a large proportion of the members of the Coalition parties had pledged themselves to resist any attempt to introduce nationalization, and had made their views known to the Cabinet in a communication which was practically an ultimatum. The parliamentary struggle assumed a positive form at first in direct relation, not to the mining industry, but to the railways. During the General Election of 1918 the Government was understood to have pledged itself to nationalize the railways, and it is admitted that Mr. Winston Churchill, in the course of his election campaign, stated explicitly that this decision had been taken by the Government. The Ways and Communications Bill, which was before Parliament during the spring and summer months, was not a nationalization Bill, but it included clauses enabling the Ministry of Transport to acquire and operate railways. Against this and other features of the

Bill, which were regarded as antagonistic to private enterprise, the whole force of the Coalition opponents was thrown, with the result that the Government's Bill was mutilated by the Government's own supporters, and every reference that seemed to hint at nationalization was expunged. It was intimated plainly to the Government that any measure for the nationalization, or such as to facilitate the nationalization, of the mining industry would meet the same fate. The coal-owners took part in this movement of opposition; but it was essentially a movement of the advocates of private enterprise generally, and not distinctly a coal-owners' movement. An attempt to nationalize one industry was regarded as a threat to others, and united resistance was accordingly offered.

On the publication of the Sankey Report, the volume of protest was re-doubled, while, on their side, the Labour organizations passed resolutions in favour of nationalization, but did not at this stage imitate the employers' bodies by instituting any campaign in its support. The Miners' Federation accepted the view that the right course was to let the Reports of the Commission speak for themselves, and to await the Government's pronouncement before taking any action. This was the tenour of its reply to an offer of assistance in securing nationalization made to it by the Labour Party. The Government, meanwhile, adopted a waiting game, and the constant reply to questions in the House of Commons was that 'the matter remained under consideration by the Government'.

Two parliamentary by-elections were at this time pending—in East Swansea, a mixed industrial constituency, and in Bothwell, in the heart of the Lanarkshire coal-field. Nationalization of the mines naturally became the principal issue in these contests, in both of which Labour candidates were opposing Coalitionists for seats held by the Government parties. On the 9th July, on the eve of the Swansea poll, the Government suddenly announced an increase of 6*s.* a ton in the price of coal, representing this as necessary on account of the concessions made to the miners under the Interim Sankey Report. The Labour bodies generally regarded this as a political manœuvre, designed to influence electoral opinion against the miners, and this view was strengthened by the fact that no intimation of the proposed increase had been made to the Coal Controller's Advisory Committee, on which the miners were represented jointly with the coal-owners. There is no doubt that the announcement, coming on the eve of the poll, did save the Swansea seat for the Coalition, although, even so, the Government majority was greatly reduced. In Bothwell the effect was precisely opposite. Labour was in any case secure of winning the seat; but the resentment of the largely mining electorate caused the Labour majority to swell to huge proportions, and Mr. John Robertson, a well-known leader of the Scottish miners, was elected by 13,135 votes against 5,967 cast for his opponent, a Scottish coal-owner.

On the first opportunity, both the Miners' Federation and the Labour Party in the House of Commons challenged the accuracy of the calculations by which the Government sought to justify the increase in the price of coal, and questioned its necessity. The Government maintained that it was rendered necessary by the low rate of output which was being secured, and sought to throw the blame for this upon the miners. The latter retorted that the decline in output was due, not to the slackening of efforts on their part but to defective organization at the collieries, the working of inferior seams in order to leave good seams for a future time when profits would be decontrolled, the lack of transport facilities which was throwing many collieries idle, failure to make good war-time arrears of maintenance and development, and similar causes outside the workers' control. They also pointed out that they had already asked the Government to institute a special and comprehensive inquiry into the causes of declining output, and that no action had been taken to do this. Questioned on this matter, Mr. Bonar Law declared the time to be inopportune for such an inquiry.

In the course of the debate concerning the 6*s*. increase in coal prices, Mr. Bonar Law, on the 14th July, made a tentative and conditional offer to withdraw the increase. The following are the relevant sentences in his speech:

> I say, then, to my honourable friends that, if they can give an equivalent for the dangers which I see in delay, if they can say to me on the floor of the House, 'If you postpone this for three months, we will

join with you and put our backs into it to increase the output, and during that time there will be a period of suspense, and there will be no stoppages or strikes for the three months ', I would be inclined to accept it, and I think the Government would do so also. I think that is a fair offer.

This ' offer ', if it was to be so regarded, came before the Annual Conference of the Miners' Federation, which began its sessions at Keswick on the 15th July. The Conference with practical unanimity refused to give any such pledge as the Government demanded, and passed unanimously the following resolution :

That this Annual Conference, having heard the report of the Members of Parliament upon the discussion in the House of Commons on the Government's proposal to raise the price of coal by 6*s.* per ton, declares that the increase is not necessary, and should be avoided. It regards the problem as one of production only. It is of opinion that production can only be increased to a point which would make the industry self-supporting, without additional charges to the consumer, if the economies set forth in the First Sankey Report are affected and the recommendations of the majority of the Commissioners as to an immediate change of ownership and control in the mining industry be passed into law. It therefore informs the Government that it is prepared to co-operate with the Government to the fullest extent to put such economies into effect and the recommendations into law.

The acceptance of Mr. Bonar Law's proposal would, indeed, have had very far-reaching results. There were still, as we shall see, important questions outstanding under the First Sankey Report, and the giving of a pledge would have disarmed the miners for dealing with these and also for bringing pressure to bear in support of nationalization. It would, moreover, have been construed as an admission that the miners were responsible for the decline in output, and would thus have damaged their case before the public. These, at any rate, were the contentions which prevailed at the Keswick Conference.

This Conference had also before it the wider issue arising out of the Final Reports of the Coal Commission. The result of the Commission had been, as we have noted, a majority recommendation in favour of public ownership and of workers' participation in management ; but the six Labour members had differed from

Sir John Sankey in proposing a greater measure of workers' control and on a number of other points. The issue now before the Miners' Conference was whether the Federation should continue to press for the acceptance of its own scheme of ownership and control, or whether it should follow the line of less resistance by agreeing to accept, for the time being, the proposals of Sir John Sankey. After full discussion it was unanimously decided to adopt the latter course, and the following resolution was carried:

> That this Conference, having noted the political and industrial pressure now being brought to bear upon the Government with a view to getting it to ignore the recommendations of the Coal Industry Commission, as expressed in the Reports of the Commissioners in the second stage of the Commission's work, therefore intimates to the Government that, whilst the miners are not fully satisfied with the Report of Mr. Justice Sankey in all its details, the miners are prepared to give their fullest support to carry out the recommendations of the Majority Report of the Commission into immediate effect.

This resolution is somewhat ambiguously worded, but clearly its general intention was to convey to the Government the miners' acceptance of the Sankey proposals, subject to a right to criticize them in detail on the lines of the Report submitted by the six Labour representatives on the Commission. Accordingly, the ensuing struggle centred rather round Sir John Sankey's proposals or the question of public ownership in general, than round the actual proposals made in the Bill drafted by the Miners' Federation.

Section 2. A Strike Interlude in Yorkshire

While the Miners' Federation was meeting in conference at Keswick, a serious dispute was developing in the Yorkshire coalfield, and on the 17th July a general stoppage of the Yorkshire pits began. The trouble arose directly out of the terms of settlement adopted after the publication of the Interim Sankey Report on the 20th March. It was agreed between the Miners' Federation and the Government that day-work rates should not be reduced in consequence of the reduction in hours from eight to seven, and that piece-work prices should be readjusted so as to enable the previous earnings to be maintained in the shorter working day.

The precise method to be adopted in giving effect to this pledge was left over for consideration, and, at a joint meeting between the representatives of coal-owners and miners, it was agreed to refer it to the separate districts for adjustment. Accordingly, negotiations began on a district basis, and, from certain areas, proposals agreed upon between the miners and the owners were submitted for ratification to the Coal Controller. Trouble soon followed. In June the Coal Controller issued to all districts a circular intimating that the advances upon piece-rates to be made in consequence of the reduction in hours must be limited to a maximum of 10 per cent. in any district. As against this, the miners contended that the increase should be the amount necessary to maintain the previous earnings, allowance being made for a fall in output proportionate to the reduction in hours, and should therefore be one-seventh, or 14·3 per cent. The Miners' Federation thereupon took the matter up nationally with the Coal Controller, and on the 9th July the Government agreed to amend its proposal so as to make the maximum rate of increase 12½ per cent., on condition that the average rate of increase over the whole country should not exceed 10 per cent.

In South Yorkshire the miners had already succeeded in getting the mine-owners to agree to an advance of 14·3 per cent., but this was disallowed by the Coal Controller. In addition, the miners in Yorkshire and in certain other areas were pressing for a further concession. In some collieries, where men had to walk long distances to their work, the actual hewing time was much less than the average, and a reduction of one hour in the working day therefore meant a larger percentage reduction in hewing time. Moreover, before the reduction of hours under the Sankey Report, the normal working day in the collieries was the legal maximum of eight hours [1]; but a number of pits, especially those working under a shift system, had already a shorter working day of seven and a half hours or less. The question which now arose was whether, in these pits, the increase in piece-rates was to be limited to one-seventh or whether a larger advance should be permitted where, owing to long walking time, the reduction in hewing time was more than one-eighth, or where the working day previously

[1] Equivalent actually, on the average, to an 8½ hour day. See p. 14.

in force had been of less than eight hours. On this latter point the Yorkshire owners had refused to give way, while they were prepared to agree to a uniform increase of one-eighth, or even 14·3 per cent.

At the Keswick Conference of the Miners' Federation the Yorkshire delegates, with some support from other districts, protested against the action of the National Executive in taking the matter out of the hands of the districts, to which it had been referred, and in endeavouring to negotiate a uniform arrangement for all districts with the Coal Controller. After a long discussion, however, it was agreed that the Executive should deal with the question, and that the advance asked for should be limited to 14·3 per cent. for a reduction of one hour, with proportionate advances for fractional reductions of less than a full hour. The Executive was instructed to negotiate with the Coal Controller on this basis, and 'in the meantime', the resolution added, 'all districts are requested to continue working until instructed to the contrary'.

This advice came too late. The Yorkshire delegates at the Conference, supported by those from Lancashire and Cheshire and from Kent, voted against the resolution, and the strike in Yorkshire, called officially by the Yorkshire Miners' Association, began on the very day on which the resolution was carried at Keswick. The Yorkshire miners thus struck with the full support of their own Union, but without the support of the Miners' Federation of Great Britain. During the first few days of the strike, the pumpmen and other safety workers remained in the pits, but the Yorkshire Miners' Council announced that, if no settlement was reached before the end of the week, these workers also would be withdrawn.

There was no settlement, and on the 19th July the safety men went on strike. The Government immediately met this action by dispatching to Yorkshire men from the Royal Navy, and placing these men at the disposal of the collieries for the saving of the pits from flooding. In the majority of the pits there was no immediate danger of this, but, under the superintendence of Sir Eric Geddes, who took up his head-quarters in Leeds on the 22nd July, the naval units were introduced wherever the colliery proprietors asked for their help. Generally speaking, the miners made no attempt to interfere with the work of the naval men, although their dispatch caused a good deal of resentment, and, when isolated attempts were made to interfere, the Yorkshire Miners' Council on the 24th July issued a special instruction that the naval units should be left unmolested. This order was generally obeyed.

Meanwhile, a vigorous campaign against the Yorkshire miners was being waged in the newspapers. Mr. Bonar Law, questioned in the House of Commons on the 22nd July as to the causes of the dispute, disclaimed knowledge, and imputed it to such questions as nationalization, the increase in coal prices, &c., although he had been fully informed of the negotiations which led up to the deadlock. The danger to the pits from flooding was, as usual, greatly exaggerated, and what was true only of a few pits was readily assumed by the press to be true of all.

Meanwhile, the strike showed signs of possible extension. The miners in the tiny Kent coal-field came on strike officially, and unofficial stoppages on a small scale took place in a number of other coal-fields. The attitude of the Miners' Federation, however, prevented any considerable extension of the conflict, and, except in Yorkshire, the stoppages came rapidly to an end. In Kent a settlement was reached by means of a compromise after a few days' cessation of work.

The Yorkshire position was far more serious. On the 21st July the Minister of Labour, Sir Robert Horne, wrote to Mr. Frank Hodges asking what steps the Federation was taking to secure that work should be resumed in Yorkshire in accordance with the Keswick decision. The Federation, however, was powerless, for the Yorkshire Miners' Association maintained—and constitutionally they were right—that the matter was within their own discretion, and that they were not bound by what the Federation might decide.

The Miners' Federation, therefore, could do no more than prevent the strike from extending, and carry out the decision of the Keswick Conference by resuming negotiations with the Government for the purpose of finding an acceptable formula for application nationally. This was done, and, as the result of the work of a joint sub-committee, a national settlement was reached at a full meeting between the Government and the Federation representatives on the 25th July. Under this agreement, which was in appearance very complicated, the Government granted practically what the Federation had asked for at Keswick—an increase of 14·2 per cent. in piece-work prices as the equivalent of an hour's reduction, with proportionate increases for fractions of an hour where the reduction was actually less. The proviso that the average rate of increase over the whole country should not exceed 10 per cent. remained, but was unlikely in practice to interfere with the working of the formula, as in several districts the reduction was considerably less than a full hour.

The press certainly supposed—and the Government may possibly have believed—that this national settlement would bring the Yorkshire dispute to an end. This, however, was not the case. The Yorkshire Miners' Council met on the 27th July, but it decided not to end the strike but to consult the members as to its continuance, for the purpose both of securing a more acceptable formula, and of clearing up certain other questions in dispute, of which the most important was one affecting the enginemen in West Yorkshire.

The miners throughout the Yorkshire coal-field are organized in a single body, the Yorkshire Miners' Association; but the coal-owners are divided between two independent organizations, one for South and one for West Yorkshire. It was with the South Yorkshire owners that the miners had reached, before the beginning of the dispute, the agreement which was disallowed by the Coal Controller. In West Yorkshire negotiations had been proceeding, but the Controller had intervened before an agreement could be reached. There, too, the position was complicated by the dispute as to wages and hours affecting the enginemen. In South Yorkshire the owners and the miners were at one, and the strike was really directed against the Coal Controller; in West Yorkshire the difference was primarily between the owners and the miners, though it was complicated by the Controller's attitude.

On the 29th and 30th July the first attempt was made to

settle the dispute by direct negotiation. The miners met the West Yorkshire owners, at the request of the latter. Sir David Shackleton, representing the Minister of Labour, proposed that work should be at once resumed on the basis of a provisional advance of 11·8 per cent., the actual amount due to be adjusted by subsequent negotiation. This was refused. The miners stood out for the full percentage claimed, and for a settlement of other outstanding issues ; the owners contended that differences could only be adjusted after a resumption of work.

The strike therefore dragged on, causing a growing dislocation of industry in Yorkshire and the neighbouring counties. The next attempt to settle it was made on the 6th August, this time in the southern part of the coal-field. On that day the miners met the South Yorkshire owners, with whom they had really no dispute. The owners agreed to send with them a joint invitation to the Coal Controller to visit Yorkshire, in order that they might put before him the grounds on which they had agreed, before the dispute, on an advance of 14·3 per cent. The South Yorkshire owners also offered a separate settlement on the terms already agreed upon. This would have left the dispute to go on in West Yorkshire, while ending it in the larger southern section of the coal-field.

These hopes of settlement, however, came to nothing. On the 7th August the Coal Controller refused to agree to the joint proposals of the South Yorkshire miners and owners, on the ground that they would involve a departure from the national formula agreed upon with the Miners' Federation. The miners, on their side, refused a separate settlement, on the ground that this would weaken their position in West Yorkshire. The strike seemed to have gained a new lease of life.

Already, however, the strain was telling. The funds of the miners were nearly exhausted, and it was clear that the deadlock could not be indefinitely maintained. On the 11th August a further attempt at agreement was made in West Yorkshire. This broke down because the owners sought to bind the miners down to give fourteen days' notice of any future strike, and because they would not agree that, if work were resumed, any settlement reached for the enginemen should be retrospective to the date of resumption.

There was thus a complete deadlock when the Yorkshire Miners' Council met on the 12th August in order to consider the position. A prolongation of the dispute did not seem likely to secure any result, at least in South Yorkshire, and the Council accordingly decided to recommend the men to resume work in South Yorkshire immediately, and in West Yorkshire as soon as the owners agreed to make the enginemen's settlement retrospective. On the 14th August the men in South Yorkshire accepted the recommendation to resume work, and the strike in that part of the coal-field ended. A few days later the West Yorkshire enginemen also voted in favour of resumption, and on the 21st August the Yorkshire Miners' Association declared the strike at an end in West Yorkshire also. Work had already started in most of the South Yorkshire pits, and West Yorkshire now followed suit. The naval men were withdrawn as soon as the settlement was reached, and only in a few cases did flooding or falling of roofs cause any serious delay before work could be resumed. Thus, the costly strike interlude in Yorkshire came to an end, but not before it had effectively confused the public mind in relation to the issues arising out of the Sankey Report, and afforded to the Government an extraordinarily convenient opportunity for pronouncing against the nationalization of the mining industry.

Section 3. The Government Rejects Nationalization

Early in July 1919 the Government introduced into the House of Commons a Coal Mines Bill amending the Eight Hours Act of 1908. The Bill, which consisted of but two clauses, was such as to give effect to the recommendation in the Interim Sankey Report that the legal working day should be reduced from eight to seven hours. Its introduction had been delayed by special negotiations concerning the position under the Report of certain classes of workers, such as deputies and enginemen, in whose case a special adjustment of hours was required. Those workers whose shift had been a maximum of nine and a half hours under the Eight Hours Act were now to have their hours reduced to eight, while the seven-hour day was to be applicable to the main classes of underground labour. The Bill was confined entirely to the question of hours, and did not deal with any of the other recommendations made either in the Interim, or in the Final, Reports of the Coal Commission. Certain attempts to increase its stringency were made in the House of Commons by the representatives of the miners, but these were defeated, and the Bill became law on the 15th August.

While this Bill was before the House of Commons, and while the events in Yorkshire narrated in the previous section were taking place, the Government was facing the wider questions raised by the Final Reports of the Coal Commission. Although the invariable reply to parliamentary questions was that the Government's policy was still under consideration by the Cabinet, rumours began to spread during the first part of July that a definite decision against nationalization had already been reached under pressure from the commercial interests. On the 24th July the correspondents of practically all the newspapers announced this decision as certain, although there was still no official intimation of it. In this condition things remained until the collapse of the Yorkshire strike. At length, on the 18th August, when work was being resumed in South Yorkshire and the West Yorkshire dispute was clearly ending, Mr. Lloyd George made in the House of Commons his official announcement of the Government's policy.

The *Star*, in its editorial comment on Mr. Lloyd George's speech, aptly described the Government proposal for the future organization of the mining industry as 'Duckham and water'. Mr. Frank Hodges, for the Miners' Federation, made practically the same comment when he said that the Government actually did not go so far as Sir Arthur Duckham. Mr. Lloyd George completely threw over Sir John Sankey's Report, and announced outright that the Government could not adopt the policy of nationalization. In doing this, he made considerable play with the argument that nationalization would not avert industrial unrest, and instanced the Yorkshire strike as a strike directed against the Coal Controller, or, in other words, against the Government. The collapse in Yorkshire thus afforded a very convenient occasion for the declaration of the Government's policy.

Throwing over nationalization, Mr. Lloyd George was almost of necessity driven back upon Sir Arthur Duckham's proposals. The Interim Sankey Report, which the Government had publicly pledged itself to carry out 'in the spirit and in the letter', had definitely condemned the existing system, and urged that 'some other system must be substituted for it, either nationalization or a method of unification by national purchase and/or joint control'. It was possible to argue that, in accepting this recommendation, the Government had not pledged itself to nationalization, even if nationalization was subsequently proposed by the Commission; but it had certainly pledged itself to carry out either nationalization or 'a method of unification'. The only method of unification without nationalization proposed by any of the Commissioners was the scheme of Sir Arthur Duckham, and upon this Mr. Lloyd George, compelled by his supporters to forswear nationalization, inevitably fell back.

The miners' spokesmen urged that this was a breach of faith, and that the Government was fully pledged to nationalization, in the event of a recommendation in its favour by a majority of the Commission. They pointed out that, when the Coal Industry Commission Bill, under which the Commission was established, was before Parliament in February 1919, the Home Secretary, speaking on behalf of the Government, had referred to the question in the following terms:

> It is a pure business proposition, and if it turns out on investigation that it is for the good of the country as a whole that the mines should be nationalized, that the people of this country would be better off if the mines were worked under a nationalized system, rather than under private ownership, then it is a good business proposition, and we should accept it. The Government desire to go into the matter to see if it is a good business proposition. . . . I should have thought myself that for any one who desired merely to do that which was best for the country, the proposal of the Government was the best, namely that the whole question should be thrashed out with expert evidence, expert opinion, expert knowledge, before a competent and highly efficient tribunal.

This statement, and also Mr. Bonar Law's words in accepting on behalf of the Government the Interim Reports of the Commission, were generally interpreted at the time as committing the Government to nationalization, if it was proposed by the

Commission. The Government was, indeed, taken to task in some quarters for delegating to an outside body the responsibility for taking so important a decision on a vital question of policy. Mr. Lloyd George and Mr. Bonar Law, however, now denied that they were in any way committed to nationalization, and urged that the responsibility for such a decision could not be delegated, but must remain with the Government, subject to the sanction of Parliament.

The miners, on the 18th August, roundly accused the Government of having broken its pledge. Mr. Vernon Hartshorn, speaking for them in the House of Commons, summed up their view of the position in the following words:

> We did not ask for a Commission. We accepted it. We gave evidence before it. Why was the Commission set up? Was it a huge game of bluff? Was it never intended that, if the Reports favoured nationalization, we were to get it? Why was the question sent at all to the Commission? That is the kind of question the miners of the country will ask, and they will say, 'We have been deceived, betrayed, duped'.

The Government's actual proposals, while they followed the general lines of Sir Arthur Duckham's Report, fell short of it in several respects. The outline of them, given by Mr. Lloyd George in the House of Commons on the 18th August, was in the following terms:

> The Government accepts the policy of State purchase of mineral rights in coal, on which subject all the reports of the Royal Commission were perfectly unanimous.
>
> That, in view of the fact that the lives and livelihood of the miners depend upon the way in which the miners are worked, means should be devised for securing their co-operation in the shaping of the general conditions of the industry, without interfering with the executive control of the individual.
>
> That the industry should be so organized as to reduce to a minimum the expenses of management and working charges, and that with this end in view the country should be divided into convenient areas, in each of which an amalgamation of neighbouring mines should be undertaken within a limited period, say, two years. That the workers in and about the mines should have directors representing them on the body controlling the policy of the area groups to which they belong.
>
> The scheme of amalgamation should be subject to the approval of the Government, and must conform to any conditions laid down by the Government for the protection of the general body of coal consumers.

The Government thus accepted the recommendation, made by all the Commissioners, that the State should assume the ownership of all mineral rights. It also followed the view of a majority of the Commissioners in proposing that these rights should be acquired by purchase.

It accepted, in somewhat vague language, Sir Arthur Duckham's proposal for the unification of the mining industry by amalgamation of colliery concerns on a district basis, but the Prime Minister made no reference to Sir Arthur Duckham's recommendation that profits should be limited, and his reference to any form of State control over the unified industry was studiously vague.

On the question of workers' control, the Government accepted Sir Arthur Duckham's scheme for workmen directors on the boards of the ' area groups ' to be created by amalgamation, and endorsed, in very general terms, the recommendation that the workers should have a say in shaping the conditions of the industry, with the proviso that this must not ' interfere with the executive control of the individual '. The scheme as a whole was propounded only in the most general outline and in such a way that its real character could in many respects hardly be made out without fuller information.

As we have seen, the policy of the Miners' Federation had been to await an explicit declaration of policy on the part of the Government before taking any step in furtherance of the demand for public ownership and workers' control. Accordingly, the Executive decided, when the Prime Minister had given his decision, to call a full National Conference, and to place the situation before the delegates. This Conference met on the 3rd September 1919, and, after a heated discussion in which immediate strike action was proposed, carried unanimously the following resolution:

> Being convinced that the Government's scheme is wholly impracticable for the future working of the mines, this Conference of Miners' Delegates rejects the Government scheme, and records its regret that the Government has no better scheme than the creation of great trusts to secure the economic well-being of the industry.
>
> We are convinced that the only way to place the industry upon a scientific basis for the purpose of giving the advantage of a maximum production to the community, consistent with the maximum economic

and social well-being of the miners, is at once to introduce the scheme of nationalization recommended by the majority of the Coal Industry Commission.

We do not at this stage recommend the miners to take industrial action to secure the adoption of the Coal Commission's Report, but we invite the Trades Union Congress to declare that the fullest and most effective action be taken to secure that the Government shall adopt the Majority Report of the Commission as to the further governance of the industry.

The Miners' Federation thus repudiated without hesitation, as they were doubtless expected to do, the 'Duckham and water' proposals of the Prime Minister, and made an unequivocal demand for nationalization on the principles recommended by the Commission. But, instead of determining to take industrial action by themselves for the achievement of their objects, they appealed to the Trades Union Congress to mobilize the whole resources of the Labour movement in support of the nationalization demand.

Section 4. The 'Mines for the Nation' Campaign

The Miners' Conference of the 3rd September was held, advisedly, immediately before the opening of the annual Trades Union Congress, to which the Miners' Executive had determined to appeal. In the following week the miners presented their case to the Congress, and asked that the issue of public ownership in the mining industry should be made one, not for the miners alone, but for the whole Labour movement. The result of this appeal was that, almost with unanimity, the Congress resolved to support the miners. The opposition, led by Mr. Havelock Wilson, of the Sailors' and Firemen's Union, a Trade Union supporter of the Government, who had long been at variance with the official Trade Union leaders, found very few supporters, and the resolution pledging the Trade Unions to aid the miners was carried by 4,478,999 votes against 77,999. Most of the minority votes are accounted for by the block vote of the Sailors' and Firemen's Union, and all the other big Unions voted in favour of the resolution, which was moved by Mr. Robert Smillie, on behalf of the miners, and seconded by the railwaymen's leader, Mr. J. H. Thomas.

The resolution, prepared by the leaders of the Triple Industrial Alliance, was worded as follows :

(*a*) This Congress, having received the request of the Miners' Federation to consider the Government rejection of the Majority Report of the Coal Industry Commission, and the adoption in its place of a scheme of district trustification of the industry, hereby declares that, in conjunction with the miners, it rejects the Government scheme for the governance of the industry as a scheme contrary to the best interests of the nation ; and it expresses its resolve to co-operate with the Miners' Federation of Great Britain to the fullest extent, with a view to compelling the Government to adopt the scheme of national ownership and joint control recommended by the majority of the Commission in their Report.

(*b*) To this end the Congress instructs the Parliamentary Committee, in conjunction with the Miners' Federation, to immediately interview the Prime Minister on the matter, in the name of the entire Labour movement, to insist upon the Government adopting the Report.

(*c*) In the event of the Government still refusing to accept the position, a Special Congress shall be convened for the purpose of deciding the form of action to be taken to compel the Government to accept the Majority Report of the Commission.

This resolution, it is to be noted, quite definitely committed the Trades Union Congress to support the miners in their demand for national ownership, while it left open the question of the means to be adopted with this object. The first step to be taken under the resolution was to make an effort to persuade the Government to change its mind, although it was difficult for the Labour leaders, with their knowledge of the influences against nationalization which had been brought to bear, to entertain much hope of such a change. But, hopeful or hopeless, the Trades Union Congress and the miners could but try, in the first instance, the effect of their united persuasions. The deputation provided for in the Congress resolution took, however, some time to arrange, and it was not until the 9th October that the Labour leaders met Mr. Lloyd George and other prominent Ministers.

The result of the meeting was precisely what had been expected. Speaking on behalf of the Government, Mr. Lloyd George announced that 'We have come definitely to the conclusion that we cannot see our way to advise Parliament to pass a measure for taking over as a business of the State the management of the mines of this country'.

This was definite enough, and the only step open to the Labour organizations, in accordance with the Congress resolution of the 10th September, was to summon a special Congress in order to consider what action should be taken 'to compel the Government to accept the Majority Report of the Commission'. This clearly implied a threat of strike action, but, after fully considering the position, the miners decided that, even if strike action might be necessary at a later stage, it would be desirable first to make a further appeal to public opinion, and to endeavour to arouse the public to a sense of the need for public ownership of the mining industry.

Accordingly, when the Special Trades Union Congress met on the 9th December, the proposal before it was not for a strike, but for an educational campaign. It was proposed that for two months the whole propagandist activity of the Labour movement should be devoted to a national campaign in support of the recommendations of the Coal Commission. The Trades Union Congress and the Labour Party both agreed to co-operate with the miners in this campaign, and, after the scheme had been approved by the Special Trades Union Congress, the Co-operative Union also appointed representatives to serve on the Committee controlling the campaign.

The 'Mines for the Nation' campaign was duly launched at a big public meeting in London on the 9th December, and continued for a period of two months. Meetings were held in all parts of the country, and everywhere resolutions in favour of public ownership and joint control of the mining industry were carried. An immense quantity of leaflets and many pamphlets were also distributed.

Despite the energy devoted to it, there is no doubt that, on the whole, the campaign was a failure. No considerable opposition to nationalization was disclosed, but it became apparent that, outside the circles directly under Labour influence, there was no keen interest in the question. The mining districts were solid enough, and Labour opinion was everywhere favourable, but it proved to be merely impossible to concentrate attention on the mining issue at the expense of the many other national and international questions which were also claiming the notice of the public.

The bodies which were responsible for the 'Mines for the

Nation' campaign therefore found themselves, as it drew to an end, in no more favourable position than they had been at its inception. Indeed, in one respect they were worse off, for the issues raised by the Sankey Report had, in the minds of many of the public, lost their immediacy. Seven months had passed since the reports were published, and nothing had been done, and it was easy to conclude that, where seven months had passed, a much longer period might pass without serious trouble.

While the campaign was in full swing, the Government introduced into the House of Commons a Bill for the regulation of the coal industry. On the 11th December 1919, the Coal Mines Emergency Bill came before Parliament. It contained no reference to the proposals for unification put forward in August by Mr. Lloyd George. These had been already abandoned as impracticable in face of the united opposition of owners and miners. The Bill proposed only to carry out one of the recommendations of the Sankey Report by limiting coal-owners' profits to 1*s.* 2*d.* per ton. The limitation was, however, to be purely temporary, extending only to March 1920; and, whereas Mr. Justice Sankey had recommended that control should continue, the Bill proposed to terminate the Government control of the coal mines in March 1920, and thus to bring about a complete restoration of private ownership and control.

This measure was vigorously attacked in the House of Commons, with the result that the debates upon it were adjourned *sine die*, and it was at length withdrawn for reconsideration by the Government.

The Miners' Executive met again on the 6th February 1920 in order to consider the situation which would arise on the conclusion of the 'Mines for the Nation' campaign. The position was that the December Special Trades Union Congress had adjourned until February, in order to allow time for a propagandist effort. The obvious course, therefore, was to move that the Congress should be recalled in order to consider its further action. This the miners decided to do, and accordingly the Parliamentary Committee of the Trades Union Congress was requested by the Miners' Executive to convene at once a further Special Congress. On the 18th February the two

Committees met and made the necessary arrangements for the Congress.

The Special Trades Union Congress duly met on the 18th March, preceded, on the 9th March, by a full delegate Conference of the Miners' Federation. The miners at their conference decided to press for direct action by the whole Trade Union movement in support of the demand for public ownership and joint control. There was, however, considerable difference of opinion, even among the miners themselves. Before the Delegate Conference the question of 'direct action' had been fully discussed in the various districts of the Miners' Federation, and each district sent its representatives to the Conference with a definite mandate. The result of the voting was that 524,999 votes were cast in favour of 'a general Trade Union strike' for nationalization, and as many as 344,000 votes against. It should be observed that, in the national Conferences of the Miners' Federation, it is the practice for each district to cast a block vote, so that the figures do not necessarily indicate the numerical division of opinion among the members. On this occasion, eleven districts, including South Wales, Lancashire and Cheshire, the Midlands, Nottinghamshire, Derbyshire, Northumberland, and Scotland, voted for a strike, and nine districts, including Yorkshire and Durham, against.

Although the actual particulars of the vote were not disclosed, it was well known at the Trades Union Congress that there had been an acute division in the ranks of the miners. This doubtless contributed to the result, and helped to determine waverers to vote against direct action. The miners had taken a vote simply for or against 'a general Trade Union strike'. At the Trades Union Congress the issue was stated differently, and the delegates were asked to decide between 'industrial action' and 'political action' as a means of compelling the Government to carry out the Coal Commission's Report. The alternative methods were presented as follows:

(*a*) Trade Union action, in the form of a general strike.

(*b*) Political action, in the form of intensive political propaganda in preparation for a General Election.

There voted for a general strike 1,050,000, and for political action 3,732,000. Intensive political propaganda, in preference to strike action, was therefore accepted as the decision of the Trades Union Congress.

Whatever may have been the intention behind the Congress decision, its effect was to shelve the whole question of nationalization. The 'Mines for the Nation' campaign had already proved conclusively that public attention could not be concentrated on this single issue, and as there was no early prospect of a General Election, the road to intensive political activity was in fact closed. This was accepted by the miners as the true situation, and they at once realized that any immediate chance of enforcing nationalization had disappeared. They therefore felt themselves free to act in other directions. While the campaign for public ownership was in progress they had refrained, despite the rapid rise in the cost of living, from making any demand for increased wages, though many of the districts had been pressing for such a demand. The collapse of the movement for direct action made a demand for higher wages inevitable.

CHAPTER VII

WAGES AND PRICES, 1920—THE MINING INDUSTRY ACT

SECTION 1. WAGES AND PRICES, 1920—THE FIRST DEMAND

ACCORDING to the official figures published by the Ministry of Labour, the cost of living advanced by only five points between January and December 1919. In January and February 1919, it stood at 120 per cent. above the pre-war level. In March, when the miners received the Sankey advance, it had fallen to 115 per cent., and it continued to fall until June, when it reached 105 per cent. Then, however, the tide turned, and the cost of living mounted again steadily, reaching 125 per cent. in December 1919, and 130 per cent. in February 1920.

The important point about these figures in relation to miners' wages is that, at the time when the Sankey advance of 2*s*. per shift for adults was offered and accepted, it was universally believed, at least among the miners, that the period of high prices was over, and that the cost of living would steadily fall. Only on this assumption could the Sankey advance be regarded—and it was generally so regarded—as conceding a positive improvement on the pre-war standard of living; for, as we have seen, the total average increase in earnings in the mining industry amounted only to 106 per cent., whereas the cost of living had risen by 115 per cent. The Sankey advance was equivalent to 30 per cent. on the average pre-war wage, and thus brought the miners up to 136 per cent. average increase. The Government subsequently contended that the Sankey advance was given both to compensate for the higher cost of living and to raise the standard of real wages; but the miners always maintained that it had been given explicitly in order to improve the standard of life, and that it must not be taken into account in reckoning the advances necessary to compensate for increases in the cost of living. There is, in any case, no doubt that in March 1919 it was generally anticipated that the cost of living would rapidly fall, and that the whole of the Sankey advance of 30 per cent. would go directly to improve the standard of life.

These hopes were speedily falsified, and, as the cost of living began to mount again during the latter half of 1919, one district after another began to press the Miners' Federation to demand a further increase in wages, or alternatively to insist that the Government should take effective measures to bring down the cost of living to a more reasonable level. While the 'Mines for the Nation' campaign was in progress, and there seemed still to be a chance that the mines would be brought under public ownership, the miners' leaders were adverse to any confusion of the issue by the bringing forward of a new wage demand. Accordingly when, in January 1920, the pressure from the districts became too strong to be longer resisted, the Federation determined to approach the Government, not with a wages claim, but with a demand that the cost of living should be reduced. This demand was accompanied by an intimation that, if the Government failed to reduce the cost of living, there would be no alternative to the making of a claim for higher wages.

Reference was made in the previous chapter to the manipulation of coal prices by the Government during the latter part of the year 1919. In July of that year, as we saw, the Government suddenly announced a price increase of 6*s*. a ton on all kinds of coal, and, after a conditional offer to withdraw the increase in return for a pledge against strikes, it was enforced later in the month. The decision to impose this increase in prices was based on certain provisional estimates made by the Government as to the financial position of the industry. These were, as we saw, at once challenged by the miners, and the events of the next few months proved the increase to have been excessive. In November 1919, therefore, a further change in prices was made. The price of industrial coal was left unchanged, and export prices were still governed purely by the market, but the price of domestic coal was reduced by 10*s*. a ton on the 25th November.

The contention of the miners at the beginning of 1920 was that excessive prices were still being charged for coal, with the result that both the owners and the Government, under the control arrangements, were taking unduly large sums out of the industry at the expense of the domestic and industrial consumers. As a means to the reduction of the cost of living, the miners accordingly proposed that the prices both for industrial and for domestic coal should be brought down. A reduction in industrial coal, it was urged, would help to reduce the prices of commodities produced by all the coal-using industries, and would thus have a considerable effect in lowering the cost of living. If living costs were not reduced in this way, the miners announced they would be compelled to demand a substantial increase in wages. They pointed out that, under the various district arrangements for varying wages, they would, in the absence of control, have received large increases in certain of the districts, for wages in the coal-fields were normally based mainly on the selling-price of coal. These district arrangements were in abeyance owing to the operation of the control scheme, but, as the miners urged, this had produced a situation in which wages were kept down while high profits were being made, and the State, owing to the reopening of the export markets, was reaping a rich harvest out of the industry in the form of the coal levy on excess profits.

On the 28th January 1920 the Miners' Federation representatives met the Prime Minister and placed these contentions before him. At once an argument arose as to the real financial position of the coal industry. The miners contended that a big and steadily increasing surplus was passing into the hands of the Government. Mr. Lloyd George replied that an independent accountant had been appointed to go into the financial position, and that, until his report was ready, it was not possible to say what the surplus was. He also contended that, in fact, the surplus was entirely due to the high prices prevailing for exported coal, and that this could not be regarded as part of the ordinary revenue of the industry, but must be treated as a 'windfall' to the benefit of which the debt-burdened Government was entitled. The meeting was finally adjourned in order to allow time for the completion of the accountant's report.

On the 19th February the miners again met the Prime Minister, and the argument was resumed in the light of the accountant's report. I do not propose to go into the extremely complicated financial questions which the report raised. It is enough for the purpose of this study to state that the existence of a considerable surplus was admitted, and that it was also agreed that, if the level of export prices was maintained, this surplus would increase very rapidly during the following months.

The miners, reinforced by these figures, repeated on the 19th February their demand for a general reduction in coal prices. The Government spokesmen, in reply, both reaffirmed their previous attitude that the surplus derived from exports was a windfall which should properly belong to the State, and pointed out that, even if the price of industrial coal were reduced, it would be impossible, in the absence of a system of control over all industries, to ensure that the benefit of the reduction would go to the consumer, or to prevent 'the foreigner' from reaping the benefit in the reduced prices of exported commodities into which the price of coal entered. The miners replied that, if control by the State was necessary, that control ought to be imposed, but to this the Government, intent at the time on removing as rapidly as possible the vestiges of war-time State control over the industries of the country, entirely refused to agree. There was, indeed, behind the difference between the miners and the Government on this point the whole broad difference between the Government policy of removing, and the Labour policy of retaining, State control. Mr. Lloyd George at the meeting made a tentative suggestion that the coal surplus might be applied to carry out the pledge to purchase the coal-measures on behalf of the State, but this was not seriously pursued.

The meeting of the 19th February therefore ended in a deadlock, and further action by the miners was postponed until after the meeting of the Trades Union Congress, already described, at which the question of direct action in support of the demand for nationalization was to be decided. The miners, as we have seen, met on the 10th March and voted in favour of asking the Trades Union Congress to declare a general strike. At this meeting, the failure to secure from the Government a reduction in coal prices was reported, but it was decided to leave over the question of further action on the wages issue until the Congress had made up its mind. On the following day the Trades Union Congress rejected direct action in favour of political action. On the next day the Miners' Conference met again in order to consider its attitude in the light of this rejection. It was decided to proceed at once, in view of the Government's refusal to reduce coal prices, with a claim for a wage increase of 3*s*. a shift for adults and 1*s*. 6*d*. for juveniles. In order that the wage negotiations might not be complicated, the question of further action in support of the nationalization demand was adjourned for later consideration. In effect, it was shelved, and the proposal for direct action in order to force the Government to nationalize the mines was not again seriously brought forward.

On the 18th March 1920 the miners again met the Prime Minister, this time with the single demand for an advance in wages. The proposal that the Government should take steps in order to reduce the price of coal was dropped for the time being, in face of the definite refusal of February, and the argument accordingly centred mainly round the question of the real amount of the surplus available in the industry, and the question whether, on the ground of increased coal prices or of the cost of living, the miners were entitled to a wage advance. Mr. Lloyd George refused to deal with the demand for direct bargaining, and referred the miners in the first instance to the Coal Controller, as the Government representative with whom they ought to open negotiations.

On the following day, therefore, the miners met the Coal Controller, and began with him a bout of negotiation which extended from the 19th to 23rd March. On the latter date the Coal Controller made his offer in the Government's name. Instead of the 3*s*. a shift for which the miners had asked in the case of adults, he offered 1*s*. 6*d*. a shift, and for juveniles 6*d*. in the place of 1*s*. 6*d*. Alternatively, an advance of 20 per cent. was offered on current wages, excluding the 'war wages' and the 'Sankey wage'. This offer, however, was made conditional on the willingness of the miners to agree to the consolidation into their standard time and piece rates of the special war and post-war additions which had been granted as additions to earnings at a flat rate.

The miners, in reply to this offer, urged both that it was inadequate in amount, and that it was undesirable to make the consolidation of wages a condition of the advance. They were not, they said, opposed to consolidation, but it would inevitably take time and raise many difficult questions. It could not, therefore, properly be made a condition of an advance which was immediately needed. One point in the minds of the miners' leaders in making this answer was doubtless the difference in the conditions under which the standard wages and the 'war wage' additions were payable. The former were paid only on shifts actually worked; the latter were payable where a man was thrown temporarily out of work by causes not under his control, such as a stoppage at the pit. The miners were very anxious to preserve this concession, and feared that it might be lost by consolidation unless special provision were made for its retention. At the same time, they did not want to complicate the straightforward wage negotiation on which they were engaged by introducing this highly controversial question. They therefore contented themselves with affirming their readiness to discuss consolidation subsequently, while objecting to the attempt to make the wage advance conditional upon it.

On the 24th March the Miners' Conference met in order to hear the report upon the wage negotiations. Without hesitation, it rejected the Government's offer, and instructed the Executive to reopen negotiations. On the 25th, therefore, the miners met the Prime Minister, and received from him an offer only amended very slightly. The offer of 6*d.* to juveniles was increased to 9*d.* per shift and the alternative offer of 1*s.* 6*d.* a shift or 20 per cent. advance on rates were amalgamated into an offer of 20 per cent., with a guaranteed minimum of 1*s.* 6*d.* a shift. This was offered in order to meet the case of those men for whom an advance of 20 per cent. on piece-work prices might otherwise mean an advance smaller than 1*s.* 6*d.* or even no advance at all. This would be the case, for example, for men working in 'abnormal places', where piece-work earnings could not reach the level of the daily minimum wage. Unless an actual addition were made to the guaranteed daily wages, an addition to piece-work prices would leave these men's earnings unaffected, as it would still leave their increased piece-work earnings below the legal minimum wage which had to be paid in any case.

This offer, reported to the Miners' Conference on the 26th March, met with no more favourable reception than the first, but the Executive was empowered by the delegates to return and negotiate a settlement with the Government, i.e. to make some modification in the original claim for 3*s*. a shift. Further negotiations were opened with Mr. Lloyd George the same day, and continued until the 29th March. The Government rejected the miners' amended claim for an advance of 22½ per cent. with guaranteed *minima* of 3*s*. a shift for those over 18, 2*s*. for those between 16 and 18, and 1*s*. for those under 16. Instead, Mr. Lloyd George offered an advance of 20 per cent., but raised the guaranteed minimum advance to 2*s*. a shift for those over 18, 1*s*. for those between 16 and 18, and 9*d*. for those under 16. This Mr. Lloyd George described as a ' final offer '.

The Miners' Conference on the 29th March decided to refer this offer to a ballot vote of the Federation. Accordingly, a vote was taken during the next fortnight, with the result that 442,000 votes were cast in favour of acceptance and 337,000 in favour of a strike. In view of these figures, the delegate Conference, when it reassembled on the 15th April, formally accepted the offer, and the crisis ended, although negotiations on points of interpretation of the agreement dragged on for a week or two longer.

Immediately the general wages question had been disposed of, consideration of another important matter which had been held over during the crisis was resumed. The miners had for some time been seeking to secure a uniform national agreement, similar to those in force in other industries such as engineering, for payment at an enhanced rate for overtime and week-end work. A national meeting on this question was arranged with the owners and the Coal Controller for the 29th April, when a full discussion took place. At an adjourned meeting on the 6th May an agreement was reached, and this was duly signed a few days later on behalf both of the Mining Association of Great Britain and of the Miners' Federation. It provided for overtime payment on ordinary week-days at the rate of time and a third, and all week-end work between the beginning of the Saturday afternoon and the beginning of the Sunday night shift was to be paid for at the rate of time and a half. More favourable customs, where they were already in existence, were not to be interfered with. The substitution of these uniform principles for the chaos of local arrangements previously in force was a considerable step forward in the regulation of conditions of work.

SECTION 2. THE MINES ACTS OF 1920

On the 12th February 1920 the Government introduced into the House of Commons a new Mines Emergency Bill in place of the measure abandoned the previous December. The miners' representatives made some attempt to amend the Bill so as to limit more rigidly the owners' profits in accordance with the recommendation of the Interim Sankey Report that the owners should be allowed to retain only 1*s.* 2*d.* per ton of coal raised, and that the Coal Mines Agreement should be amended accordingly. These proposals, however, were resisted by the Government, and the Bill passed into law almost unamended on the 31st March. Its passage through Parliament thus synchronized with the wage crisis, which served, to some extent, to divert attention from it.

The Coal Mines (Emergency) Act of 1920 was a purely temporary measure, and was to lapse automatically at the end of August 1920, unless steps were taken for its renewal. It dealt only with profits and the financial conditions of Government control, and was in form a measure amending, or rather replacing, the Coal Mines Agreement (Confirmation) Act of 1918, some of the clauses of which it re-enacted without change. The main alterations were in the methods to be adopted for the allocation of profits. Under the new Act, all profits from the coal-mines were to be aggregated: the profits to be distributed by any colliery concern were limited to the standard profits[1] *plus* one-tenth of the standard. If the aggregate profits amounted to less than nine-tenths of the sum of the profits standard, and it could be shown that the deficiency was caused by any order or regulation of the Government made by virtue of its control over the

[1] See p. 54, *ante*.

industry, the Government was to make good the deficiency up to nine-tenths of the profits standard. The owners thus received a minimum guaranteed profit on the one hand, while, on the other, although profits were limited, the amount to be retained largely exceeded in most cases the 1*s.* 2*d.* per ton recommended by Sir John Sankey.

The Coal Mines (Emergency) Act, it will be seen, settled nothing with regard to the future conduct and control of the industry, and the Government was therefore still under an obligation to produce and pass into law its promised alternative to the nationalization schemes of Sir John Sankey and the Miners' Federation. This, moreover, had to be done before the 31st August, the date on which the Emergency Act was due to expire; or, otherwise, the whole system of control would lapse without any substitute for it being provided. It would, of course, have been possible merely to prolong the life of the Emergency Act, but it was clearly desirable that the future status of the industry should be settled without further delay, and the collapse, in March, of the Labour threat of direct action had left the way open for the Government to produce its scheme.

The last official pronouncement of the Government as to its intentions for the future of the mining industry had been Mr. Lloyd George's 'Duckham and water' proposal of August 1919. Nothing further had been heard of this, and it was rightly assumed to have lapsed in face of the opposition of both miners and owners. There was accordingly no surprise when it was found that the new Government proposals, brought forward in June 1920, provided neither for public ownership of the mines nor for unification under private ownership. On the 21st June 1920 the Government introduced into Parliament the Ministry of Mines Bill, which subsequently, on the 16th August, became law under the name of the Mining Industry Act, 1920. The change of name was due mainly to the whittling down of the Bill in the House of Commons, and the making of the Mines Department a section of the Board of Trade instead of a separate Ministry.

The Mining Industry Act falls into three parts. Part I established the Mines Department of the Board of Trade on a permanent footing, and defined its powers and constitution. It also included certain temporary provisions, continuing up to the end of August 1921 the power to control coal exports and coal prices originally assumed under the Defence of the Realm Act, and also maintaining in force the general provisions of the Coal Mines (Emergency) Act up to the same date. The effect of these clauses was to continue for a year longer the Government control arrangements which would otherwise have lapsed in August 1920, while bringing the variation of the control scheme laid down in the Emergency Act within the power of the Government.

Part II of the Act embodied the Government's alternative scheme to that of the Sankey Commission for conferring upon the miners a share in the management of their industry. Part III contained a number of miscellaneous provisions, including a clause establishing a 'Miners' Welfare Fund', to be raised by a levy on the owners of all coal-mines of 1*d.* per ton raised, and to be applied to approved purposes 'connected with the social well-being, recreation, and conditions of living' of mine-workers, and with 'mining education and research'. Another clause empowered the Board of Trade to make schemes for the joint execution of drainage schemes for groups of mines. These provisions were, of course, based on the proposals made by the Sankey Commission, from which the Government, having rejected the main recommendations, borrowed certain features not inconsistent with its alternative plan. Nationalization of royalties, however, was still unprovided for, although it had been unanimously recommended by the Commission. In the course of the negotiations described in the preceding section, Mr. Lloyd George at one time, on the 19th February, tentatively suggested that the surplus revenue of the mining industry which passed to the Government might be applied to the purchase of royalties, but the suggestion was not followed up.

The powers of control conferred upon the Mines Department under Parts I and III of the Act were inconsiderable. The powers to restrict exports and to regulate compulsorily profits and wages were limited to a period of one year, at the end of which control by the State was to lapse. Apart from these, the only power of importance which the Act conferred was that dealing with schemes of drainage. The general powers of the Mines Department only continued those already exercised by the Board of Trade under earlier Acts.

From the first, the controversy over the Act centred round two points. In the first place, sins of omission were urged against it. It wholly failed, said its critics, to carry out the Reports of the Sankey Commission, or to make any real change in the pre-war system of administration and control. It amounted to a restoration of private enterprise unrestricted. Secondly, it was argued by the spokesmen of the Miners' Federation that the Act was an Act clearly designed to defeat the miners' demand for the national regulation of the industry, and to bring about the disruption of the Miners' Federation. The case against it was argued on these lines by the Labour representatives when the Bill was before the House of Commons; and the Annual Conference of the Miners' Federation, held at Leamington on the 6th July and the following days, unanimously passed, after a discussion in which the Bill was vigorously denounced as disruptive of the Federation, the following resolution:

> That this Conference, having examined the terms of the Ministry of Mines Bill, hereby decides to refuse to operate the Bill should it become law, and urges the Labour Party to use every means at its disposal to prevent its passage through the House.

The reasons for this strong hostility of the miners become evident on a reading of Part II of the Act, which was passed in spite of their opposition. The object of Part II was to provide for the establishment in the mining industry of a system of Joint Committees and Boards representing the owners and the workers. It prescribed that, at each mine where a majority of the workers so desired, a Joint Pit Committee should be established, representing the management and the workers, the representatives of the latter to form at least half the membership of the Committee, and to be elected by ballot of the workers employed, whereas the representatives of the management were to be nominated by the owners. The main functions of the Pit Committee were to 'make recommendations' concerning safety, health and welfare, output, &c., and to deal with 'disputes arising in connexion with the mine, including disputes as to wages'. Certain powers of inspection of the pit were conferred, and also a very limited power to call for information.

Above the Pit Committee the Act proposed to set up in each district defined by the Act (usually co-extensive with the County Miners' Association) a Joint District Committee of members appointed by the owners and elected by the workers in a manner which the Board of Trade was left to prescribe by regulation. The District Committee was to deal with matters of the same character as the Pit Committees, where they related to the district as a whole, and also with any question referred to it by a Pit Committee or by one of the superior bodies still to be described.

At the next stage was to stand the Area Board, appointed for an area including as a rule several county districts. Thus Scotland was to form one area, divided into five districts; the Midland area included fourteen districts, and was practically co-extensive with the 'Federated Area' of the English Coal Conciliation Board [1]; and the Southern area included four districts. Northumberland, Durham, South Wales, and Ireland, on the other hand, were to form each an area co-extensive with a district.

The Area Board was to consist of representatives of the 'owners and management' nominated by their representatives on the District Committees, and of miners' representatives similarly chosen by the miners on the District Committees. The general functions of the Area Boards were defined in much the same terms as those of the District Committees, but with the following important addition:

> Section 10, sub-section 3. An area board shall formulate, at such intervals as may be prescribed by the National Board, schemes for adjusting the remuneration of the workers within the area, having regard among other considerations to the profits of the industry within the area, and any such scheme when formulated shall be submitted to the National Board for their approval, and, if approved by that Board, shall be referred to the Board of Trade, and for the purpose of this sub-section the owners of mines in the area shall furnish to accountants appointed by the area board such information as they may require in order that they may ascertain for the information of the area board particulars of the output, cost of production, proceeds and profits in the area as a whole.[2]

A further section laid down that any powers exercised by

[1] See p. 9.

[2] There was a proviso that the accountant should not disclose information with respect to any particular undertaking. To this proviso the miners unsuccessfully raised objection.

a Conciliation Board or by a Joint District Board under the Coal Mines (Minimum Wage) Act of 1912 might be transferred to an Area Board or District Committee under the new Act.

The structure established by the Act was completed by a Joint National Board consisting in equal numbers of representatives of coal-owners and of miners, the method of appointment being reserved to be laid down by regulation of the Board of Trade. The principal function of the National Board was to deal with questions, including wages questions, affecting the coal-mining industry as a whole; and it was also empowered to deal with any matter referred to it either by an Area Board or by the Board of Trade. It was explicitly directed to lay down the principles on which the Area Boards were to work in settling wages, and to review the schemes drawn up by the Area Boards.

The effect of this whole complicated system of Joint Boards and Committees is evident enough. The intention behind it was that wages and conditions of employment should, subject to the national determination of very broad questions of principle, be adjusted, and varied, on an area and district basis. This was the case before the War, when advances and reductions were negotiated by the various area Conciliation Boards, and rates and conditions varied from district to district, even within the area of each Conciliation Board. As we have seen, the miners, even before the War, had declared their hostility to this system, and their desire for a National Board which would deal with all advances and reductions on a national basis. During the period of control a part of their desire had been realized, and, from 1917 onwards, wage advances had been granted nationally to all districts at a flat rate. The miners desired to make this system permanent, and to carry it further by working gradually towards the establishment of national wage-rates and conditions for each class of workers as well as national variations in the rates from time to time paid. They saw, not without cause, in Part II of the Mining Industry Bill an attempt to defeat their claim for a real National Wages Board, and to thrust them back upon the pre-war system of district or area negotiations and settlements of wages. This it was which, they urged, would make for the disruption of the Miners' Federation.

Objection was also taken to the Bill on the ground that, from start to finish, it extended no recognition to the Miners' Federation or its component parts, and provided for the choice of the workers' representatives, not through their Trade Unions, but by separate ballot vote or nomination quite apart from the Trade Union machinery. In this too, it was claimed, the desire of the Government to go behind and ignore the Miners' Federation was plainly shown.

These objections were fully known both to the Government and to the public while the Bill was before Parliament; and the known opposition of the Miners' Federation and its certain intention to boycott the Act when it became law resulted in the insertion in Part II of a special section providing for this eventuality. It was enacted that

> If at the expiration of one year from the passing of this Act it appears to the Board of Trade that the scheme of this part of the Act has been rendered abortive by reason of the failure on the part of those entitled to appoint representatives as members of the pit and district committees, area boards, and the National Board to avail themselves of such right, the Board of Trade shall issue a report of the circumstances, and that report shall be laid before Parliament, and at the expiration of thirty days during the session of Parliament from the date when it is so laid all the provisions of this part of this Act shall cease to have effect unless in the meantime a resolution to the contrary is passed by both Houses of Parliament.

The intention of the Miners' Federation to boycott the Mining Industry Act was soon put to the test. No attempt was made, in face of its hostility, to put Part II of the Act into immediate operation. But Part I made provision for the appointment by the Board of Trade of Advisory Committees to work with the new Mines Department and the Secretary for Mines, who was to be a subordinate Minister under the President of the Board of Trade. The principal of these committees was to be a Coal Industry Advisory Committee of twenty-four appointed members under a chairman appointed by the Board of Trade. Of the twenty-four, four were to represent mine-owners, four mine-workers, three employers in other industries, and three workers in other industries. Two were to be colliery managers, under-managers, or agents, one a mining engineer, one a coal exporter, one a coal factor or merchant, one a person with commercial experience outside the coal trade, one a co-operative expert, and three 'persons with an expert knowledge of medical or other science'.

In accordance with these provisions, the Mines Department, in the autumn of 1920, approached both the Miners' Federation, as representing mine-workers, and the Parliamentary Committee of the Trades Union Congress as representing workers in other industries, and requested them to nominate persons to serve on the Coal Advisory Committee. The Parliamentary Committee of the Trades Union Congress thereupon asked the Miners' Federation for its advice, and, having been officially informed that the miners' policy was that of boycotting the Act, refused to make any nomination. The Miners' Federation, on the 9th December 1920, also finally decided to make no nomination either for the Advisory Committee or for the Miners' Welfare Committee established to administer the welfare fund under Part III of the Act.[1]

The provisions made in the Mining Industry Act for the future organization of the industry were thus, despite the passage of the Act, largely impossible of operation, and their fate remained to be settled by the dispute of 1921. For the immediate future, however, the Act had made provision by enabling the control established under the Emergency Act to be continued, at the discretion of the Government, up to the end of August 1921. This continuance of control was, however, optional, and it was left within the power of the Board of Trade to terminate it at any earlier date after the end of August 1920, if it saw fit. The importance of this legal discretion left in the power of the Government will be fully realized when we come to consider the history of the stoppages of 1920 and 1921.

SECTION 3. THE LEAMINGTON CONFERENCE—THE INTERNATIONAL MINERS' FEDERATION

Reference has already been made to the decision of the Miners' Federation at its Annual Conference of 1920 to boycott the Mining Industry Bill should it become law. The Conference, which was

[1] These decisions were revised, and the whole attitude of the Miners' Federation towards the Act was reconsidered, after the end of the national dispute of 1921. See *post*, p. 238.

held at Leamington on the 6th July and the following days, also took a number of other important decisions. It had to face the fact that the agitation for the immediate transference of the coal industry to public ownership had definitely collapsed for the time being, and that, for some time at least, 'direct action' in support of the demand was out of the question. This was generally admitted, and the resolution carried on the question of nationalization was therefore of almost an academic character. It was worded as follows, and was carried by a unanimous vote :

> This Conference views with regret the failure of the Government to introduce legislation for the purpose of nationalizing the mining industry, and reiterates its conviction that the industry will never be placed upon a satisfactory basis in the interests of the community until it is publicly owned and worked between the representatives of the State and the technical and manual workers engaged in it, and resolves to continue to educate and organize working-class opinion until the Government are compelled to bring about this fundamental change in the ownership and management of the industry.

While they thus definitely recognized that the changes in the conduct of the mining industry which they advocated could not be immediately realized, the miners in 1920 were still determined to oppose to the best of their power the virtually complete handing back of the mines to private control contemplated in the Mining Industry Bill. In conjunction with the above resolution, the Conference therefore adopted another, in the following terms :

> That we demand continuance of Government control of the mining industry until the mines are nationalized.

The Conference, among many other resolutions, also declared in favour of standardization of wages and conditions on a national basis, and instructed the Executive to take steps for the attainment of this object—a decision which led up directly to the policy adopted by the Federation in the great dispute of 1921.

It also declared for the abolition of the 'butty' or 'contract' system of working, still largely operative in certain of the coalfields, and demanded the amendment of the Coal Mines (Minimum Wage) Act of 1912, so as to make it universally applicable to surface-workers as well as to those working underground. Its decisions on the question of a new wages claim and a new demand for a reduction in prices are described in the next chapter.

During the year 1920, the British miners took an active part in the re-creation and strengthening of the International Miners' Federation, and attempted, through it, to place the movement for public ownership and democratic control of the mining industry on an international basis. The International Miners' Federation was originally formed in 1890, and the British Miners' Federation from the outset took a leading part in its development. The head-quarters were in Great Britain, and the secretary of the International Federation was the secretary of the Miners' Federation of Great Britain. The War temporarily interrupted the work of this, as of other International Trade Union Federations; but already in 1919 steps were being taken for its resumption.

A full international Conference of Miners was held at Geneva in August 1920. The number of members represented was 2,614,215, as against a pre-war membership of 1,374,000. The countries represented and the membership of the various national Trade Unions was as follows:

Country	Members	Country	Members
America	500,000	Great Britain	900,000
Austria	22,000	Holland	4,000
Belgium	123,540	Hungary	25,000
Czecho-Slovakia	123,000	Jugo-Slavia	10,000
France	130,000	Luxemburg	4,000
Germany	768,675	Poland	4,000

At this Conference the British miners raised the question of nationalization, and the following resolution was unanimously adopted:

Considering that the nationalization or socialization of the mines is the only way to obtain the practical re-organization and regulation of the conditions of work, as well as equitable remuneration for the efforts of the producer; that on this new re-organization and regulation of work depends the increase in production which is indispensable in order to satisfy the needs of the peoples; that by these means alone it will be possible to recommence the economic life of all countries under normal conditions, through granting to each of them, by means of an international organization, the distribution and exchange of the products of the nationalized or socialized mines, which is necessary for their free development;

Considering that it is also the only way to put the peoples on an equal footing and to allow the producer and consumer in every country to obtain proper respect and recognition for their reciprocal rights;

The Congress declares that the International Committee of Miners shall meet within two months after the closing of this Conference to re-examine the claims of every country in this matter.

The Congress entrusts the International Committee with the duty of continuing from this time and with full powers and by all possible means, including international general strikes if it becomes necessary, to work for the prompt realization of this demand in every country.

By means of reports from each country, information will be distributed concerning the general situation, and will be used as a guide as to the future conduct. If it be considered indispensable, in order to attain the end desired, to have recourse to extreme measures, it will be necessary to make sure beforehand, by means of clearly worded engagements, of the co-operation of the different federated countries whose duty it will be to carry out fully the decisions come to. The different countries must henceforth prepare their members for all possibilities, so that they may be ready at any time whatever to carry out the decisions of the International Committee.

This definite threat of international strike action, which, if it were carried into effect, would initiate an altogether new form of industrial activity, was not intended to be immediately operative. Its effect has been to produce a closer co-ordination of policy between the Miners' Trade Unions in the various countries, which are now united in demanding public ownership and a form of democratic control in which the workers would largely participate.

CHAPTER VIII

THE MINING STRIKE OF 1920

Section 1. An 'Indivisible Demand'

On the 10th June 1920 the Miners' Delegate Conference had already decided in principle on a fresh wage demand, and had referred to the Executive the task of formulating a definite claim. On the 21st June the Executive accordingly issued its proposals to the districts for their consideration. These proposals dealt not only with wages, but also with coal prices, and thus recalled the abortive plans of the first months of 1920. On this occasion, as on that, the case for this double claim was based on the Government's action in fixing coal prices. On the 12th May 1920 the Government had put into force further advances of 14*s.* 2*d.* a ton in the price of household coal, and 4*s.* 2*d.* in the case of industrial coal, thus cancelling the 10*s.* reduction in household coal prices made in December 1919, and adding a further 4*s.* 2*d.* to the price of all kinds of coal consumed in Great Britain. This brought the standard national rise in coal prices since 1914 to 20*s.* 8*d.* per ton, and the rise in South Wales to 23*s.* 2*d.* The actual changes were as follows:

Changes in Coal Prices, 1914–20

	s.	*d.*
1915, standard increase under Limitation Act	4	0
1916, June 1st (South Wales and Forest of Dean only)	2	6
1917, October 12th	2	6
1918, June 24th	2	6
1918, July 8th	1	6
1919, July 21st	6	0
1919, December 1st, decrease in household coal	10	0
1920, May 12th, increase in household coal	14	2
1920, May 12th, increase in industrial coal	4	2

As on the occasion described in the previous chapter, the miners contended that the price advances made in May were unnecessary, and that there were ample resources in the industry to pay not only the advance in wages granted in March, but also the new advance now to be demanded, without any increase in prices. The Executive, therefore, proposed to ask for a reduction of 14*s*. 2*d*. per ton in the price of household coal, leaving untouched the increased price of industrial coal. One reason for this discrimination undoubtedly was that, during the previous negotiations, the Government had insisted that any reduced price for industrial coal would affect the cost of production of manufactured goods, and, therefore, the price at which they could be exported. In order to prevent 'the foreigner' from getting the benefit of this, it was stated, a vast control of exports would be required, and this the Government had refused to consider. This objection, however, could not apply to a reduction in the price of household coal, such as the Government itself had made in December 1919; and to this the Miners' Executive accordingly proposed to limit their price demand. Together with this the Executive advised the miners to claim a wage advance of 2*s*. a shift for adults, with proportionate advances for juniors.

The case advanced in support of this wage demand was largely based on the cost of living. In March 1920, when the previous advance came into force, the cost of living stood at 130 per cent. above the pre-war level. In July it had risen to 152 per cent., and it was still sharply rising. Negotiations would inevitably take some time, and it would, therefore, have been not unnatural to claim enough to offset the further rise which was immediately anticipated. The claim, however, according to the miners' view, was practically limited to meeting the rise in prices which was already in being.

Miners' wages, according to the statement made by Sir Robert Horne on the 26th July in reply to the miners' claims, had risen by 154 per cent., including all advances up to that date. But, as we have seen, the miners claimed that, in any calculation based on the cost of living, the special Sankey advance of 1919, amounting to 30 per cent., must be excluded, on the ground that it had been given for the purpose of improving the pre-war standard of living. Wages, therefore, according to the miners' contention, should be regarded as having risen by 124 per cent., as against a rise of 152 per cent. in the cost of living, which was still going up, and in fact reached 164 per cent. before the negotiations were concluded.

The proposals of the Miners' Federation came before the Annual Conference at Leamington, and were there approved in the character of an 'indivisible demand'. This meant that the claims in respect of prices and wages were not to be taken separately, but together, and that a failure to grant the demand for a reduction in prices would be treated as a reason for making a larger wage demand. There was, indeed, at the Conference, very strong pressure from certain of the districts, notably South Wales, in favour of a larger wage demand, and the acceptance of the 'invisible demand', carrying with it a restriction of the wage claim, was adopted largely owing to Mr. Robert Smillie's personal advocacy.

The miners thus set out once more to make a demand, not only on their own behalf, but also on that of the consumer. They were compelled, they said, to demand higher wages because the cost of living had risen; but they disliked the 'vicious circle' of prices and wages, and made their proposal of a reduction in coal prices with the definite object of bringing down the cost of living. The industry, they held, could afford to bear the burden, and the surplus revenue available ought to be applied to reducing prices rather than passed into the Exchequer.

On the 15th July, the miners met the Coal Controller and presented their claims. This, however, was merely a preliminary meeting; for it was clear from the outset that the question would be one for the Government as a whole to deal with. Accordingly, the Controller passed the miners on to his official superior, the President of the Board of Trade. Sir Robert Horne, who then held this office, met the miners on the 26th July, and delivered to them the Government's reply. On the question of wages, the Government contended that the claim for an increase had not been made out, basing its calculations on the existing wages, including the Sankey advances which, the miners held, ought not to be taken into account. The demand for a reduction in prices was also rejected absolutely. Sir Robert Horne argued that the British coal consumer was paying, even after the increase, considerably less than the world price for his coal, that any differentiation between industrial and household prices would involve more control by the State, and heavier book-keeping expenses, and that, in any case, the surplus derived from the industry was in the nature of 'excess profits', and ought to pass, neither to the miners nor to the consumers, but to the Exchequer in relief of taxation. He did not dispute the miners' contention that the surplus available was then at the rate of something like sixty-six million pounds a year, but pointed out that this was dependent on the maintenance of export quantities and prices at the existing levels. It further emerged in the discussion, when the miners challenged the necessity for the price increases of May, that these had been made with the object of placing each coal-producing district, and, as far as possible, each individual mine, on a profit-making basis. This, the miners contended, was obviously being done with a view to the early decontrol of the industry. Sir Robert Horne, while disclaiming any intention of immediate decontrol, hardly disputed that this was the tendency of the Government's policy. The only sign of any disposition on the part of the Government to agree to concessions was a hint, dropped by Sir Robert Horne towards the end of the discussion, that higher wages might be granted in consideration of increased output, if the miners could see their way to a scheme on these lines.

A complete deadlock thus seemed to have been reached, and, in the circumstances, the Executive decided to report the position to a Special Conference for the purpose of determining future policy. A National Miners' Conference accordingly met in London on the 12th August. The business placed before the delegates was to determine whether, in view of the Government's rejection of the demands, a strike ballot should be taken throughout the coal-fields. After a short discussion, two resolutions were almost unanimously adopted. The first ordered the taking of a ballot vote for and against a strike; the second recommended the miners to vote in favour of strike action. At the same sessions, the attitude of the Miners' Federation to the proposed general strike against British intervention on behalf of Poland against

Russia was discussed, and it was agreed without a division to support the proposal for a strike, if it was made by the Council of Action.[1] In the event this resolution did not lead to strike action, and the threat of war with Russia was averted. The incident is mentioned here only in order to point out the coincidence of the two crises in the world of Labour.

On the 31st August, the result of the miners' strike ballot was declared; 845,647 votes had been cast in favour of a strike, and 238,865 against. On the same day, a Conference of the three Executives composing the Triple Alliance of Miners, Railwaymen, and Transport Workers was held, and the Alliance decided, at an adjourned meeting held on the following day, to give all possible support to the miners' claims. This did not amount to a definite declaration in favour of a sympathetic strike. Indeed, the Transport Workers' Executive held the view that they had no power to call a strike, and could only recommend their affiliated Unions to take action. The Railwaymen's Executive had the power to call a strike at once, without appeal to a ballot vote or to a Delegate Meeting; but actually they restricted themselves to a conditional threat, and emphasized their willingness to open negotiations with the Government on behalf of the Triple Alliance, in the hope that a strike might still be averted. The positive action of the Triple Alliance was, then, limited to the establishment of a joint Publicity Committee to take charge of propaganda, and to an expression of faith in the justice of the miners' cause. This did not mean that the Alliance would do no more, but that a further meeting would be required before a definite decision could be taken. Meanwhile the Publicity Committee got to work, and its efforts were seconded by the Labour Research Department, which, on this occasion as during the Coal Commission and subsequently in the dispute of 1921, was called by the miners to their aid.

The Miners' National Conference met on the 2nd September, and, on receiving the report on the result of the ballot vote, fixed

[1] The Council of Action was established jointly by the Labour Party and the Trades Union Congress on the 9th August. On the 13th August a National Labour Conference endorsed its appointment and policy, and declared in favour of a general strike, if necessary, for the prevention of war with Russia.

the 25th September as the date on which a national strike should begin, and instructed all sections of the Federation to see to the tendering of strike notices. The question whether or not the safety men and certain other sections should be called out on strike was raised, but was left to be settled later. Meanwhile notices were to be sent in for all without exception.

On the day following the Conference, the Government at last made a fresh move, and Sir Robert Horne published the suggestion that the miners' claim, so far as it related to wages, should be referred to arbitration. On the price demand, no concession was offered, the Government still maintaining that this was a matter outside the miners' jurisdiction. Sir Robert Horne's proposal was at once rejected, and the deadlock remained in being.

The following week was the week of the Annual Trades Union Congress, held this year at Portsmouth. Here, on the 8th September, Mr. Frank Hodges was allowed to make a special statement on behalf of the miners, and an emergency resolution was carried in these terms:

> This Congress, having heard the statement of the miners' case for a reduction in the price of domestic coal of 14*s.* 2*d.* a ton and an advance in wages of 2*s.*, 1*s.*, and 9*d.* per shift for adults, youths, and boys respectively, is of opinion that the claims are both reasonable and just, and should be conceded forthwith.

On the same day, after this resolution had been carried, Sir Robert Horne wired to the miners' leaders at Portsmouth, asking them to meet him in London on the following day.

All this time, a great press controversy had been raging round the issues which the miners had raised. The Press, assiduously fed with official and semi-official statements from the Government side, was at first strongly hostile to the miners. The latter accordingly took steps, even before the appointment of a Publicity Committee by the Triple Alliance, to place their side of the case before the public. A special full statement, subsequently published under the title *Facts about the Coal Dispute*, was prepared by the Miners' Federation in conjunction with the Labour Research Department, and placed first of all in the hands of journalists at a newspaper conference called by the miners. Thereafter, regular statements were issued to the Press under the names of the Triple Alliance and the Miners' Federation, and an increasing amount of other publicity work was done. The effect became evident in a changed, and more judicial, attitude on the part of most of the newspapers.

On the 9th September, the miners again met Sir Robert Horne, in response to his invitation of the previous day. For those who had hoped that this meeting would be the prelude to a settlement, the result was more than disappointing; for Sir Robert Horne merely reiterated the Government's refusal to consider the demand for a reduction in prices, and renewed the proposal that the wage demand should be referred to arbitration, designating the Industrial Court, established at the end of 1919 to take over the functions of the war-time Committee on Production, as the appropriate body to adjudicate. The suggestion that the price demand should be referred to an inquiry was rejected on the ground that this was a matter solely within the Government's discretion. The miners, in reply to the proposal that the wages question should go to Government arbitration, expressed their distrust of arbitration machinery under Government control, and emphasized the fact that their experiences after the Coal Industry Commission had not disposed them to place much faith in Courts established by the Government.

The deadlock, therefore, continued. But on the 15th September, a material change took place in the situation. In the meantime, the official figures relating to the financial position of the coal industry for the quarter ending with June 1920 had been issued. These showed, on the basis of the quarter's work alone, but after allowance had been made for the price increase of May, a balance in the industry at the rate, not of £66,000,000, but only of £33,000,000. These figures were, from the standpoint of the miners, gravely suspect. Compared with the figures for the March quarter, on which the estimate of £66,000,000 had been largely based, they showed a very large increase in working expenses. Wages costs had risen by 12 per cent. only, in consequence of the March advance; but stores and timber had risen by 14 per cent., and other costs, including repairs and management, by no less than 46 per cent. This had taken place despite a fall in the cost of timber, and was held by the miners to be due to the carrying out and charging to cost of production of an abnormal amount of development work, in anticipation of decontrol. The tonnage raised had fallen by nearly four million tons from the level reached in the March quarter. It was also shown that export prices had risen by 5*s*. a ton since the *June* quarter, thus again swelling the surplus even if the increased costs were accepted as legitimate.

Even, however, if the miners had an answer to the apparent deduction from the June figures that the anticipated surplus of £66,000,000 would not be realized, the publication of the return undoubtedly made it far more difficult for them to argue the case effectively before the public, which would be almost certain to take the figures at their face value. The public, moreover, had not at any stage shown itself particularly enthusiastic in favour of the reduction in prices. With these two facts in mind, the Miners' Executive, on the 15th September, modified its 'indivisible demand' and, leaving the wages claim unaffected, substituted for the unequivocal demand for a reduction of 14*s*. 2*d*. a ton in household coal prices the claim that the question of possible reductions in price should be referred to a specially constituted Committee of Inquiry.

It was accordingly decided to ask for an immediate meeting with the President of the Board of Trade, and the following amended schedule of demands was drawn up for presentation to the Government:

1. The Government to concede forthwith the advance in wages as per our own proposals.
2. The Government to agree that the cost of such advance shall not be added to the price of home-consumed coal.
3. A competent and representative tribunal to be appointed to inquire into and determine whether, in view of the financial position of the industry, a reduction in the price of domestic coal should take place, and, if so, to what extent.
4. The tribunal referred to above to report not later than October 31st, 1920.
5. The Government to adopt the recommendations of a majority of the tribunal.
6. The Government to accept a proposal for the establishment of a competent Committee to be appointed to inquire into the cause of declining output and to make recommendations with a view to rectifying same.

The 'indivisible demand' was thus dropped or modified; and the negotiations entered on a second phase.

Section 2. The Second Phase—The Triple Alliance

On the 16th September 1920, the Miners' Executive once more met Sir Robert Horne, and presented to the Government their modified demands. The fresh negotiations thus initiated lasted until Monday, the 20th September, when they ended in a further deadlock. The new proposals of the Miners' Federation proved to be no less unacceptable to the Government than the original 'indivisible demand'. The proposal that the question of coal prices should be referred to a Committee of Inquiry was unequivocally rejected, on the ground that the price increases of May had received the sanction of Parliament, and therefore could not be questioned by any tribunal. On the question of wages, Sir Robert Horne repeated his previous suggestion that the miners should submit their claim to arbitration by the Industrial Court, or to a tribunal consisting of miners' and mine-owners' representatives under an impartial chairman with power to decide. But, in view of the miners' rejection of this proposal, the Government now brought forward the alternative scheme of making an advance in wages dependent on the securing of increased output. By this was intended, not simply that the piece-worker would actually earn more if output increased, but that an advance upon the rates paid should be granted in return for an increased total output actually secured. If x tons were taken as the output to be related to the present wages, then, it was proposed, if this tonnage rose to $x+y$ the miners should receive an advance of so much per shift. This scheme was not, at this stage, elaborated by Sir Robert Horne as a definite proposal, but was put forward as a basis for consideration. He also suggested that the whole system of wage-payment in the coal-fields should be reconsidered, with a view to the merging of all the advances then in operation into standard rates of wages, related as far as possible to output, and urged that the miners should meet the owners and discuss this matter in relation to the present claim. He stated that he did not believe the wage claim to be justified, on the basis of the existing output, but that the Government would accept the decision of the Industrial Court. With an eye to public opinion outside, he also pointed out that whatever surplus there might be in the industry would be speedily destroyed by a strike, which would also probably involve a rise in the price of coal.

Faced with this answer, the miners again refused to go to the Industrial Court. On the question of wages in relation to output, they affirmed their desire to do everything possible to help in increasing output, but stated that the causes of low output were, in the main, outside their control. They pointed out that the reduced output of 4,000,000 tons for the June quarter coincided with an increase of 10,000 in the number of persons employed in the mines, and with a largely increased expenditure in timber and repairs. The owners, they held, instead of getting coal, were employing men and material on development work with a view to having their pits in good order when decontrol came, and were thus postponing larger output until prices were decontrolled. They, therefore, pressed for an assurance that the Government would not decontrol the industry, and received from Sir Robert Horne the statement that the Government had no present intention of doing this, and would not do it as long as the existing differences between home and export prices continued to exist.

Holding that the power to increase output rested mainly not with them, but with the owners, the miners rejected the proposal that any increase in wages should be made to depend on output, and reiterated their demand for the advances of 2*s*., 1*s*., and 9*d*. which they had claimed in June. At the same time they pressed for a full inquiry into all the circumstances affecting output, but received only the reply that this would be one of the matters to be dealt with by the new Coal Advisory Committee under Part I of the Mining Industry Act.[1]

There was thus no sign of an approach towards agreement; and, on the breakdown of the negotiations, the Miners' Executive at once proceeded to report the position to their full Delegate Conference, which met again on the 21st September. After a long discussion, in which a number of delegates questioned the wisdom of the Executive's action in modifying the original demands, the policy adopted by the Executive was endorsed. The Conference then carried a resolution that 'nothing has emerged during the negotiations between the Executive Committee and the Government to

[1] For the miners' attitude towards this body, see pp. 136 and 238.

justify the Conference in advising the miners to continue work '. This was carried by 105 votes against 73 votes for a more extreme proposal that unless the wage demand was granted in full by the end of the week, the miners should be advised to strike. The policy of the majority was to leave the door open for further negotiations.

Meanwhile, the necessary steps had been taken to bring the machinery of the Triple Alliance to bear upon the dispute. On the 21st September, the day of the Miners' Conference, both the other sections of the Alliance assembled their full Delegate Meetings in order to consider their attitude to the crisis. Each section passed a resolution reaffirming its belief in the justice of the miners' demands ; but each deferred any definite decision as to its own line of action until after the full meeting of the Alliance itself, which had been fixed for the following day.

Accordingly, on the 22nd September, the Triple Alliance met in full Delegate Conference. Each section first reported on its own proceedings of the day before, and the Conference then proceeded to discuss what action it should take. On behalf of the railwaymen, Mr. J. H. Thomas at once made it clear that, if they were expected to strike in sympathy with the miners, they would also expect that the control of policy should pass from the Miners' Federation to the whole body of the Alliance. This point was not discussed, and, on Mr. Thomas's motion, the Conference passed a resolution appointing a deputation to wait upon the Prime Minister and urge the immediate concession of the miners' demands. The joint Conference was, meanwhile, to remain in session, and to decide upon its policy when it had heard the result of the meeting with the Prime Minister. The press statements concerning the attitude of the railwaymen and transport workers at that stage indicated that considerable doubt was already entertained as to the likelihood of a Triple Alliance strike, even if no settlement was reached. There were rumours, well or ill founded, of differences in the ranks of the Alliance, and these doubtless influenced the Government's attitude.

The Triple Alliance deputation met Mr. Lloyd George on the afternoon of the 22nd September. The meeting was fruitless. Mr. Lloyd George's reply was practically identical with that made previously by Sir Robert Horne. The alternatives offered were still reference of the dispute to the Industrial Court, or an advance in wages conditional upon, and related to, an increase in output. The deputation, which had power, not to negotiate, but only to plead for the concession of the advance, could only report that the attitude of the Government was unchanged.

Before the joint Conference discussed the position created by the report of the deputation each section met separately, on the morning of the 23rd September, in order to discuss its policy. The Miners' Executive, which had met the previous night, had before it, and rejected by a majority, a proposal that the question of allowing the wages claim to go to arbitration should be submitted to a ballot vote. This course, both at the Executive meeting and at the Delegate Conference, was supported by Mr. Robert Smillie, who urged that the miners' case was a strong one, and that this way of dealing with it might be the means of preserving the principle that wages in the industry should be nationally regulated. The attitude of the supporters of this point of view was also undoubtedly influenced by the fear that the proposed intervention of the Triple Alliance would in fact end in a fiasco. The Miners' Conference, however, rejected the proposal, on a card vote, by 545,000 votes to 350,000. This meant that, unless negotiations were reopened, the strike notices would take effect on the 25th September.

While the miners' Conference was in session, the railwaymen and transport workers were also in conference. The first business of the resumed Triple Alliance meeting was to receive the reports of the three sections. When the miners had announced their decision, Mr. Thomas, on behalf of the railwaymen, stated that a resolution in favour of sympathetic strike action by them on the 25th September had been defeated in their Conference, and that they were in favour of a further effort at mediation to be made by the Triple Alliance. Mr. Thomas explained that there was some doubt, even if a strike were called, as to the response which their members would make, and referred to the dangers of an unsuccessful movement. Mr. Harry Gosling, on behalf of the transport workers, intimated that they had come to no decision on the question of a strike, and that, in their view also, a further effort towards a settlement ought to be made by the Triple Alliance.

These statements were immediately understood to mean that there would be no sympathetic strike; and Mr. Hartshorn and Mr. Hodges, acting on their own behalf and not officially on that of the Miners' Federation, at once moved that the joint Conference should be dissolved. This course was objected to by some of the transport leaders, who pointed out that no definite decision against a sympathetic strike had been taken. It was then late at night, and it was finally agreed to adjourn the Conference until the following morning.

When the Alliance met again on the 24th September, an immediate adjournment took place in order to enable the miners to hold a separate meeting. On the advice of their Executive, the miners decided that their leaders should at once go to see Mr. Lloyd George, and should intimate to him personally that the decision to strike on the following day still held good. The clear intention behind the decision was to afford an opportunity for a reopening of direct negotiations, which the miners greatly preferred to an attempt at mediation by the other sections of the Alliance, especially in view of their ambiguous attitude on the question of sympathetic action.

At the meeting which followed, Mr. Lloyd George followed up his proposals for a wage advance based upon increased output with the suggestion that the miners' representatives should meet the coal-owners, with or without the Mines Department, and discuss the position with them, and that meanwhile the strike notices should be suspended. The miners endeavoured to get a pledge that, in the event of their succeeding in coming to an arrangement with the owners in favour of the wage advance they demanded, the Government would accept a joint recommendation from both parties. Mr. Lloyd George refused to give this pledge, but said that a joint recommendation would, of course, carry great weight. In the circumstances, the Miners' Executive felt compelled to accept this qualified assurance; and they accordingly recommended to their Conference, when it met again later in the day, that they should be empowered to negotiate with the owners, and that meanwhile the strike notices should be suspended for a week. After some discussion, the Miners' Conference accepted this proposal, and also agreed that it should be communicated to the other sections of the Alliance. Instead, therefore, of a full resumption of the Triple Alliance deliberations, Mr. Smillie and Mr. Hodges, on the miners' behalf, met the other two sections, and informed them of the change in the situation. After a short discussion, the railway and transport sections of the Alliance thereupon dispersed, on the understanding that they could be called upon again if they were required. For the time being, however, they passed out of the dispute.

Section 3. Negotiations on Wages and Output

In agreeing to meet the coal-owners, the miners had practically admitted their willingness, under the circumstances which confronted them, to agree that, for the purposes of a temporary settlement, the wages to be paid should be brought into relation to the total output of the collieries. They were prepared to negotiate on this basis, not because they liked it, but because it seemed preferable to the reference of the dispute to a tribunal, and to be worth considering as the sole remaining alternative to a strike. They had, however, no intention of abandoning or modifying the wages claim previously made; and, when they met the owners on the 25th September, it was in order to ask them to make, with the Miners' Federation, a joint recommendation to the Government that the advance of *2s.*[1] asked for should be granted immediately, on the basis of the existing output. If this were done, they would agree to a temporary settlement, which, it was suggested, should run on to the end of the year, involving the dependence of further wage advances on the increase of total output.

To this proposal the owners refused to agree. They insisted that the Government had already refused to grant the proposed advance, and that they were met to discuss only an advance conditional on increased output. After some days of negotiation, the owners at last put forward a definite proposal, intimating at the same time that, if output was to be increased so as to raise

[1] The figures mentioned in this section are the advances for adults. For those between 16 and 18 every shilling would mean *6d.*, and for those under 16, *4½d.*

wages, they would demand an 'incentive' to increase it in the form of higher profits than the Government allowed them to retain.

The owners' proposal was that no increase in wages should be given unless total output reached a rate of 242 million tons a year. At this point, they offered to recommend a wage advance of 1*s*. per shift. If output reached the rate of 250 million tons, they would recommend 2*s*. advance, and at 260 million tons 3*s*. For the purpose of calculating the annual output, a week's output was to be multipled by 50, in order to allow for holidays.

The miners at once submitted counter-proposals. They urged that the 2*s*. claimed should be given on the basis of the output for the September quarter, which was at the rate of 235 to 236 million tons (estimated) per annum. At 244 million tons they asked for 2*s*. 6*d*., and at 248 million tons for 3*s*.

There was thus a wide gap between the two sets of proposals; and this gap was still as wide as ever when the negotiations ended on the 29th September. The miners were due to meet their Delegate Conference the following morning, and the strike notices were due to run out two days later. Accordingly, on the 29th September, both the owners and the miners reported to the Government their failure to agree. This led to no suggestion, except that they should meet again and make a further effort.

The Miners' Conference met on the 30th September, and adjourned, after a full day's discussion, in order to enable the Executive, in the light of what had been said, to bring up a proposal on the following morning. The Executive at once decided to endeavour to meet the Government again, and a joint meeting with the coal-owners and the Prime Minister was arranged for the morning of the 1st October. At this meeting, both parties brought forward amended proposals. The miners now suggested that the 2*s*. advance should be related to an output of 240 million tons, which was actually being more than realized during the last weeks of September. The proposal for a further increase of 6*d*. at 244 million tons was dropped, but, as before, a further 1*s*. was asked for at 248 million tons. The owners' new proposal was to pay 1*s*. advance at 240 million tons (instead of 242 millions), 2*s*. at 246 (instead of 250), 2*s*. 6*d*. at 252, and 3*s*. at 256 million tons. The gap was thus slightly narrowed, but there was still a considerable difference, especially on the vital point whether the 2*s*. advance should be granted at once.

At the joint meeting, no further progress than this was made. Mr. Lloyd George expressed the view that the only alternatives to a strike were: (1) further negotiations with the owners; (2) the reference of the dispute to a tribunal; or (3) the submission of the owners' offer to a ballot vote of the miners.

The Executive reported this situation to the Miners' Conference the same afternoon. After some discussion, it was agreed by 530,000 votes to 401,000 to take a ballot vote of the men. The question being raised whether the ballot should be taken solely for or against the owners' offer, or whether the proposed reference to a tribunal should be also placed before the men, the former course was upheld by 619,000 to 226,000. The Conference then agreed to suspend the strike notices for a further fortnight, in order to allow time for the vote to be taken. It was also agreed that no recommendation should be made by the Conference either for or against acceptance.

The Miners' Conference reassembled on the 14th October, in order to hear the result of the vote and to determine upon its policy. There had voted for acceptance of the owners' offer 181,428, and against 635,098—a majority of 458,886 in favour of rejection. The only bodies in the Federation which showed majorities for acceptance were the small craft Unions of cokemen and enginemen. Every district Miners' Association showed a substantial majority for rejection.

In face of these figures only one course seemed to the majority of the delegates to be open. An attempt was, indeed, made by a few delegates to raise again the question of referring the dispute to arbitration; but this found little support, and it was decided to intimate by letter to the Prime Minister the decision that the strike notices must take effect in accordance with the result of the ballot. Meanwhile the Conference remained in session for the discussion of other business not connected with the dispute.

The Prime Minister replied the same evening in a long letter, which he sent to the press. His letter was obviously written for publication; and the greater part of it consisted of a recapitulation of the offers made to the miners, with a severe censure on their attitude in rejecting them. Mr. Lloyd George referred to the alternative proposals for arbitration or an advance conditional on increased output. It was well known that Mr. Smillie had from the first favoured the reference of the dispute to arbitration, and that, on the rejection of this proposal, he had advocated the temporary acceptance of the owners' offer. He and many of the leaders had, while the preparations for the ballot were being made, strongly urged acceptance. Mr. Lloyd George, in appealing to the public against the miners' decision, made full use of these facts.

> 'In facing', he wrote, 'the trials which the decision of your Conference has imposed upon our people, the country will no doubt be fortified in its determination to endure by the fact that the proposals made by its elected Government have received the support of the most responsible and experienced minds within your Federation.'

It should, however, be pointed out that Mr. Smillie and the other leaders who urged acceptance of the offer did so most unwillingly, not because they thought the offer a good one, but because they hoped, by accepting a temporary settlement, to allow time for the negotiation of a more satisfactory agreement on a permanent basis.

Mr. Lloyd George added these words at the end of his letter:

> 'Upon our part we have explored, and are still ready to explore, every avenue that might lead to a peaceful solution of this difficulty. I can only express my profound regret that proposals which all must regard as supremely reasonable have received a final rejection at the hands of your Conference.'

It is a disputed point whether this enigmatical sentence, of which the latter part appears to cancel the former, could have been regarded as an invitation to resume negotiations. The Government certainly attempted to give the public to understand that they had left the door open, and that the closing of it was the act of the miners. The miners, on the other hand, saw in the letter only an appeal to public opinion against them, and believed that it had been deliberately worded in such a way as to place them in a difficulty. Accordingly, when the letter was read to the Conference on the 15th October, although a few delegates raised the question of attempting to negotiate further, the general feeling was that there was nothing to justify the course, dangerous to the morale of the miners and likely to result in unofficial stoppages, of further postponing the strike notices.

On the 16th October, therefore, the Miners' strike began. It was complete in all districts ; but the men essential to the safety of the pits and to the keeping of them in good order for resumption were allowed to continue at work.

At the Conference on the 15th October, when the business of the strike had been disposed of, the President of the Miners' Federation, Mr. Robert Smillie, tendered his resignation, on the ground that, on the questions both of reference to a tribunal and of the acceptance of the owners' offer, his view had proved to be at variance with that of the majority. He was requested by delegates of all shades of opinion to retain his office, and informed that he retained the full confidence of the Federation. The proposed resignation was then withdrawn. The incident was supposed to be private ; but some reports of it appeared in the press, and some attempt was made to use it in order to damage the miners' case during the dispute.

Section 4. The Strike and the Settlement

The national miners' strike of 1920 began on the 16th October and lasted until the Miners' Conference on the 3rd November ordered work to be resumed. During the first week of the strike, no direct negotiations took place, although there were informal attempts at mediation almost from the beginning. Direct negotiations began again with the second week of the strike, and before the week ended proposed terms of settlement were being submitted to a ballot vote. But, short as the strike was, there was time for many important events to take place during its continuance.

From the first, it was evident that the Government had made very elaborate preparations for dealing with the situation. Coal exports had been restricted, and big reserve stocks built up in anticipation of the stoppage. Emergency arrangements had been fully made for the provision of foodstuffs and other necessaries in the event of a sympathetic strike of railwaymen or other transport workers, and preliminary measures had been taken for the conferring on the Government of exceptional powers. Many of these preparations were not actually required; but some parade was made of their existence, possibly with a view to deterring other workers from taking sympathetic action.

On the 19th October, a debate on the mining situation took place in the House of Commons. Sir Robert Horne, who stated the Government case, was answered by Mr. William Brace, on behalf of the miner members of Parliament. Mr. Brace made the suggestion that, if the *2s.* advance was at once conceded, joint committees could at once be established to increase output, and a National Wages Board set up with the duty of preparing, before the end of the year, a permanent scheme for the regulation of wages and for the complete revision of the existing bases of wage payment. These proposals were well received in the House; but the Prime Minister, who spoke later in the debate, said that an increase in wages could not be given unless increased output was absolutely guaranteed. Pressed by the Labour Party to call a further joint conference with the owners and miners, Mr. Lloyd George replied that he could not do this without consulting the Cabinet, and that, in his opinion, it would be useless to call a conference unless there were a good prospect that a settlement under which wages would be based on output would be accepted by the miners.

The debate in Parliament, if it had no other effect, caused an almost general demand in the press for mediation. But, although he held some indirect negotiations with certain of the miners' M.P.'s., Mr. Lloyd George still refused to call a conference.

At this point in the dispute, the Triple Alliance suddenly came again on the scene. On the 20th October, a special Delegate Meeting of the National Union of Railwaymen met in order to consider its action in view of the miners' dispute. On the same day, the Executive Committee of the Transport Workers' Federation also met, partly on its own business, but also in order to deal with the mining dispute. The road transport sections of the Federation were themselves involved in a dispute which, unless a settlement was reached, would mean a strike on the 23rd October in all parts of the country. The Parliamentary Committee of the Trades Union Congress also held a meeting.

The meetings of the 20th October were adjourned until the following day. The railwaymen then, in view of the continuance of the deadlock, determined to take action, and announced that, unless the miners' demands were conceded in full before the end of the week, they would call a national strike for midnight on Sunday, the 24th October. The transport workers still came to no decision; but their General Secretary, Mr. Robert Williams, issued a strongly worded statement in favour of a general strike.

The strike threat of the railwaymen had the effect of ending the deadlock; for, although Mr. Lloyd George declared in the House of Commons on the evening of the 21st October that it had made the resumption of negotiations far more difficult, there can be no doubt that it caused the mediators to redouble their efforts, or that it was speedily followed by a change in the Government's attitude. On the one hand, the Government intensified its preparations: on the other, it made an overture towards negotiations.

First, it made a display of firmness. On the 22nd October, the Emergency Powers Bill was introduced into the House of Commons. This measure, designed to confer large exceptional powers upon the Government, had been prepared some time before, in anticipation of the earlier threatened action of the Triple Alliance. It was now again hurried forward in face of the new threat. On the same day, the 22nd October, the Parliamentary Committee of the Trades Union Congress summoned, for the following Wednesday, an emergency Conference of all Trade Union Executives in order to deal with this critical situation which seemed to be developing.

But, while the Emergency Powers Bill was being brought forward, the unofficial negotiations were already being converted into official negotiations. On the 23rd October, as a result of the mediation of Messrs. Brace and Hartshorn and other leaders, the Miners' Executive, which had scattered to the various districts during the strike, met again in London. To it were presented, not only letters from the National Union of Railwaymen announcing their decision to cease work, and asking the miners to meet them in order to discuss the situation, but also a letter from the Prime Minister proposing that negotiations should be resumed, and that, as a first step, he should meet the officers of the Federation.

The Miners' Executive accepted both invitations, and decided to request the railwaymen, in view of the reopening of negotiations, to postpone strike action for the time being. They then met the railwaymen, who agreed to postpone their stoppage, and to await events. Meanwhile, the strike threat of the road transport workers was disposed of by an agreement to refer their wage dispute for settlement in the various districts, and no further action had been taken by the Transport Workers' Federation, which was not a party to the strike threat of the railwaymen.

On the Sunday and Monday, the 24th and 25th October, the miners' officials were in conference with the Prime Minister. An agreed basis was not reached ; but enough progress was made to enable full negotiations to be resumed on the 26th October.

These negotiations were still in progress when the Special Trade Union Conference met on the 27th October. In view of the situation, it was clearly impossible for any decision to be taken, and the Conference, after registering a strong protest against the Government's action, adjourned until the following morning. Despite this protest, the Emergency Powers Bill received the Royal Assent, and became an Act, later in the day.[1]

On the 28th October, the miners' representatives reached with the Government a provisional settlement, and at once determined to refer this to a ballot vote of the miners throughout the country. This decision was immediately reported to the Special Trade Union Conference, which then dispersed without taking any further action. The railwaymen's delegates also dispersed. Acceptance of the proposed terms was regarded almost as a forgone conclusion, and the crisis seemed to be at an end. The Miners' Executive strongly advised the men to accept.

The terms thus recommended were, briefly, as follows. The advance of 2*s*. for which the miners had contended was to be granted at once, and was to remain in force to up the end of December. The owners and miners were to meet and advise a permanent scheme, which was to be submitted to the Government not later than the 31st March 1921. Temporarily, a scheme was to be in force under which wages would vary according to the total output of the mines and with the value of that output. The advance of 2*s*. a shift was made to correspond to an output of between 246 and 250 million tons, and to an increased value of £576,000. An increase or decrease in output of four million tons and in value of £288,000 was to carry with it an advance or

[1] For the text of the Emergency Powers Act, see Appendix C, p. 258.

reduction of 6*d.* per shift. The owners were to receive or lose for each similar variation a sum equivalent to one quarter of the profits which they were allowed to retain in excess of the standard. Somewhat complicated financial arrangements, which need not be described here, were involved in this proposal, and incorporated in the agreement. In order that the values realized might not fall below the amounts estimated as corresponding to the various levels of output, the Government undertook to guarantee an export price of 72*s.* a ton. The whole scheme was to remain in force only until the establishment of a National Wages Board for the mining industry.

The ballot vote on these terms was concluded on the 2nd November, and on the following day the Miners' Conference met again. There had voted for acceptance 338,045, and against 346,504—a majority of 8,459 in favour of rejection. It should be noted, however, that no less than sixteen districts voted for acceptance, in most cases by small majorities, while only four voted against, and only two, South Wales and Lancashire, showed large majorities against acceptance.

The Miners' Federation has a rule under which a two-thirds majority is necessary, not only before a strike can be declared, but also for its continuance, if a vote is taken at any time during its progress. The Conference accordingly put this rule into operation, and, although there was a small hostile majority, accepted the Government terms, and ordered an immediate resumption of work. The strike, therefore, ended on the 3rd November, and work was fully resumed during the following two days.

But, though the strike was over, the large vote against the terms of the settlement showed the deep hostility of the miners to any arrangement under which wages would be related to output. It was clear that the temporary settlement would furnish no basis at all for a permanent system, and that the Negotiating Committee of miners and owners, which had now to determine the future method of fixing and adjusting wages, would have to get to work along quite different lines. As was soon to appear, the peace of the 3rd November was a patched-up peace, which settled none of the big outstanding issues.

CHAPTER IX

THE STRUGGLE OF 1921

SECTION 1. THE LULL BEFORE THE STORM

I COME now to the story of the great mining struggle of 1921. That struggle brings to a close the war history of the mining industry. During 1919 and 1920 the industry was existing under artificial conditions. A system of control, designed only to meet the urgent needs of war, was being continued into the post-war period : artificial prosperity was being maintained by reason of the coal famine in Europe, which enabled Great Britain to exact an absurdly inflated price for exported coal : of the coal consumed in home markets much was being sold at a loss, the balance being far more than made up out of the profits of the export trade. The State was receiving a large share of these surplus profits, which were also enabling the coal-owners to receive very large dividends and the miners comparatively high wages. There was a general illusion of prosperity, exemplified above all in the settlement of 1920, under which both miners and owners were offered additional renumeration in return for a larger output —soon to prove a drug in the market. The whole edifice was bound to collapse as soon as the inflated export prices had to be reduced. At the beginning of 1921 the imminent prostration of the export market could be clearly forseen. State control was on the point of turning from a source of large profit into a serious drain on the Exchequer. The Government, which had reckoned on a continuance during 1922 of the artificial conditions of prosperity, rapidly reversed its policy, and left the coal industry to shift for itself under circumstances which made chaos and disaster inevitable. The illusion that war was fruitful of lasting economic benefits could be no longer sustained: the War, and the unstable conditions of half peace which followed the Armistice, at length showed their real results in economic collapse. The dispute of 1921 and its aftermath are the real working out of the consequences of war. They round off the tragic story of shattered hopes which was soon to become the story of almost every industry in the country.

The first scene of this last act of the tragedy is staged in the conference room.

The Joint Committee of coal-owners' and miners' representatives lost no time, after the temporary settlement of 1920, in setting to work upon their task of drafting a permanent scheme for the regulation of wages and conditions. The miners had made it clear, before entering upon negotiations, that they proposed to insist upon a National Wages Board and a national system of wage regulation; and, although the precise meaning to be attached to these claims was not made clear, there can be no doubt that negotiations began on the basis of a common endeavour to find a mutually acceptable national system. This, at any rate, was certainly understood by the Miners' Executive, as can be seen from the reports of its discussions with the delegates appointed to carry on the actual negotiations.

At first, reassuring statements were issued to the Press concerning the progress of these negotiations, and it was generally understood that a substantial advance towards a settlement was being made. In fact, both parties seem to have agreed to tackle first the questions least likely to lead to a deadlock. Attention was therefore at first concentrated on such questions as the principles on which the rate of wages in the industry, in its relation to other claims such as the claim to profits, should be settled, and the thorny question of the precise constitution and functions of the National Wages Board was left over for the time in the hope that an agreed solution might emerge from agreement on the other questions to be decided. It is now clear that, in doing this, the two parties had different conceptions. The mine-owners regarded a National Wages Board as, at the most, only an appeal court to which difficulties over wages fixed on a district basis might be submitted for adjustment: the miners meant by a National Board a body with powers to fix wages, and make advances and reductions on a national basis.

Unless, therefore, as some of the miners' leaders maintained, the owners fundamentally changed their attitude in the course of the discussions, the two parties were largely at cross-purposes from the outset. This, however, was not plain to the miners' leaders, and did not at all appear in the brief published reports on the negotiations. Until well after the date on which the Government discharged its bombshell concerning the immediate decontrol of the industry, the public supposed that the negotiations for a lasting settlement were proceeding well and smoothly, and that there was every probability of an agreement by the 31st March, the date fixed for the expiration of the temporary settlement of 1920.

The two problems round which the earlier stages of the negotiations mainly centred were, first, the method to be employed in consolidating wages on a post-war basis, and secondly, the principles which should govern wage variations in the future. The wage-system in the mining industry was, as I have pointed out, quite extraordinarily complicated, and the actual wage received by each man was made up of a number of different elements, each calculated in a different way.

First, there was for each grade a *basis* wage, or standard on which percentage advances were calculated. This basis or standard remained in some areas the same as before the War; but in South Wales, as we have seen, a new standard had been negotiated during the War, and in other areas changes had been made in the standards of particular grades, usually for the purpose of levelling up the minimum rates of the lower-paid workers.

Secondly, in each district there were percentage advances calculated on the standard. These varied from district to district, both in nominal amount and in real value; i. e. a 30 per cent. advance might be less on a low standard than a 20 per cent.

advance on a high standard, and, further, the value of the advances given differed from case to case.

Thirdly, there were the flat-rate advances conceded under control. These were on a uniform national basis, and amounted in all to 3*s.* per shift. This 3*s.*, known as the war wage, had the advantage that it was payable even for shifts which were not actually worked; i. e. if a man was under a contract of employment, he could claim the war wage even for days on which the pit was shut down, or he was prevented from working through circumstances beyond his own control. The monetary value of this form of out-of-work pay, averaged over all shifts, was estimated at 2*d.* per shift.

Fourthly, there was the Sankey wage, the flat-rate national advance of 2*s.* per shift granted in 1919 on the advice of the Coal Commission.

Fifthly, in the case of piece-workers only, there was the adjustment, varying from case to case, but usually approximating to 14·2 per cent., granted in order to compensate the piece-workers for the fall in earnings which might otherwise have resulted from the shorter working day inaugurated in 1919. This was calculated as a percentage of the basis rate *plus* the percentage advances on the basis; e. g. basis rate 8*s.* and percentage advance 50 per cent. = 12*s.*, on which the 14·2 per cent. adjustment would be calculated.

Sixthly, there was the national advance of March 1920, which was an advance of 20 per cent., calculated on the basis *plus* district percentages *plus* piece-work adjustment, but not on the war wage or the Sankey advance. The position of this part of the wage was further complicated by the fact that, if in the case of adults the 20 per cent. advance did not yield an actual advance of as much as 2*s.* a shift, it had to be made up to this sum in the case of each individual.

Seventhly, there was, from October 1920 up to and including February 1921, the datum-line advance conceded at the end of the 1920 stoppage. At its inception, this was 2*s.* a shift: it rose in January to 3*s.* 6*d.*, fell again to 1*s.* 6*d.* in February, and disappeared altogether with the decline in output and values in March 1921.

Thus, even if we leave this last factor out of account, the miners' wage, quite apart from special allowances and payments for special work, was made up of no less than six elements. For example, a highly paid piece-work miner in South Wales might be earning 21*s*. 5*d*. per shift. This would be made up as follows:

	s.	*d.*
1. Price-list earnings (equivalent to basis wage of time-workers) . . . . (say)	8	0
2. District percentages (50 per cent.)	4	0
3. Piece-work adjustment for shorter hours (14·2 per cent.)	1	8·4
4. Advance of March 1920 (20 per cent. on above with 2*s*. minimum)	2	8·8
5. War wage	3	0
6. Sankey wage	2	0
	21	5

In the case of day-workers, item 3*s*. would be missing; but all the other items would be present.

It was agreed by both parties that this intolerable complication of rates and advances could not be allowed to continue, and that the system of paying wages must somehow be simplified. It was further agreed that the first step towards simplification was the consolidation of some part of the advances into a new standard rate, which would take the place of the old basis rate, and that the second step was the determination of some uniform method of computing all advances on the new consolidated standard. But there were differences both as to the amounts to be consolidated into the new standard rates, and as to the method of computing advances upon them.

The points here at issue must be kept clearly distinct from the controversial question whether advances were in future to be made nationally or locally. This issue, as I have pointed out, was being kept in the background, and did not directly arise at the stage now under discussion. The miners did not demand that the new consolidated rate should be on a uniform national basis. On the contrary, they accepted the position that a new rate should be set up in each district, based on the standard rates already in existence, but merging in them certain of the advances conceded. Two alternative methods of doing this were considered by them.

The first was to start from the total sum payable in wages, and to divide this into two parts, without regard to the basis on which it was calculated. Thus, if it were agreed that 30 per cent. of the total wage should be treated as a floating margin, subject to increase or decrease, and the remaining 70 per cent. consolidated into a new standard rate, then, in the case given above, a new standard wage of 16*s.* 5·7*d.* per shift would be reached, and just under 5*s.* would remain as a floating margin. The second method was to consolidate into the new standard all percentage advances, including the piece-work adjustment (No. 3) and the March advance (No. 4), leaving as a floating margin the war and Sankey flat-rate advances. This, in the same case, would give a new standard of 16*s.* 5*d.*, and would leave 5*s.* as a floating margin.

In the consideration of these alternatives the miners had to take into account not so much the amount to be arrived at in the new consolidated wage, as the basis on which the floating margin was to be dealt with in future. This margin might be treated either as a flat-rate addition to the standard of so much a shift, liable to flat-rate increases or reductions. Or it might be treated as an addition of so much per cent. to the standard, liable to increase or reduction in terms of percentages. This was an important question of policy. As I have pointed out, the effect of flat-rate advances equally applicable to all grades of workers is to diminish the real difference in standard of life between low paid and the more highly paid workers, whereas percentage advances give the more highly paid workers larger actual advances than the low paid, and keep the grades at the same proportionate distances. But, when wages fall, the effect is reversed. A flat-rate reduction means a larger percentage reduction for low paid than for the more highly paid workers: a percentage reduction means for the more highly paid a larger actual reduction in terms of money.

During the earlier stages of the negotiations the miners had not made up their minds definitely, either between the alternative methods of consolidation, or on the question whether future advances and reductions should be flat rates or percentages. Their policy on these points was not finally settled until the 22nd February, when a National Conference, the second held to deal with the question, had before it the votes of the district associations on this and certain other questions arising out of the negotiations with the owners. The decision was in favour of consolidation by the second of the methods outlined above, the merging of all percentage advances with the old standards into new district standards, and the retention of the war and Sankey advances as a flat-rate addition, subject to variation by a method of flat-rate advances or reductions. Certain districts, of which Northumberland and Durham were the most important, favoured the percentage system ; but all the other large districts were for a system of flat-rate advances and reductions in the future.

The question of the method of consolidation and of determining future advances and reductions was, however, hardly pressed to an issue in the negotiations. The owners were, it is true, strongly in favour of the percentage, as against the flat-rate, system. But this point was not pushed to a decision, for it proved to be impossible to reach anything like an agreement as to the amounts to be consolidated into the new standard wage. The owners appear at the outset to have given the miners to understand that they could on no account agree to any rate embodying more than half the wages payable under control. When they put their proposal in definite form, it was that the new standard rate should be, in nearly all cases, the rate which had been actually payable in July 1914, and that all advances conceded during the war period, whether as percentages or at flat rates, should be excluded from the standard. The only exceptions were to be actual readjustments in the standard rates themselves reached since 1914. In certain areas, especially Cumberland and North Wales, the owners intimated that, owing to financial exigencies, they might not be able to agree to rates as high even as those in force in 1914. As neither party would depart from its claims on these points, a deadlock was reached, and no new consolidated rates could be agreed upon.

The second group of questions round which the earlier negotiations turned was the future method of determining variations in wages, and the relation of wages to profits, selling prices, and costs of production. Under the pre-war system, as we have seen, the principal, and often the only, factor taken into account by the district Conciliation Boards in determining changes in mining wages had been the selling-price of coal. This system fell into abeyance during the war, when the rise in the cost of living and the control of the industry and of coal prices by the Government made it unworkable. The question was whether it should be revived, either locally or on a national basis, with the termination of price control, which came to an end in February 1921.

Selling-prices alone, it is clear, could not be more than a rough indication of the profit-making capacity of the coal industry. Comparatively low prices, with large output, might yield greater aggregate profits than high prices with low output. If, therefore, the principle that the miners' renumeration should depend on the capacity of the industry to pay was to be accepted, it was clearly desirable to work out some more accurate system of correspondence between wages and capacity to pay than could be secured by variation in accordance only with changes in selling-prices. Accordingly, the owners and the miners began to work on the outlines of a scheme which was virtually one of profit-sharing, under which a fixed ratio between wages and profits would be determined, and wages and profits would both vary automatically in accordance with the ability of the industry to pay.

Out of the discussions the following proposals emerged. It was suggested that not only a new consolidated standard wage, but also a standard profit, expressed as a percentage of the standard wage, should be laid down. In other words, whatever might be the total amount of the standard wages (not including any variable flat-rate or percentage additions) payable to all grades of mine-workers, the owners should be entitled, in correspondence to the standard wage, to a total standard profit amounting to x per cent. of the standard wage. Under normal conditions there would remain in the industry a substantial sum after payment of the standard wage, the standard profit, and all costs of production other than wages. This ' surplus ', it was proposed, should also be allocated to wages and profits in fixed proportions, y per cent. to wages and z per cent. to profits, the amount payable in wages being added to the standard wage either as a percentage (owners' proposal) or as a flat-rate addition (miners' proposal).

It was clearly a moot point on the Labour side whether such a principle as this, marking the open recognition of profit-sharing throughout the industry, should be accepted. But it was contended that virtually the mines had been worked for many years past under a bad system of profit-sharing, based on the variation of wages in accordance with selling-prices, and that it would at least be better to have a real system under which the miners would effectually share in the prosperity of their industry. Together with the question of consolidation already discussed, the question of accepting or rejecting the profit-sharing basis was submitted in February to the district Miners' Associations, with the result that, subject to certain conditions, it was approved by an overwhelming majority of the districts voting. Kent alone voted against: Scotland, South Wales, Yorkshire and seven other districts voted in favour. Durham decided to leave the question to the Federation as a whole: eight districts, including Lancashire and the Midlands, abstained from voting. There was, however, a clear majority in favour of acceptance, subject only to the condition—all-important in the sequel—that any such arrangement should be subject to the acceptance by the owners of a national system of wage regulation—in other words, to the National Wages Board and the National Pool.

While the principle of a fixed relationship between profits and wages was thus conditionally accepted by the miners as well as the owners, there was no agreement as to the proportions in which the sums available should be divided. Two questions were involved—first, the relation which the 'standard profits' should bear to the 'standard wage', or basis wage; and secondly, the apportionment of any surplus. On both these points there was a wide gulf between the proposals of the two parties. The miners proposed that the standard profits should be 10 per cent. of the standard wage, and that a slightly higher proportion of the surplus, one-tenth as compared with one-eleventh, should go to increase profits, nine-tenths being credited to wages. Debenture charges, depreciation, &c., would count as costs of production, and the sums available for wages and profits would be calculated after they had been deducted.

The owners, on the other hand, began with a demand for a standard profit at the rate of 2*s.* per ton. As the average profit of the five pre-war years was under 1*s.* per ton, this meant a demand for a standard profit increased, on the same output, by over 100 per cent., whereas the proposed increases in the standard wage were not at all in proportion. This can hardly have been more than a preliminary bargaining demand; and, when the owners definitely formulated their written scheme, their claim was for a standard profit equivalent to 17 per cent. of the standard wage.

The difference between this 17 per cent. and the 10 per cent. proposed by the miners is not so large as might appear; for a lower percentage on a higher standard wage might yield more in the aggregate than a higher percentage on a lower standard. Thus, if the standard wage was 15*s*. a shift, a 10 per cent. basis would yield a profit of 1*s*. 6*d*., whereas, on a wage of 10*s*. only, 17 per cent. would yield only 1*s*. 8*d*. The standard percentage for profit would clearly depend on the level of the standard wage; and, until this was fixed, it could not be fixed either. But, as we have seen, a deadlock was reached on the question of the standard wage.

There was not the same obstacle to agreement as to the disposal of the surplus available after meeting cost of production, standard wages, and standard profits; for here it was only a matter of determining the proportion in which the sum should be divided. Here the miners, as we have seen, offered the owners one-tenth; but the owners demanded one-quarter of the total surplus. The estimated pre-war wage bill (for 1913) was £91,000,000: the profits were £22,000,000 in 1913, but only £13,000,000 on the average for the five years 1909–13. On the other hand, during 1919 and 1920 wages represented a much larger proportion of the total outgoings, and the nine to one ratio proposed by the miners approximately represented the actual position existing in 1921. The one-tenth which the miners suggested was clearly less than the normal pre-war proportion of profits to wages: the one-fourth proposed by the owners was clearly much in excess of it.

One further point in connexion with the wages issue needs to be mentioned. It has been pointed out that the war wage was payable for days when a pit was stopped or a man was otherwise prevented from working through circumstances not under his control. The value in money of this concession was estimated at 2*d*. a shift. The question arose whether, if the new wage was to be either consolidated or placed on a new footing as either a percentage or a flat rate advance on a new standard, it should continue to be paid for 'idle days' as under control, or whether the *2d.* should be added to the amount of the war wage and merged in the new consolidated rate or in the floating advance payable on it. The miners demanded that payment for 'idle days' should continue: the owners strongly urged the abolition of this special payment.

On these and similar points the negotiations between the owners and the miners dragged on. The conditional acceptance by the latter of the principle of a fixed relation between profits and wages was hailed in the press as a good omen for the success of the negotiators in coming to an agreement which would eliminate wage disputes for the future. The importance of the fact that the miners attached to their acceptance the condition that the owners should accept the National Wages Board and the National Pool was not appreciated until later, and it was not until March that the practical certainty that the parties would fail to reach an agreement became known.

Meanwhile, the Government had made definitely public its decision, which is discussed in the next section of this chapter, to complete the decontrol of the coal industry by the end of March. This decision profoundly affected the later course of the negotiations. I have tried, in this section, to describe them only up to the point to which they can be described without raising the issues arising out of the termination of control. It will be seen that, even had there been no question of decontrol, agreement would not have been easily reached. Decontrol made the reaching of any agreement, in time to prevent a serious crisis, practically impossible.

Section 2. Decontrol

It was, we have seen, in the midst of the joint negotiations for a permanent national settlement that the Government suddenly announced its decision to advance the date of decontrol. Under the Mining Industry Act of 1920, control was to continue until the 31st August 1921, and accordingly both the modified arrangements guaranteeing certain profits to the owners and the national system of wage regulation established under control were to continue in force until that date. These facts had been repeatedly affirmed by Ministers, and had been the whole basis of the relations between the miners, the owners, and the Government. Moreover, the provision that control was to continue was embodied in a statute, and although the Government had taken power by Order to modify or even remove control before the appointed date, the financial provisions of the Act of 1920 in fact made complete decontrol impracticable without fresh legislation. No one, at the beginning of the negotiations between the owners and the miners, or probably even at the outset of 1921, had any idea that such legislation was contemplated.

At some time, however, almost at the beginning of 1921, the Government decided to advance the date of decontrol. Its reasons for this far-reaching decision, which was clearly a breach of pledges repeatedly given and was inevitably destined to throw the coal industry into chaos, cannot be stated with certainty. Undoubtedly, however, two important considerations were in the minds of the Ministry. The first was the sudden and unforeseen reversal in the fortunes of the industry itself. The Government, in common with the owners and the miners, had been basing its calculations on the continuance, for some time at least, of the abnormal prosperity of 1920, which was dependent on the inflated prices secured for coal exported to Europe. But these prices could not be maintained, and, by the beginning of 1921, the policy, systematically pursued under the sanction of the Government, of exploiting by heavy charges the need of Europe for coal, was bringing retribution upon the industry. American coal, attracted into the European markets during the dispute of 1920, became a powerful competitor, and every success in wringing reparations, in the form of coal exports, from Germany helped to bring down the prices which British coal could command. France naturally preferred cheap or free coal from Germany to dear coal from Great Britain, and other countries could do better by buying from France or America than by continuing to use British coal. Consequently the drain upon the profits pool created by the pooling of part of the excess profits under the control scheme grew alarmingly, and it became clear to the Government that the sums in the pool would be exhausted by the end of March, and that, if further payments of guaranteed profits were to be made to the owners, they would fall upon the Government itself.

In the second place, the dates originally fixed for the decontrol of mines and railways coincided. Especially in view of the existence of the Triple Alliance, this coincidence was felt to be dangerous, as it might lead to a labour dispute in which the groups of workers affected would make common cause. There was, from this point of view, a positive advantage in making a change, and the mines, rather than the railways, were singled out because there the financial motive was also strongly present.

That there were weighty reasons, even of a kind to appeal to the Government, against decontrol will appear plainly enough in the course of this chapter. Decontrol took the coal industry at a very awkward moment, when the force of the depression was just being felt. It was carried through so suddenly as to leave almost no time for readjustment or for an attempt to devise new machinery to deal with the situation. It disappointed expectations legitimately entertained, on the strength of many Government statements and of an Act of Parliament but recently passed into law. And it made practically impossible the success of the negotiations in which the coal-owners and the Unions were engaged at the Government's own request.

This was made plain by the comments which immediately followed the announcement.

The attitude of the owners at that time is indicated by a statement made by Mr. Evan Williams, on behalf of the Mining Association, on the 2nd March :

> 'We recognized that, while financial control remained, it was inevitable that settlements of wages should be national, and we hoped after March 31st to find a scheme by which wages would be brought in relation with the capacity of the *industry as a whole*. We worked towards such a scheme in the belief that, by August 31st, the industry would have found its feet, and that all difficulties in the way of districts in applying the principles of the scheme would have gone.'

It is thus clear that, during the earlier part of the negotiations, both the miners and the owners were working definitely and explicitly for a national scheme. Before the negotiations were finished, but after months of work had been spent upon them and the general principles which were to govern the proposed agreement largely determined, there was a sudden change in the whole situation, followed by a change of attitude on the part of the owners. This caused all the work which had been done to be scrapped, and led directly to the disaster which came upon the industry.

The cause of this change was, simply and solely, the decision of the Government to remove financial control of the coal industry on the 31st March. That and nothing else, was the immediate cause of the great dispute of 1921.

The owners, as well as the miners, agreed that this decision was definitely contrary to the pledges which had been given. General Hickman, one of the spokesmen of the coal-owners, said in the debate on the Second Reading of the Coal Mines Decontrol Bill, that he agreed with the miners that decontrol 'is a breach of promise to the owners and the men'. Nevertheless, he and his colleagues agreed to decontrol.

How, then, did it come about that the coal-owners agreed to accept the Decontrol Bill although they regarded it as a breach of faith, and that the Bill passed the House of Commons with hardly any opposition, except from the Labour benches? The full story is both important and instructive.

It seems to have been during the latter part of December 1920 that the Government definitely conceived the idea of advancing the date on which decontrol was to take effect, and determined to approach the mine-owners and discuss the proposal with them. On the 5th January 1921 the Miners' Executive was summoned to the Board of Trade, and given the first private intimation in quite general terms of the Government's changed intention. A further meeting on the question was held on the 13th January, when the President of the Board of Trade definitely announced that the Government control of coal prices and of distribution would be removed from the 1st March, but gave the miners to understand that the profits pool, on which the arrangements for the payment of the wage advances conceded under control were dependent, would be continued probably until the end of June. On both these occasions the miners' leaders strongly protested against any proposal to remove control before definite arrangements had been made by the men and the owners for the future regulation of the industry ; and on the 26th January the miners, invited to attend a further meeting for the discussion of decontrol, informed the Board of Trade that, as they were totally opposed to the suggestion, no good purpose would in their opinion be served by a further meeting. This protest against decontrol was endorsed by their Conference which met on the same day, and by subsequent Conferences on the 22nd February and the 10th March.

So far, decontrol had been discussed privately with the owners, and the Government's intention had been intimated, not very clearly or definitely, to the miners. The first public and official mention of the new policy was, however, not made until Sir Robert Horne's speech in Glasgow on the 2nd February. He then announced that the Government was anxious to complete the decontrol of the industry at the earliest possible moment, but that the actual date of decontrol was still undecided. He also stated that it was calculated that the whole of the 'pool' under the control scheme 'would have disappeared into deficiencies by the end of March' (i. e. that the whole of the excess profits paid into a 'pool' by the more prosperous concerns would have been used up in making the profits of the less prosperous collieries up to the standard guaranteed profit).

From this point events marched rapidly. On the 15th February legislation for the removal of control was announced in the King's Speech on the opening of Parliament, but still no definite date was given. It was on the 22nd February that Sir Robert Horne called both the miners and the owners into conference, and announced to them the definite decision of the Government that complete decontrol should take effect not on the 30th June, but as early as the 31st March. Thus, hardly more than a month's notice was given of a decision which would inevitably upset the whole financial basis of the industry.

Commenting upon the decision on the following day, Mr. Evan Williams said that 'the Government proposal to end control on the 31st March creates for the owners the gravest situation they have ever been called upon to face'. He said also that 'the unexpected removal of control will affect very considerably the possibility of arriving at an agreement with the men'.

It is clear that, for some time before the Government definitely announced its decision, negotiations had been proceeding between the Government and the owners. At the Annual Dinner of the Mining Institute of Scotland on the 5th February, Dr. Charles Carlow, of the Fife Coal Company, said that ' delicate negotiations would be brought about very shortly between the Government and the coal-owners, and to some extent the miners, but chiefly between the Government and the coal-owners. Sir Robert Horne had indicated that decontrol on the financial side should take place on the 31st March, instead of the 31st August. Speaking that evening with a feeling of great responsibility to the members of the Mining Institute of Scotland, he wished to say that the coal-owners of the country would not submit to this '. (*Colliery Guardian* of the 11th February 1921.) The *Colliery Guardian* also stated in the same issue that colliery owners were asking for a continuance of the guarantee, i. e., of the Government guarantee of ' standard ' profits.

In the *Compendium*, a well-known industrial monthly, for February, the desire of the Government to decontrol the industry on the 31st March was referred to. The Editor added: ' Some little time must be allowed for readjustment. It is impossible to decontrol without some upheaval, and therefore it may be found to be necessary to continue the financial arrangement for a few months longer.' Reference was then made to differences of opinion among the colliery owners on the question of decontrol. The *Colliery Guardian* of the 4th February 1921 stated that ' the alternative (to some continued State help) of leaving the poorer districts to fend for themselves at the present time is unthinkable, and the industry had hardly been emancipated for a sufficient period to devise efficient measures itself to meet the situation adequately '. Yet this ' unthinkable situation ' is precisely that in which the Government decided to place the industry.

The *Compendium* for March stated that, after the Government had announced decontrol from the 31st March, ' at the meeting of the Executive Council of the Mining Association which followed, it was pointed out that the unexpected lifting of financial control would affect very considerably the possibility of arriving at an agreement with the men *already discussed* '.

It is therefore clear (1) that the putting forward of the date of decontrol was the action not of the coal-owners, but of the Government; and (2) that this step immediately upset the whole basis of negotiations between the owners and the miners. This was because the industry was at the time in a condition of quite abnormal depression, which made impossible any satisfactory national agreement on the wages question, if control were removed. The continuance of control until the date originally promised, the end of August, would, on the other hand, have given time for the industry to put its house in order, and have thus made an agreement possible.

Why, then, did the owners, who expressed opposition when earlier decontrol was first announced and prophesied the breakdown of negotiations as a result of it, rapidly change their attitude, and withdraw their opposition? This was partly explained in the course of the discussions on the Decontrol Bill which took place in the House of Commons. In the debate on the Second Reading on the 8th March, the owners withdrew their opposition; but, in speaking on behalf of the owners, Sir Clifford Cory made it plain that they did so only on the understanding that a financial agreement which had been arrived at between them and the Government should be strictly adhered to. Sir Clifford Cory referred to the pledge given by Lord Peel to Lord Gainford in the House of Lords, in connexion with the Coal Mines Emergency Bill, that no order or regulation should be issued varying the profits payable to the owners up to the 31st August without the consent of the Mining Association. He stated that the Government was getting round this pledge by making the variation by means of a new Bill instead of by an Order, and he expressed the dissatisfaction of the Mining Association, and its view that the industry, out of which the Treasury had received such large sums under control, was entitled to help from the Treasury in its present difficulty. He then continued as follows:

'However, having regard to the present condition of national finances, the Mining Association have decided not to press the claim of the coal-owners for their full standard up to the end of August, but they will accept an arrangement that the full standard should be paid up to the end of December, and, unwillingly, nine-tenths to the end of March. If there should be sufficient in the pool to pay the full amount of the standard for these three months, of course they will be paid. The coal-owners have agreed to accept the Bill if it is in the form which I have indicated; but I think on every ground they are entitled to more consideration than they have been given.'

In speaking on the Committee Stage of the Decontrol Bill on the 11th March, Sir Clifford Cory made the owners' reasons for acceptance a good deal clearer, and brought out that there were other causes besides 'the financial embarrassments of the country' which led them to agree to a course which was bound to plunge the industry into chaos. He said that the coal-owners realized that, if they got control extended, there 'would not be very much in it'.

'The Government brought in the clause in the Coal Mines (Emergency) Act which stated that, if any deficiency appeared not to have been caused by an Order, regulation, or direction issued by the Controller or the Board, the Government would not make up the guarantee. It was held by the Government that the losses were due, not to any order or regulation issued by the Government, but to the ordinary course of trade, owing to there being a slump in trade. The coal-owners did not take that view. They said that, in their view, the losses were due to the action of the Government in one way or another. The Government took the opposite view. Their (the coal-owners') only remedy would be to take some action against the Government. But action against the Government was not very successful as a rule. Under these circumstances, they thought it would be better to make sure of the nine-tenths guarantee up to March than nothing at all. If the owners were not going to have the nine-tenths pre-war profits on the current quarter they would be bound to feel the pinch. There had been some benefit in making this arrangement with the Government. The Government was at any rate liable for this quarter. If they prolonged control, it was the Government's view that they would not be liable even for the nine-tenths. There would not, therefore, be much benefit in continuing control. It was no good having an illusory guarantee for a further period.'

The motives of the coal-owners in agreeing to decontrol could not have been more candidly stated. It was for them purely a financial question, and they treated it as such, although as we have seen, they fully recognized that it was likely to upset all their negotiations with the miners for a new agreement. It was not, in the view of the coal-owners, their business to look after the miners' interests.

General Hickman, the coal-owners' second spokesman in the House of Commons on the 8th March, carried matters some steps farther. After saying that he blamed the Government and the owners for forcing export prices up so high that the Americans captured the market, he went on to complain of the Government's action in decontrolling the industry without first taking off war wages. This Government action, he thought, made it difficult for the owners and the miners to come to a friendly arrangement. 'Therefore', he said, 'I have a great quarrel with the Government on that point, and, if they had any courage or backbone, before they decontrolled the industry they should have taken off all the flat rates which they had put on, and allowed the owners to make their own arrangements with the men.' Sir L. W. Llewelyn, presiding at the meeting of the Cambrian Combine on the 3rd March, followed the same line of argument, and accused the Government of putting the unpopularity of reducing wages on to the owners by insisting on immediate decontrol. Nevertheless, all these spokesmen of the coal-owners, having reached their financial arrangement with the Government, accepted decontrol without regard for its effect upon the miners.

The Labour Party was almost alone in resisting the Decontrol Bill in the House of Commons, and the Bill, after passing its Second Reading on the 8th March, its Committee Stage on the 11th and 15th March, and Report and Third Reading on the 15th March, was accepted without amendment by the House of Lords, and speedily received the Royal Assent. It thus appeared to have secured almost universal assent outside the ranks of Labour; but an interesting commentary on the way in which this assent was secured was furnished by the account given by Mr. Alfred Bigland, a Unionist M.P., of the manner in which he was persuaded to vote for the Bill. 'I gave', he wrote to the newspapers in March, 'my vote with the Government after a conversation with the Minister of Mines, who assured me that the mine-owners were prepared with a generous response, and that the terms offered to the men were such that the Ministry of Mines had no doubt that they would be accepted.' The making of this statement does not seem to have been denied; but it is clear that it was a complete travesty of the position. Apart from the question whether the terms submitted by the owners to the miners were or were not reasonable, there was certainly no warrant for supposing that they were likely to be accepted. From the moment when decontrol was announced, the problem of a settlement in the mining industry became practically insoluble within the time available and under the conditions existing at the time.

What is clear is that, in deciding on a step which involved a definite reversal of policy and breach of promises made to the industry, the Government consulted, and reached a financial accommodation with, the coal-owners, but did this without any attempt to offer any form of financial aid to the miners, who were even more deeply affected by the proposal, since the rates of wages which they were receiving, and the system under which these wages were paid, were dependent on the continuance of control. The owners, on their part, came to an agreement with the Government, without in any way consulting the miners, although it was manifest that the effect of this agreement would be to upset altogether the negotiations upon which they and the miners were at the time engaged. The Government caused the situation which led to the dispute: the coal-owners acquiesced in it. When the Government had reached its arrangement with the owners, the miners found themselves confronted with an ultimatum. They protested immediately, and continued to protest, against decontrol; but, when the Decontrol Bill became an Act, they were left, face to face with the owners, to deal with the wages question as best they could, and with only a week or two before the termination of the temporary agreement.

Section 3. Rival Schemes—The Question of a Subsidy

On the 16th February 1921, the day following the announcement of decontrol at the opening of Parliament, the *Daily Herald* published, in a prominent position, the statement that the mine-owners had determined upon a national lock-out, to take effect at the end of March, and that secret communications were being sent to all owners advising them of this decision and urging that reserves of coal should be built up in view of an impending national stoppage. It appears that, as early as December 1920, a communication was circulated among the Scottish coal-owners urging them, in view of a probable emergency in March, to build up stocks of coal to the greatest possible extent. This circular made no direct reference to a lock-out; but the inference was clear that serious danger of a stoppage in March was considered to exist. A little later, similar circulars, variously worded, appear to have been issued in other districts; and some of these, falling into the hands of miners, were naturally interpreted as indications that the owners were preparing for a possible stoppage.

It is, indeed, clear enough from certain of the quotations made in the previous section that the question of the future level of wages entered largely into the negotiations between the owners and the Government on the question of decontrol. As we have seen, some at least of the owners took the view that the Government should, before decontrolling the industry, have reduced wages by taking off the advances which it had conceded during the period of control. The Government, however, maintained that the future level of wages was a matter for the owners to deal with in the light of the new conditions created by decontrol. This being so, there can be no doubt that the owners had already in February made their calculation of the wages which, in their opinion, they could afford to pay in the absence of State assistance, and had definitely made up their minds that decontrol must be accompanied by very large reductions in many of the districts, and especially by the withdrawal of the national flat-rate advances paid during the period of control. It cannot be stated precisely at what date they decided that the best method of enforcing these reductions was by the issue of notices terminating existing wage-contracts to all mine-workers; but it seems probable that this decision was reached at least by the beginning of February, and that the 'secret circulars' referred to by the *Daily Herald* were the directions issued to their members by the mine-owners' organizations in pursuance of this policy.

The *Herald's* allegation that a national lock-out was to be declared was immediately denied; but the point at issue was less a point of fact than a point of interpretation. The decision to issue notices terminating all wage-contracts had undoubtedly been taken, and this would, of course, be the procedure necessary to enforce a lock-out. But the owners maintained that the object of the notices was not to declare a lock-out, but to bring about a necessary reduction of wages in the light of the changed conditions. This, the miners said, amounted to a lock-out; for it was a refusal on the owners' part to give employment save on new conditions imposed by them. The dispute on the question whether the mining stoppage was to be regarded as a strike or a lock-out continued throughout its duration, and was at times acrimonious in the extreme.

We, however, are concerned here, not with this question, but with the precise methods adopted by the owners. The industry, without Government assistance, clearly could not afford, on its existing basis, to continue to pay the rates of wages which had been in force during the period of control. These wages varied in part from district to district; but over and above the varying district rates in force before the war and the comparatively small percentage advances upon them granted before the imposition of control there were the flat-rate advances conceded by the Government on a national basis. These had been paid under control by means of a virtual pooling system, so that even if the coal raised in one district was being sold at a loss, the deficit could be made up out of the surplus realized by the more profitable districts, especially those which were producing largely for export. But, with the abolition of control, the owners were determined to revert to a system under which there would be no pooling, and the wages in each district would be determined solely by the financial position of that district alone. Even if there had been no depression, this system would have meant wage reductions in many of the districts: in face of the depression, it meant large reductions in almost every district.

While the mine-owners were determined to go back to a system of fixing wages on a district basis, in accordance with the financial circumstances of each district, the miners were no less determined to do everything in their power to secure the continuance of a national system. They did not, indeed, demand that the existing district variations in basic wages should be swept away and a national scale of wages fixed for each grade of colliery workers. But they did demand that in future, as during the period of control, advances and reductions in wages should be uniform throughout all the coal-fields. They realized clearly that this would involve a change in the financial conduct of the industry and a departure from the pre-war system ; and they urged that the best method, short of public ownership, of providing for a national wage system was the institution, not only of a National Wages Board with power to make uniform advances and reductions, but also of a National Pool, into which the various colliery concerns would pay out of their surplus in accordance with their ability, and from which they would receive according to their needs. In other words, the miners demanded that the system of pooling which was in force under control should be continued on a permanent basis, as the means to a national wage system for the whole industry.

This was the position when, at various dates during the month of March, the owners gave notice to all mine-workers in their employment to terminate their wage-contracts from the end of March. The procedure adopted was that these notices were given without, as a rule, any definite statement as to the wages which, after March, the owners would be prepared to pay. Only after the notices had been given did the coal-owners' associations in the various districts, in some cases right at the end of the month, publish the amended scales of wages which they were prepared to offer on the basis of the most recent ascertainment of the financial position in each district. In some cases at least the owners also attempted to open up with the district Miners' Associations direct negotiations as to the amount of the wages to be paid. By decision of the Miners' Federation as a whole, the district associations refused to enter into discussions on this basis, which would have involved the abandonment of their claim to a national wage system. Accordingly, the owners published without negotiation their district schedules of the wage-rates which would rule in their collieries from the 1st April.

The mining industry was thus drifting rapidly towards the total stoppage threatened for the beginning of April, and no apparent effort was being made to avert the catastrophe. The complete failure of the protracted negotiations between the owners and the miners had become evident by the beginning of March ; and, on the 10th March, the Miners' Conference accepted the fact of failure, and instructed the Executive, after a final attempt to secure acceptance of their claims by the owners, to lay directly before the Government the scheme for the future regulation of the industry which they had drawn up. Accordingly, on the 10th March, the miners obtained from the owners their final proposals in writing, and, on the instructions of a further Conference held on the 18th March, submitted them for acceptance or rejection to the district Miners' Associations, asking of each district whether or not it was prepared to recommend the temporary abandonment of the demand for a National Pool, and the opening up of negotiations for a settlement on a district basis. Meanwhile, on the 11th March, the Miners' Executive had already submitted to Sir Robert Horne its own scheme, duly approved by the Conference of the 10th March, for the future regulation of the industry, and the owners had also placed their 'final proposals' in the hands of the Government. The result of the district deliberations on the owners' scheme and the proposal that the demand for a national settlement should be temporarily abandoned was its decisive rejection by most of the districts of the Federation. Two important districts, Yorkshire and Northumberland, and five small groups voted in favour of a temporary settlement on a district basis; South Wales, Scotland, Lancashire, Durham, the Midlands, and eight smaller districts voted against. This decision was reported to the Miners' Conference on the 25th March, and it was left in the hands of the Executive to press forward the proposals already forwarded by the miners to the Government.

The Government had thus before it, instead of a plan agreed upon by owners and miners, two rival schemes for the future regulation of the industry. These schemes presented certain features of similarity; but the divergences between them were fundamental. The miners' plan involved the continuance of wage variations on a uniform national basis, under the auspices of a National Wages Board and with the aid of a National Pool into which a proportion of profits would be paid: the owners refused to consider at all any method of regulating wages except on a district basis.

The two schemes are so important that they are here set out side by side in their essential features. The italics are mine.

COAL-OWNERS' SCHEME

Mining Association of Great Britain

Heads of Proposed Scheme for the Future Regulation of Wages and Profits in the Coal Industry.

It being agreed that wages in the industry must depend upon the financial ability to pay, the owners propose that the following principles be adopted by the Mining Association of Great Britain and the Miners' Federation of Great Britain for application to the determination of the *wages payable in each district upon the financial position of such district:*

MINERS' SCHEME

Miners' Federation of Great Britain

Draft of Agreement proposed to be entered into between the Mining Association of Great Britain and the Miners' Federation of Great Britain, hereinafter referred to as the parties.

It is hereby agreed that the regulation of wages and profits in the coal industry of Great Britain shall be determined for the duration of this agreement upon the basis set forth below.

1. For the purpose of securing the most effective means for the distribution of profits and wages in the industry, there shall be established *a National Board* (to be known as the National Coal Board), and *all powers and duties of the several district Conciliation Boards now in existence, relating to the fixing of the general district rates, shall hereafter be exercised by the National Coal Board.*

2. The National Coal Board shall consist of representatives of the owners and workmen, 26 of whom shall be representatives of the owners and 26 shall be representatives of the workmen, the manner of their election to be determined by the parties.

3. The National Coal Board shall determine all questions of wages and profits affecting the coal-mining industry as a whole.

1. That the base rates now existing at each colliery, with the percentages (or the equivalents in any district where there has been a subsequent merging into new standards) which were paid in July 1914, shall be regarded as the point below which wages shall not be automatically reduced.

Note.—All additions which have since been made to the base rates prevailing in July 1914 shall be maintained, and the percentages which have been added to pieceworkers' rates consequent upon the reduction in hours from eight to seven shall continue.

In lieu of the standard basis, or minimum wage, of each workman prevailing at the respective collieries prior to the date of the signing of this agreement, *a new standard wage for each workman shall be established, by incorporating therein the whole of the existing district percentages,* provided the alteration in such standard, basis, or minimum wage, shall not itself cause a change in wages.

The new standard thus created shall be known as the 1921 Standard wage which standard wage shall operate as a minimum wage during the lifetime of this agreement. In the case of those workmen for whom the advance in wages of 20 per cent. (known as the March 12th, 1920, advance in wages) did not yield an advance of 2*s.* extra per shift in the case of adults, 1*s.* per shift for persons of 16 up to 18 years of age, and 9*d.* per shift for persons under 16 years of age, upon the gross earnings, exclusive of the war wage and the Sankey wage, a percentage shall be incorporated which will result in 2*s.*, 1*s.*, and 9*d.* respectively being incorporated in the new standard before mentioned.

Wages known as the war and Sankey wage, and any other flat rate advances in addition to the 1921 standard, and which were in existence on or before March 31st, 1921, *shall be combined into one flat rate to be added to the 1921 standard,* until such combined flat rate is advanced or reduced in accordance with the terms of this agreement.

That portion of the *war wage payable for time lost* through circumstances at the colliery over which the workmen have no control shall not be incorporated in the new combined flat rate, but *shall be continued as heretofore* in accordance with the rules governing the payment as set forth in the war wage agreement of September 17th, 1917, and any subsequent orders and decisions by the Coal Controller or the Ministry of Mines.

Where the customary number of war wage or Sankey wage payments are in excess of the actual number of shifts worked by the workmen, such additional war wage or Sankey wage payments shall be included in the combined flat rate payment hereafter to be paid in addition to the 1921 standard.

The 1921 standard wage shall be reckoned as the principal element of the cost of production, and shall be payable before any profit is allocated to the coal-owners, additional wages in excess of the standard wage to be payable in accordance with the principles set forth in this agreement.

Any advance in wages above the 1921 standard, *or reduction* in wages to the standard made in accordance with the terms of this agreement, *shall be* in the form of additions to, or deductions from the combined flat rate in excess of the standard, as *flat rate advances or flat rate reductions respectively.*

The colliery owners shall receive in the aggregate as profits one-tenth of the amount paid as wages.

2. *That the owners' aggregate standard profits in each district in correspondence with the above shall be taken as 17 per cent. of the aggregate amount of wages payable as above.*

4. That if at any period of ascertainment the owners' standard profit is not realized, the amount of the deficiency shall be carried forward as a prior charge against any surplus available for the payment of wages in excess of the basis of wages provided in No. 1 above.

When wages are at or on the standard the owners shall receive as a minimum profit one-tenth of the aggregate wage paid at the aforesaid standard.

Where, however, the quarterly certificate of the joint auditors shows that the balance available for distribution as profit, after costs have been met as set forth in the first schedule to this agreement, does not provide a sufficient sum to ensure a payment of one-tenth of the aggregate wages standard as profits, the owners agree to forego the minimum profit until subsequent ascertainments show available balances sufficient to enable them to be paid any arrears of profit due from previous quarters.

The workmen undertake to make no application for wage advances above the standard as long as arrears of owners' minimum profit remain unpaid.

3. That *any surplus* remaining of the proceeds of the sale of coal at the pit-head after such wages and profits and all other costs have been taken into account *shall be divisible as to 75 per cent. to the workmen and 25 per cent. to the owners,* the workmen's share being expressed as a percentage on the standard rate of the district.

Note.—To meet the present abnormal situation the owners are prepared to accept a temporary departure from the strict application of the above principles to the extent of waiving their share of the surplus in favour of the workmen, on condition that ascertainments

The amount payable in wages in excess of the standard, which standard is an element of cost as set forth in Schedule 1 of this agreement, *shall be the whole of the income of the industry, after costs have been met* as hereinafter scheduled, *less one-tenth thereof, which shall be payable to the owners as profits* in addition to the minimum profit as set forth in paragraph 1.

are made at monthly periods to determine the wages payable during such time as the above concession on the part of the owners continues to operate.

The owners agree to maintain in production by means of a National Profits Fund all the collieries and all collieries hereafter to be developed, until such times as the National Coal Board decides to the contrary.

These rival schemes, we have noted, were placed in the hands of the Government on or about the 11th March. On that day, Sir Robert Horne, as President of the Board of Trade, met separately both the owners and the miners, and received their reports as to the position reached in the negotiations between them. The discussion with the miners centred mainly round two points, the effect of the owners' action in issuing notices for the termination of contracts, and the question of the National Pool. Sir Robert Horne showed plainly the Government's opposition to the proposal of a Pool, which, he affirmed, would involve the continuance of control. A day or two later he spoke in the same sense in the House of Commons, and on the 15th March he summed up his and the Government's attitude in a letter addressed to the miners.

After asserting that it was not for him or for the Government to pronounce an opinion on 'the proper division of the proceeds of the coal industry between the wage-earners and the owners', and after stressing the 'agreement on principle' which he understood to exist between them on this point, he went on to deal with the question of the Pool, or, as he put it, 'the proposal that the less profitable collieries should be subsidized out of the earnings of those which—whether from better management or greater natural advantages—succeed in realizing better results'. Sir Robert Horne announced that, after full consideration, he had come to the conclusion that the Government could not introduce legislation to put the Pool into effect, as 'it would not only be contrary to the principles upon which we believe the commercial success of this country to be based, but it would be disastrous to the coal industry itself '.

On the 24th March, as we have seen, the Coal Decontrol Act became law, and the miners by district vote, ratified by Conference decision, finally rejected the proposal that they should temporarily give up the demand for the National Pool, and attempt to negotiate a wage settlement on a district basis. From this point a crisis at the end of the month seemed to be inevitable. But no further step was made by either the owners or the Government. The miners wrote on the 24th March to the Prime Minister, enclosing their proposals for the future regulation of the industry, and at the same time drawing the attention of the Government to the impossible situation caused by the termination of control. The letter is important as showing the clear recognition that, with the industry in the condition to which it had been reduced, it was out of the power of the miners and owners to reach unaided a workable settlement, and in its insistence that it was for the Government, which by decontrol had placed the industry in an intolerable situation, to come at once to its assistance, in time to prevent the otherwise inevitable stoppage.

> ' It is clearly impossible ', Mr. Hodges wrote, ' to arrive at any agreement of anything like a permanent character and for normal times which can be made applicable to the present abnormal situation in the industry. The situation caused by the Government's decision to decontrol the trade on March 31 instead of August 31 is of a character which has made general agreement impossible. Only the Government can render assistance to the trade at the moment, and my Committee confidently expect that the Government will render such assistance to the trade as will enable it to live through the present crisis.
>
> ' As you are aware, the contracts of service between ourselves and the owners terminate on March 31, the owners having duly given notice to terminate such contracts. A lock-out is, therefore, unavoidable unless the workmen are prepared to accept such terms of employment as would reduce them, in many instances, to very nearly the pre-war level of wages, with the cost of living at 141 per cent. above pre-war prices. In our judgement, it would be a national calamity to have the trade brought to a standstill on Friday next.
>
> ' My Executive Committee will hold themselves in readiness to meet you at any time to discuss the situation with you, and it appears to us that such a meeting is highly desirable before the actual lock-out takes place.'

To this urgent letter no reply seems to have been received until five days later, only two days before the notices were due to expire. Then at last, on the 29th March, a request came from Sir Robert Horne that the miners should meet him on the following day. On the 30th March, *The Times* published a long article by Mr. Frank Hodges. The Miners' Secretary began by referring to the financial position of the industry. The official figures for February, published by the Mines Department, showed, he said, an unquestioned loss of £4,500,000 for the four weeks. Some collieries were still paying their way : the great majority were not. This deficiency could not be met out of wages and profits without reducing wages far below the pre-war standard of living. 'It is easily within the power of the parties'—despite the differences between them—'to agree on a scheme for the normal working of the industry, but the conditions of the moment are so abnormal that disaster cannot be averted unless some temporary expedient is provided.' This expedient, in Mr. Hodges's view, could only take the form of temporary Government aid, such as would have been available if control had been continued until August. He then went on to argue that the Government should provide cheap coal and so help trade revival by 'placing the credit of the nation at the disposal of the mining industry for such a time as is necessary to resuscitate our national trade'. The article ended with the following significant paragraph, which must be taken as expressing the author's personal opinion, rather than the official view of the Miners' Federation.

> 'The question of the relation of profits to wages, of the unification of the trade, of the National Wages Board *versus* the District Wages Board, of new standard wages, can all be left over to a much deeper and closer study than the owners and workmen have hitherto been able to give it. It may be that outside expert assistance would have to be sought and imported judgement exercised before a permanent satisfactory arrangement could be fixed up. Such are questions, however, for future regulation. For the moment it is our business to prevent a stoppage of work on Friday, and the only authority that can render help in this direction is the Government itself.'

In this article, Mr. Hodges was clearly making a bid for an offer of Government assistance which would enable a temporary settlement to be reached, and the big questions of principle at issue between the owners and miners to be left over for future adjustment. The importance of this personal view of Mr. Hodges, shared by other leaders among the miners, will become obvious at a later stage.

Mr. Hodges, however, received no encouragement for his attempts to prevent the stoppage when, later in the day, the Miners' Executive met Sir Robert Horne at the Board of Trade. Sir Robert, speaking for the Government, brusquely rejected the claim for a subsidy, on the ground that, if Government aid were given to the mining industry, almost every other industry would speedily come forward with a similar claim. He did not meet the point that the crisis in the mines had been created by the Government's own action in enforcing decontrol, and so disappointing the legitimate expectation that assistance would be continued up to the date fixed originally by Act of Parliament. He merely asserted that the State could not afford to give a subsidy, and that other industries would inevitably hold that they had an equal claim. Yet before long, as we shall see, the State did offer a subsidy, and the dispute was finally settled only by means of a subsidy, the granting of which did not lead to any claims from other industries for similar aid. The situation in the mines was utterly abnormal, and, by refusing to recognize this fact in good time, the Government made the stoppage inevitable, and the situation infinitely worse than it need have been. Probably the offer of a subsidy on the 29th March would have prevented the whole disastrous dispute.

No subsidy was offered. On the 31st March, Government control of the coal-mines came to an end. On the same day, the notices given by the owners took effect, and the national stoppage began.

Section 4. In Terms of Wages

What the public wanted most to know, when the imminence of a national mining struggle became evident, was the actual extent of the reductions which the coal-owners were seeking to enforce. But on this point it was by no means easy to obtain accurate information, or to express in a really intelligible form the information that could be secured. The owners stated that they were prepared to offer wages reckoned on the basis which they had proposed to the miners and the Government for the future regulation of the industry. This meant that their wages offer would be different for each district, and also of course for each grade within the district, the district standard being based on the ascertained capacity of the district to pay. This capacity would be measured by equating the standard wage proposed—roughly, the wage of 1914—with the standard profit, taken by the owners as 17 per cent. of the standard wage, and adding to the standard wage for the district a percentage equivalent to three-quarters of the surplus available after payment of standard wages, other costs of production, and standard profits. The sum available would be temporarily increased if the owners acted on their offer, mentioned above, to forgo for the time being their share in the surplus.

Clearly, then, the owners' offer was conditional on the financial position of the industry in each district, and they professed themselves unable to make any definite wage offer for April until the ascertainment of the financial position for the month of February was complete. This was not the case until almost the end of March, and until a few days before the stoppage there was no means of knowing what wages the owners were prepared to offer.

Gradually, however, figures came in from the various districts. But it was exceedingly difficult for the public to make much of these figures, beyond seeing at a glance that the reductions demanded were, in the majority of cases, very large indeed. This difficulty arose out of two causes. In the first place, the number of separate figures proposed for different grades in different districts was so large as to be confusing. In the second place, there was apparently no correspondence at all between the statements issued by the owners and the miners respectively as to the severity of the cuts proposed.

This discrepancy arose mainly from the different methods adopted by the two parties in reckoning the wages payable. Both purported to state what the weekly wages would be under the new conditions offered by the coal-owners; but, whereas the former, in order to arrive at the weekly wage, took the wage offered per shift and multiplied this by five, the coal-owners multiplied by six, and so seemed to be offering a wage larger than the miners were prepared to admit.

Which basis of reckoning was right? The reader can be left to determine this point with the aid of the following facts. The average number of shifts worked in a week by each miner under normal conditions was just under five. The average number of shifts for which the pits were open in a week under normal conditions was about five and a half. In some districts the pits were only open five days a week, in others eleven days a fortnight, in yet others six days a week. The average was five and a half shifts, and this was the maximum number that could be worked without a change of custom, and without any allowance for absence owing to illness or other causes. In fact, absenteeism, avoidable and unavoidable, brought the actual shifts worked down on the average to less than five a week. The coal-owners contended that, by eliminating avoidable absenteeism and agreeing that the pits should be everywhere working six days in the week, the miners could work more than five days. But, even so, it is clear that they could not possibly have brought the average up to six, on which the owners based their reckoning of the wages offered. The miners, on their side, contended that an average of five shifts a week was quite as much as could reasonably be aimed at in so heavy and hazardous an industry as coal-mining.

In order that we may avoid this controversy, it will be most convenient, wherever possible, to speak of the wages proposed in terms of single shifts, leaving the reader to multiply by five or whatever figure he may choose in order to arrive at the weekly equivalents. It will also be best to express the reductions as percentages of the wage-rates paid in March, and not only as actual amounts. No more than a few specimen figures need be given, illustrating the reductions demanded in a few typical districts.

Let us take first South Wales, one of the hardest hit—through the failure of the export trade—among the large districts. In South Wales the piece-work hewer was receiving in March 1921 a rate of 17*s*. 10·2*d*. per shift. The coal-owners offered for April, 10*s*. 8·5*d*. per shift, a reduction of 7*s*. 1·7*d*., or of 40 per cent. The March wage for labourers was 14*s*. 9·5*d*. per shift: the April offer was 7*s*. 9·9*d*., a reduction of nearly 7*s*., or of 49·5 per cent. These represent the two extremes, the reductions proposed for most of the grades being about 7*s*. a shift, or between 40 and 50 per cent. off the March rates.

In Lancashire and Cheshire, the colliers' pre-stoppage rate was 16*s*. 5·3*d*., and the rate offered for April, 12*s*. 10·2*d*. per shift, a reduction of 3*s*. 7*d*., or 22 per cent. For day-wagemen, the corresponding rates were 14*s*. 6·8*d*. and 10*s*. 4·1*d*., a reduction of 4*s*. 2·7*d*. or 26·7 per cent. The reductions in Lancashire ranged from 18 per cent. to 30 per cent. in the case of adults.

In Scotland, colliers earning 17*s*. per shift before the stoppage were to be reduced to 12*s*. 10*d*., a drop of 4*s*. 2*d*. Surface-workers were to be cut down from 15*s*. and 14*s*. a shift to about 7*s*. 6*d*., or from 45 to 50 per cent.

In Durham, hewers were to drop from 16*s*. 6·5*d*. to 11*s*. 11*d*. per shift, or by 28 per cent., and labourers from 13*s*. 8·9*d*. to 8*s*. 3·4*d*. per shift, or by nearly 40 per cent. In Nottingham, on the other hand, the cuts only ranged from 10 per cent. to 25 per cent., and in South Yorkshire, while reductions were proposed in the case of the lower-paid grades, the piece-work hewers were actually in some cases to receive a small increase.

The larger cuts proposed for the lower-paid grades were, of course, due to the return to a percentage basis, instead of a flat-rate basis, in the calculation of advances over the proposed new standard rates. This pressed very heavily on the less skilled grades in many of the districts.

The accompanying table, published on the Miners' behalf as a leaflet early in the dispute, shows, on the basis of five shifts a week, the effect of the proposed reductions in a number of typical grades and districts. The figures were disputed by the owners, but only, I think, on the ground that six, instead of five, shifts should have been made the basis of the calculation.[1]

It will be understood at once that reductions on such a scale as this were most unlikely to be accepted without a struggle, even if the wages proposed were the most that, out of its current income, the mining industry was able to afford. When this argument was

[1] It was also suggested that, by working hard, men might increase their piece-work earnings, and so make good some of the loss.

WAGE REDUCTIONS PROPOSED BY THE COAL-OWNERS FOR APRIL 1921 (on the basis of five shifts per week)

District and grade	*Owners' offer*	*Reduction*	*Percentage reduction*	*Real value of owners' offer at 1914 prices*
	Per week of five shifts.			
SOUTH WALES	£ s. d.	£ s. d.	Per cent.	£ s. d.
Colliers (piece rates)	2 13 6	1 15 9	40	1 2 2
Colliers (day rates)	2 10 7½	1 15 1½	41	1 1 0
Labourers	1 18 11½	1 15 0	49	16 2
SCOTLAND				
Colliers	3 4 2	1 0 10	24	1 6 7½
Underground firemen	3 9 2	1 0 10	23	1 8 8
Roadmen	3 0 5	1 0 10	26	1 5 1
NORTHUMBERLAND				
Coal hewers	3 8 4	1 5 10	27	1 8 4
Trolley and timbermen	2 7 3	1 7 1	37	19 7
Pumpers	2 2 11	1 7 11	39	17 9½
Boiler firemen	2 4 2	1 7 1	38	18 4
NOTTS.				
Colliers (contract)	4 6 8	10 4	10·7	1 16 0
Labourers	2 14 3	18 5	25	1 2 6
NORTH STAFFORD				
Colliers (contracting)	3 7 6	18 7	21	1 8 0
Other colliers	3 2 8½	19 7	24	1 6 0
Loaders	2 17 11	1 0 8	26	1 4 0
FOREST OF DEAN				
Colliers	2 3 4	1 12 11	43	18 0
Surface labourers	1 10 5	1 13 9	52	12 8
Trammers	1 13 9	1 13 4	49	14 0
NORTH WALES				
Colliers and timbermen	1 12 0	1 9 7	36	1 1 7
Hookers (head)	2 10 8	1 9 11	37	1 1 0
Hookers (others)	2 4 0	1 10 3	41	18 3
Fillers (ordinary)	2 2 8	1 11 1	42	17 8½
SOMERSET				
Colliers	2 6 8	1 6 4	36	19 4
Labourers and hauliers	2 0 5	1 7 6	40	16 9
Carters	2 3 1½	1 6 10	38	17 10½
DURHAM				
Coal-getters	2 19 7	1 3 1½	28	1 4 8½
Labourers	2 1 5	1 7 3	40	17 2
CUMBERLAND				
Colliers	2 0 10	1 19 2	49	17 0
Labourers	1 13 4	1 18 0	53	10 5
LANCASHIRE				
Colliers	3 4 3	18 0	22	1 6 9
Labourers	14 2 to 2 0 10	12 7 to 1 4 4	47 to 37	5 10 to 17 0

put forward, the miners replied that they would sooner see whole coal-fields go out of production for the time being than accept wages which would bring them down far below the pre-war standard of life. Moreover, they pointed out that the severity of the proposed cuts was greatly increased by the determination of the owners to revert to a district system, since it would no longer be possible to use the surplus profits of one district to aid another, even under the quite abnormal conditions caused by the break in export prices and the sudden termination of the Government guarantee. The miners insisted—and in this they carried a large measure of public sympathy with them—that the proposed reductions were out of all proportion to any actual or anticipated fall in the cost of living, and that, on this ground as well as in others, it was quite impossible to accept them.

But, if the miners rejected the terms proposed by the owners, what were they willing to accept ? They desired, as we have seen, the establishment of a new consolidated rate including all the wages payable in March 1921, except the Sankey wage of 2*s*. and the new wage of 3*s*. per shift. There was thus a sum of 5*s*. a shift left as a floating margin liable to reduction under the miners' own scheme. How much of this 5*s*. they would retain would depend, under the scheme itself, on the financial position of the industry as a whole, and not of each district ; but, owing to the severe depression, the miners held that the full operation of the permanent scheme was, for the time being, impracticable. They demanded, accordingly, some State assistance, a recognition by the Government that its obligations could not be simply evaded by the putting forward of the date of decontrol. This Government aid, they held, should be available during a transition period, while the industry was setting its house in order, for the maintenance of wage rates at a reasonable level. What was this reasonable level to be ?

From the outset, the miners made it clear that they were willing to accept some reduction in wages, provided that this was spread fairly over the different coal-fields, and did not result in reduction of the standard of living. Between November 1920 and March 1921, the Government cost-of-living index figure had fallen from 276 to 241, that is by 35 points towards the 1914 level of 100. This fall was referred to again and again during the negotiations, and the miners made it plain that they would be prepared to recommend the acceptance of a corresponding wage reduction, but not of more than the fall in the cost of living would justify. At a later stage, a definite offer to accept a reduction of 2*s*. per shift was made, and on the 11th April, in order to remove misunderstandings, the Miners' Executive passed a resolution definitely affirming its willingness to recommend the acceptance of a reduction corresponding to the change in the cost-of-living index number.

The dispute, however, could not be settled on this basis as long as the owners and the Government maintained their positions. Without either a system of pooling or a Government subsidy it was obvious that acceptable wages could not be paid, and that either the miners would have to accept a standard of living cut down, in most districts, far below the pre-war level, or the coal industry must be brought to a standstill.

When the stoppage began on the 1st April 1921, the actual wage position was by no means so clear to the public as it is possible to make it now. The miners were publishing tables giving their estimate of the reductions proposed; but, as these were based on an average working week of five shifts, the coal-owners were busily issuing denials of the accuracy of the figures. The consequence was that the public was largely bemused; and only gradually, during the first weeks of April, was the severity of the proposed cuts at all widely realized. As it came to be understood, public opinion was undoubtedly swinging round to the miners' side, despite the hostility created in some circles by the threat of an extension of the stoppage. Then the events of the 15th April caused, as we shall see, a sudden reversal of fortune, and the miners were left alone to face a hopeless position. The question of wages fell into the background; the public forgot how severe the proposed reductions had been. Public opinion exerted no appreciable influence on the subsequent course of the dispute.

Section 5. Enter the Triple Alliance

The national stoppage in the coal industry began on the 1st April, and was more complete than any previous stoppage. When notices to terminate contracts of employment were given out in March by the coal-owners, they were given to workers of all grades, including those men whose continuance at work was essential to the safety of the pits. Under normal conditions, such men had not been previously affected by stoppages in the mining industry, and the usual policy of the Miners' Federation had been, while calling out most of its members, to instruct the essential ' safety men ' to remain at work. In this case, however, the conditions were not normal ; for what the miners regarded as lock-out notices had been issued by the owners to the ' safety men ' as well as to the others. On the 30th March there was a discussion in the Miners' Executive on the question whether or not these men should be instructed to remain at work ; but, in view of the fact that these grades, like the rest, were under notice, it was decided that they also must cease work. A minority favoured the proposal that the safety men should be allowed to remain at work, provided that no alteration was made in their wages or conditions until after the termination of the dispute.

Accordingly, on the 1st April, the majority of the ' safety men ' left work. Many of these were included in Unions outside the Miners' Federation ; but most of the other Unions with members in the mining industry had issued instructions to these members to stop work with the rest. Such instructions were issued, for example, by the National Union of Enginemen, the Amalgamated Engineering Union, the Electrical Trades Union, and a number of the associations of Colliery Deputies and Firemen. The Winding Enginemen, some of the deputies, and the Cokemen, were members of the Miners' Federation ; and these grades, of course, stopped work.

The withdrawal of all labour from the mines would have created, if it had been completely effective, a very serious position in many of the pits. The ' safety men ' are primarily those whose task it is to keep the mines safe from flooding. The danger of flooding, and the loss likely to ensue from it, vary widely from pit to pit. In many mines the danger hardly exists : in many more such water as may find its way in can be easily pumped out again. But in other cases, of mines more liable to flooding, damage either irreparable or reparable only at a great cost and after considerable delay may be done. These last are not a high percentage of the total number of mines ; but they are enough to be of considerable account.

The decision of the Miners' Executive that the 'safety men' must accept the notice terminating their employment caused an immediate storm. The Government and most of the newspapers declared that, in taking up this position, the miners had declared war on the community. During the first days of the stoppage the newspapers were full of alarming reports about pits which were either already flooded, or in imminent danger of destruction. In fact, a few small pits were so badly affected as to make their re-entry into production improbable, and a number of pits were more or less seriously flooded. But the damage done was at no time anything like so grave as the newspapers made it appear.

This was partly because safety work was by no means completely suspended. A number of safety men remained at work, and the colliery officials, with the aid of clerks and of workers brought in from outside, kept the pumps at work in the vast majority of instances. In a few cases, attempts were made by bodies of miners to prevent the carrying on of this work; but in far more cases, and in practically all after the 9th April, when the Miners' Federation sent out special instructions that pumping should not be interfered with, the work was carried on without hindrance. Consequently, the actual damage done was not very serious, and, with a very few exceptions, was such as could be rapidly repaired after the termination of the dispute.

Actually, then, the main effect of the cessation of work by the pumpmen was to alienate sympathy from the miners, and to divert attention from the real issue of the dispute—the question of wages. Whether this would have been so if the miners had carried their policy further, and seriously tried to prevent pumping operations from being carried on, is a moot point. Almost certainly, such a policy would have led to widespread violence, and caused a far speedier end to the dispute, whether the miners had succeeded or failed in their object. Actually, however, after the 9th April, the safety of the mines was assured, and the struggle became one of endurance, in which the miners, unless help came from outside, were certain to be worsted in the long run.

Meanwhile, the Government was taking the most elaborate precautions in order to deal with the situation. On the 31st March was issued a Royal Proclamation under the Emergency Powers

Act,[1] declaring the existence of a 'state of emergency', and arming the Executive with the drastic powers which the Act confers. On the 4th April the Emergency Regulations, defining the scope of the powers assumed by the Government, was published. Power was taken to assume possession of any land, buildings, works, plant, or material (including gas, electricity, and water undertakings), to regulate and restrict road transport and to take control of vehicles, light railways, and canals,[2] to take possession of food and forage, to close or regulate any port and to requisition ships and give directions as to the cargoes that might be transported, to take possession of coal-mines and give directions as to their management and use, to regulate the price and distribution of coal, &c. The Postmaster-General was empowered to 'direct that telegraphic messages of such classes or descriptions as he may prescribe shall not be accepted for transmission', i. e. to prevent intercommunication by telegram among the workers affected. Any area could be proclaimed with a view to the prohibition of the sale of firearms, and the carrying of arms could be prohibited. It was made an offence against the regulations not only to injure any vital industrial plant, but 'to do any act calculated to cause mutiny, sedition, or disaffection among any of his Majesty's Forces, or the police force or the fire brigade, or to impede the distribution of food, fuel, or water'.

Very drastic powers of arrest, and of restricting the right of public meeting, were also assumed. 'A Secretary of State, a mayor, or a magistrate or chief officer of police may make an order prohibiting the holding of meetings when there is reason to apprehend that the assembly will give rise to grave disorder and will thereby cause undue demands on the police or military forces.' And further, 'any police constable may arrest without warrant any person who so acts as to endanger the public safety, or who is guilty or who is suspected of being guilty of an offence' against the regulations. Powers of search, and of closing premises, were also assumed. These powers of search and arrest were widely used, and many persons were imprisoned and subsequently convicted under them, during the stoppage.

[1] See Appendix C.

[2] The railways proper were, of course, still under Government control, which was not due to expire until August 1921.

At the very beginning of the dispute, there were considerable movements of troops into the areas affected by the stoppage. On the 8th April, important further measures were taken. On that day four further Royal Proclamations were issued. The effect of these, as Mr. Lloyd George explained in the House of Commons, was that all classes of army and naval reservists were called to the Colours, special measures were taken to strengthen the Air Force by the re-enrolment of discharged officers and men, and a new body, the Defence Force, was specially created. In addition, steps were taken throughout the country to enroll special constables in the largest possible numbers.

The Defence Force, which rose in ten days to a strength of 80,000 men, at which point further re-enlistment was stopped on the 18th April, was a fully armed and uniformed body of a military character. It was placed at once in camp under full military training, and was kept in existence until the termination of the dispute three months later. It was undoubtedly recruited very largely from the ranks of the unemployed, who regarded it as a means of livelihood. In some areas, miners even joined it in considerable numbers. Its reliability was never tested; but it is somewhat doubtful whether the Government could have placed much reliance on it. The calling up of the reserves, of course, also brought many Trade Unionists, including miners, into the armed Forces, and the Government expressed its surprise at the large proportion of reservists who obeyed the summons. It is hardly possible to say whether the presence of a number of Trade Unionists in the ranks of the Army would have exercised any appreciable influence on its action if it had been called upon to act. As it turned out, no action on its part, beyond simple patrolling duty, was required.

In addition to these large military preparations, elaborate measures were adopted for securing the food supply of the country. As during the national railway dispute of 1919, motor vehicles were largely called into use, and the public parks were turned into food supply dépôts, where they were not used as military camps. The Government held itself ready, in case of a stoppage of all ordinary methods of transport, to keep the country supplied with food, and to assure the means of communication. Plans for a general system of rationing were made out, and an elaborate hierarchy of special officials arose in every area to deal with the emergency.

These elaborate steps were, of course, taken not merely because there was a general stoppage in the mining industry, but far more because an extension of the trouble to other industries was seriously threatened. A complete stoppage of coal production exercises, indeed, a very serious effect on the general economic life of the nation ; but this effect is somewhat slow to make itself widely felt. In some industries which use coal in large quantities and are not able to lay in large stocks in advance a coal stoppage rapidly causes the closing of kindred enterprises : it reacts at once on the agencies normally engaged in the transport and distribution of coal. But, especially if there is some warning that a stoppage is coming, a great deal can be done by the building up of stocks to minimize the effect of the stoppage in interfering with vital services or throwing large bodies of workers out of employment. On this occasion there had been, at least for the Government itself and the agencies under its control, ample warning of the likelihood of a stoppage, and very large stocks of coal had been accumulated, especially on the railways. Thus the immediate dislocation caused was less considerable than it would have seemed reasonable to expect.

But, of course, a widening of the area of dispute, such as to involve in the stoppage any or all of the vital branches of the transport services, would have at once changed the situation. Stocks of coal would be of no use unless they could be moved from place to place, and in the event of a stoppage by railwaymen and transport workers every available means of transportation would have to be concentrated on the distribution of food and other vital necessaries of life. The Government had improvised a gigantic organization in order to deal with such a situation during the railway stoppage of 1919 ; and this organization had subsequently been kept together and greatly improved in view of possible disputes on an even larger scale.

It was, indeed, clear from the first that the area of dispute might extend far beyond the mining industry. From the outset, the miners were keeping their colleagues in the Triple Alliance—

the railwaymen and transport workers—fully informed of the progress of negotiations, and it was being freely stated that, if the stoppage occurred, it would be 'now or never' for the Triple Alliance as a whole. On the 30th March, the day before the actual termination of notices, the Miners' Federation Executive passed a resolution definitely calling upon the Triple Alliance to take action. A joint meeting of the three Executives was held, and the railwaymen's and transport workers' Executives both issued statements affirming their belief in the justice of the miners' case, and announcing their intention to call more fully representative meetings for the discussion of their course of action.

We have seen, in a previous chapter, some of the difficulties which stood in the way of effective action by the Triple Alliance as a whole. The loose federal structure of the Transport Workers' Federation, composed of a large number of practically independent societies, made a collective decision on its part difficult both in the making and in the execution. The National Union of Railwaymen was not faced by this difficulty, but there were powerful elements in it which would certainly be opposed to a stoppage save in the absolutely last resort. In the dispute of 1920, the attempt to bring the Triple Alliance into play had ended in a fiasco, and many were in doubt whether better success was likely to attend the miners' appeal on the present occasion.

The failure of 1920, and the memories which it had left behind, undoubtedly served at the outset to push the Alliance towards decisive action. It was felt that, if yet again the Alliance failed to bring its strength to bear, there would be an end of it, and a grievous blow would be dealt to the hope of greater solidarity of the Labour forces. There was, moreover, good reason for the railwaymen and the transport workers to feel alarm at the attack levelled at the Miners' Federation; for they, like the miners, had built up during the war national systems for the determination of wages and conditions, and it might appear that the return to local settlements in the mining industry would be followed by attacks on the national wage arrangements of the other sections of the Alliance. The railwaymen especially, having built up their national system under Government control and in face of the reluctance of the railway companies, were in danger of being confronted by a situation very like that of the miners on the termination of railway control.

These and similar special arguments, as well as the general plea for Trade Union solidarity in helping the Unions to resist the demand for greatly excessive wage reductions which had been made of them, were employed by those who sought to bring the other sections of the Triple Alliance into the struggle. Their effect was speedily seen. On the 4th April, the Executive of the Transport Workers' Federation declared itself in favour of action in support of the miners unless negotiations were at once resumed on terms which both parties could accept as a basis for discussion. A full Conference of all the Executives of the Unions comprising the Transport Workers' Federation met in London on the 5th April, and on the following day this Conference declared its willingness to assist the miners by every means in its power. A Delegate Meeting of the National Union of Railwaymen met on the 6th April, and on the following day this body also declared in favour of action to support the miners. On the 8th April, the full Triple Alliance met in Conference. The miners definitely asked the other sections to take strike action in their support, and both the railwaymen and the transport workers issued a strike order for midnight on Tuesday, the 12th April. Apparently, the great machine of the Triple Alliance was at last to be brought into action.

During these days, while the Triple Alliance was deciding upon its policy, *pourparlers* were proceeding between the Miners' Federation and the Prime Minister with a view to the reopening of negotiations. On the 5th April, there was a debate on the situation in the House of Commons, and the Government was strongly urged to take the initiative in reopening negotiations. In accordance with his intention expressed in Parliament, the Prime Minister on the following day issued to both coal-owners and miners an invitation to meet him for the resumption of negotiations, but attached to his invitation the condition that, before negotiations could begin, the men required to ensure the safety of the mines must resume work. This demand the mine-owners also affirmed in their reply to the invitation. To this course the miners refused to agree, on the ground that, as the owners had locked these men out with the rest, they must take the consequences of their action. On the 7th April, the Miners' Executive met the Prime Minister, who again urged them to order the safety men to resume work, but now offered to call a conference if the miners would agree that the question of the safety of the pits should be dealt with and disposed of before any other question was raised. In rejecting this proposal, the miners affirmed their willingness to enter a conference unconditionally, and to discuss at once the question of the safety men provided that other questions were not ruled out of consideration. To this Mr. Lloyd George would not agree. On the next day came the Triple Alliance strike decision, and on the Government side the calling up of the Reserves and the formation of the Defence Force.

The railwaymen and transport workers could now be regarded as parties to the dispute, and laid claim to some share in its direction jointly with the miners. On the morning of the 9th April, a deputation from the N.U.R. and the Transport Workers' Federation met the Prime Minister, and endeavoured to remove the deadlock. As a result, a compromise was reached. The miners, under pressure from their colleagues, agreed to issue telegraphic instructions to all their districts that there should be no interference with the steps taken by the owners and the Government to preserve the mines from flooding, and, on this understanding, the Prime Minister agreed to a reopening of negotiations. As we have seen, the actual effect of this decision, which was generally observed, was to remove the danger of flooding, and also to eliminate the chief factor which would have necessitated a speedy settlement of the dispute. It is by no means certain, even from a national point of view, that the resumption of work by the safety men was an unmixed blessing.

There is no doubt that this assurance by the miners against interference with any steps that might be taken to ensure the safety of the pits was largely the result of pressure exercised by the other sections of the Triple Alliance, whose leaders seem practically to have made some such action the condition of their continued support. The railwaymen and transport workers had not taken their strike decision with unanimity, and they were by no means certain of the response with which it would meet. The reports which appeared in the Press that large sections of the workers affected would refuse to obey the strike call were undoubtedly exaggerated, and much was made of every meeting, no matter how unrepresentative, which passed an anti-strike resolution. But that there was much lukewarmness and some positive opposition, such as that of the Sailors' and Firemen's Union, was evident enough ; and, even if the strike call were generally obeyed, it was by no means certain that the strike could be long maintained in face of the elaborate preparations made by the Government. It was known that the railway companies were prepared to run an efficient skeleton service if only 40 per cent. of their staffs remained available, and at this time the attitude of the key-group of railway workers, the drivers and firemen organized in the Associated Society of Locomotive Engineers and Firemen, who were outside the Triple Alliance, was still undetermined. Some of the leaders of both railwaymen and transport workers were from the first definitely against a strike, and others were in a condition of nervousness which was liable to turn to panic in face of an actual emergency. Even when the strike decision was taken, and before there was any sign of a resumption of negotiations, there were many who doubted whether the great Triple Alliance strike would in reality ever come off.

For the time, however, the strike call stood, even after the decision had been taken to resume negotiations. These began unpromisingly on the 11th April, with a joint meeting at which the Government, as well as the miners and the coal-owners, were represented. Each side expounded its case to the Government, and each adhered firmly to its previous position, with the exception that the miners made a definite offer to accept a reduction in wages, provided that this reduction was not more than proportionate to the fall in the cost of living as recorded in the official figures. On the following day, the negotiations were continued, and, in view of this fact, the railwaymen and transport workers issued an announcement postponing the strike until their outcome was known. On this day the Prime Minister made what were the first proposals to come from the Government. In the main, they followed the lines of the owners' scheme, and rejected the basis put forward by the miners. The National Pool was dismissed as 'impracticable', and it was proposed that wages should be fixed separately for each district in accordance with the financial position of the district. The 'standard wage', of an amount to be subsequently decided for each district in accordance with principles determined nationally, was to be the first charge on the industry: the shares of owners and miners in the surplus were to be determined nationally by negotiation. There was to be a National Wages Board, but it was to deal with principles, which would be applied in each district separately. The only new feature in the Government proposals was the intimation that 'If and when an arrangement has been arrived at between the coal-owners and the miners as to the rate of wages to be paid in the industry, fixed upon an economic basis, the Government will be willing to give assistance, either by loan or otherwise, during a short period, in order to mitigate the rapid reduction in wages in the districts most severely affected'. Thus the subsidy, which only a week before, the Government had still been declaring to be impossible, was coming already to be admitted as the necessary condition of a tolerable settlement.

The Miners' Executive, having retired in order to consider these proposals, rejected them without hesitation, since they failed wholly to meet the main points in the case for which they were contending. Only a few hours after the Triple Alliance had issued notices postponing the strike on the ground that negotiations were proceeding, the negotiations completely broke down, and deadlock ensued.

Section 6. 'Black Friday'

When the Triple Alliance reassembled on the 13th April, it was faced with a complete breakdown of negotiations. The miners were still demanding a wage settlement on a national basis and, as the indispensable condition of such a settlement, the pooling of a proportion of the surplus: the Government had definitely ranged itself with the owners on the side of district settlements, and had denounced the demand for the National Pool as an attempt to secure a political end by means of industrial action. In these circumstances, there was nothing for it but to issue the strike call anew; and the railwaymen and transport workers accordingly reaffirmed their decision, and fixed the date of the proposed strike for the 15th April. This time the two bodies which had so far acted with the miners were no longer alone. The Associated Society of Locomotive Engineers and Firemen had also taken a decision in favour of strike action, and their representatives joined those of the Triple Alliance at this and subsequent meetings. The London District Council of the Electrical Trades Union also decided to strike; and both the E.T.U. Executive and the Executive of the Union of Post Office Workers met the Triple Alliance in consultation during the day. The latter body had already obtained from the Postmaster-General a pledge that, if a transport strike took place, its members would not be called upon to undertake any work ordinarily done by men who were on strike. The Executive of the Railway Clerks' Association, representing not only the clerical but also the principal supervisory grades of railway employees, also made for submission to its members a recommendation in favour of a stoppage. The Co-operative Wholesale Society too offered its aid, and the National Union of Distributive and Allied Workers, who were affiliated to the Transport Workers' Federation, submitted plans for a scheme of food distribution through the Co-operative Societies to workers involved in the dispute. Preparations for the impending stoppage were set on foot, and occupied during the next two days the attention of the Alliance and other delegates assembled at the head-quarters of the N.U.R.

There can be no doubt that, during these critical days, whether despite or because of the strike threat of the Triple Alliance, public opinion was coming round to the miners' side. The abortive negotiations had at least resulted in the actual wage reductions proposed by the coal-owners becoming more widely known, and there was an almost general opinion that these were too drastic for their acceptance to be reasonably expected. The failure of the meetings and the renewal of the strike threat brought into the field numbers of would-be mediators, who set on foot various attempts to bring the parties together again. An influential group of Coalition members of Parliament, who considered that the House of Commons had played too small a part in dealing with the crisis, determined to invite both owners and miners to state their case before it, and to consider their course of action in the light of the arguments advanced.

Accordingly, on the afternoon of the 14th April, Mr. Evan Williams, the chairman of the Mining Association, addressed in the House of Commons a largely attended meeting of members. He was considerably heckled, especially with regard to the magnitude of the wage cuts which the coal-owners were demanding, and his replies left many of the members dissatisfied. Mr. Hodges, with other miners' leaders, was in the House of Commons that day, attending a joint meeting of the Labour Party and Trades Union Congress Committees and of the Parliamentary Labour Party—a meeting which pledged its support to the miners. With the agreement of Mr. Herbert Smith,[1] the acting president, and other Miners' Federation leaders, Mr. Frank Hodges agreed to address the gathering of M.P.'s in the course of the evening.

Mr. Hodges's speech on this occasion had momentous consequences. He began by stating, clearly and forcibly, as he had often stated it before, the full case of the miners, laying stress on the demand for a national settlement backed by a National Pool, and also temporarily by aid from the Government. Then he submitted to the heckling, and found himself bombarded with questions from every side. Almost at the end of the meeting, in reply to a question which he subsequently stated to have been, in his opinion, carefully prepared in advance, Mr. Hodges made the statement which proved to be the turning-point of the dispute. No shorthand note of the proceedings was taken, but Mr. Hodges's own account of the incident, in reporting it to the Miners' Conference on the 22nd April, was as follows:

> 'The first question asked on the point was—"Are you prepared to consider a temporary settlement of the wages question, leaving the question of the National Board and Pool to be later determined?" My reply was—there was no such proposition had ever been put forward by the owners or the Government, the only settlement suggested to me during the whole of the discussions being one of a permanent settlement on a district basis. I was then asked—suppose such a proposition

[1] Mr. Robert Smillie, disappointed and in ill health, had finally resigned from the presidency shortly before the beginning of the struggle.

P 2

was made, what attitude would we take? My answer was that the Executive were prepared, were always prepared, to hear and consider any proposal as to wages, but it must be clearly understood that any such consideration was not dependent on giving up the fundamental principles for which we stood. I was then asked—suppose an offer were made to effect a temporary settlement on the basis that wages shall not fall below the cost of living, what would be our attitude? I replied that any such offer coming from an authoritative source would receive very serious consideration at our hands, and I repeated that we had only one proposal from the Government, that is, a permanent settlement on a district basis. They refused any temporary national settlement.'

This account, which represents Mr. Hodges's recollection of the incident eight days later, can be accepted as substantially, though perhaps not verbally, accurate. Whatever may have been his exact words, there is no doubt about the impression which he conveyed to his audience. A large part of that audience was disposed to consider that the wage-cuts proposed by the mine-owners were far too drastic; but few among it had much sympathy for the miners' proposal of a National Pool, which they regarded as implying either a continuance of Government control or the institution of a form of joint control in the industry. They were anxious, therefore, to find some way of settling the dispute by securing, at least temporarily, a mitigation of the proposed reductions in wages, without the concession of the principle of financial unification of the industry for which the miners were contending. Mr. Hodges's answers seemed to open the way, on the miners' side at least, to a settlement on these lines, and, when the meeting adjourned, the group of Coalition members present decided at once to send to the Prime Minister a deputation with instructions to press him to endeavour to bring about a temporary settlement on the basis suggested.

The Prime Minister, having heard what the deputation had to say, at once took action, and on the morning of the 15th April, sent to the Miners' Federation the following letter:

10 Downing Street,
London, S.W.1.
15th April, 1921.

Dear Mr. Hodges,

Several members who were present at your House of Commons meeting last night have conveyed to me the purport of your concluding offer.

They had not taken down the actual words you used, but the general impression made on their minds was that you were now prepared to discuss with the owners the question of wages without raising the controversial issue of the pool, provided the arrangements to be made were of a temporary character, and without prejudice to a further discussion of proposals for a National Pool when a permanent settlement comes to be dealt with.

If this is a fair representation of your suggestion, I invite you and your fellow delegates to meet the owners at the Board of Trade at 11 this morning to consider the best method of examining the question of wages.

Yours sincerely,
D. LLOYD GEORGE.

The Miners' Executive considered this letter the same morning, and dispatched, after an eventful meeting, a reply stating that 'the only conditions upon which a temporary settlement can be arrived at is one that must follow the concession of the two principles already made known to you, viz. a National Wages Board and a National Pool'. 'In these circumstances', the letter went on, 'my Committee feel that no good purpose would be served in meeting the owners to-day on the basis suggested.'

In face of this decision, Mr. Hodges immediately tendered his resignation to the Miners' Executive, but withdrew it subsequently at their unanimous request.

It is not easy, at first thought, to penetrate the meaning of this startling series of incidents. In the first place, what exactly did Mr. Hodges mean by the answer which he made in the House of Commons. What manner of temporary settlement was he contemplating? His own explanation, given to the Miners' Conference, on the 22nd April, was as follows: 'I answered the question [1] the more eagerly, because these inspirations come to you sometimes in critical moments, because I knew, as you must know, that any temporary settlement *of a national character* [2] which brings wages down to the level of the cost of living implies a continuance of the control—it implies financial control of the industry by the Government during the temporary period, because you cannot have a uniform reduction at one time when you have such a tremendous variation in the case of districts without the Government assuming or reassuming control.'

[1] That is, the last of the questions quoted above. [2] Italics mine.

Mr. Hodges, then, on his own showing, when he spoke of a temporary wages settlement was contemplating a settlement on a national basis, providing for a uniform wage reduction in all the coal-fields corresponding to the fall in the cost of living. But he did not make this clear to his auditors, and what Mr. Lloyd George in his letter interpreted him as meaning was something different from this. It will be remembered that the miners had refused to negotiate with the owners on a district basis concerning the amount of their reductions. Mr. Lloyd George seemed to imply that Mr. Hodges had expressed willingness to waive this objection, and this was also the interpretation placed upon his statement by most of the newspapers. A settlement on the basis of wage reductions varying from district to district, but subject to a maximum based on the cost of living, the deficit in any district being made up by a Government subsidy, was equally consistent with what Mr. Hodges had actually said, though not apparently with what he meant. But a settlement on these lines would not have involved any continuance of control, and would have involved the temporary giving up of the claim for a national settlement and a National Pool. It was, indeed, precisely the proposed basis of negotiations which the miners' organizations had rejected in March on a district vote.

It may be doubted whether the issues, and the difference between the two possible forms of temporary wages settlement, presented themselves as clearly as this to the Miners' Executive on the morning of the 15th April. They saw themselves invited to resume negotiations on a basis which would involve the temporary giving up of their claim to a national settlement, and, knowing the profound opposition of both owners and Government to the National Pool, they had little hope of securing it later by negotiation if they once returned to work without having the principle definitely conceded. A settlement such as Mr. Hodges appeared to have contemplated would, indeed, by ensuring that the temporary arrangement should be on a national basis, have gone some way towards conceding the principle, but Mr. Lloyd George's letter did not suggest that this was what he had in mind.

Wisely or unwisely, therefore, the Miners' Executive rejected

Mr. Lloyd George's invitation, and thus appeared to place itself in the unfortunate position of repudiating what Mr. Hodges had said.

The consequences of this episode were much more far-reaching than the miners at least expected them to be. The decision was not reached without keen disagreement among the members of the Miners' Executive; and the existence of this disagreement, and the fact that Mr. Hodges had offered his resignation, speedily became known. The first business of the miners, after dispatching their answer to the Prime Minister, was to report their decision to their partners in the Triple Alliance, and they seem to have done this without any idea that it would influence the contemplated strike action of the Alliance and the other unions associated with it. The unions assembled at Unity House, the railwaymen's head-quarters, when the miners had made their statement and left, went on to debate the position among themselves. They decided to send a deputation to meet the Miners' Executive, with the object of persuading them to reverse their decision, and to agree to meet the Government on the Prime Minister's invitation. This, however, the miners refused to do, intimating to the deputation that they expected the strike to take place as arranged. The deputation then returned to Unity House, and the Triple Alliance thereupon resumed its deliberations without the miners. The result was that early in the afternoon, Mr. J. H. Thomas made to the assembled pressmen, from the steps of Unity House, the laconic announcement that the strike order was cancelled. The railwaymen and transport workers and the other unions which had joined them during the preceding days, had decided, in face of the changed situation, to call off the strike. The great Triple Alliance had once more failed at the critical moment to fire the heavy artillery, and the miners were left to fight on alone.

The day on which this decision was taken, the 15th April 1921, has come to be generally known in the Labour movement as 'Black Friday'. In a moment, the whole situation was changed. What had threatened to be by far the greatest upheaval in the history of the Labour movement in Great Britain had ended in ignominious collapse; and instead of a struggle in which all the forces would be mobilized on one side or the other, and a rapid issue was certain because of the very magnitude and paralysing character of the conflict, the dispute sank into a trial of endurance between the miners on the one side and the mine-owners, with all the resources of the Government behind them, on the other.

The impression created by the collapse was, throughout the country, one of bewilderment. The rapid changes of the preceding four-and-twenty hours had not been easy to follow, and Mr. Thomas's brief and unexplanatory announcement did nothing to enlighten either the rank and file Trade Unionists or the general public. For the time being, the wills of the trade unionists were paralysed. An explanatory announcement would certainly have led to immediate controversy, and probably to sporadic strikes, led by those who disapproved of the Alliance's decision. But the mere announcement that the strike was cancelled was such as to make action impossible, and there were in fact no sectional stoppages. This probably was the effect on which Mr. Thomas calculated, and explains his reason for making the announcement in an otherwise surprising manner.

What caused the rapid change of front on the part of the miners' partners in the Triple Alliance ? In seeking the answer to this question, let us see first of all what were the explanations subsequently offered by the leaders of the Alliance. They held that the miners ought to have reopened negotiations on the basis suggested by the Government, and that their action, in pledging themselves to strike in support of the miners, gave them the right at least to advise the miners very strongly as to the policy which they should pursue, if not actually to determine their policy for them. Now, the railway and transport leaders, while they held that the wage reductions which the miners were asked to accept were intolerable, were not at any time, it appears, very enthusiastic supporters of the demand for the National Pool. The Government, from the first, had used every endeavour to persuade the public that the Pool was a political and not an industrial issue, and the contention seems to have found some support among the Triple Alliance leaders themselves. Moreover, they urged, even if they could successfully bring their members out on strike in support of the miners purely on an issue of wages, it was far more doubtful whether their members would fully appreciate the arguments advanced by the miners in favour of the Pool, and probable that they would be influenced by the Government's repeated asseverations that the struggle was of a political, and not of a legitimate industrial, character. This being so, they maintained, the miners' refusal to meet the Government and the owners on the wages issue alone made it impossible for them to rely on an adequate response to the strike order, and left them no alternative to either cancelling the strike or going out to inevitable defeat.

These arguments, and others like them, were used in the conference at Unity House on the 15th April. There was undoubtedly a widespread impression in the minds of the railway and transport leaders that the events of the day had wrecked the chances of a successful strike. The morning papers had spread abroad the impression that the reopening of negotiations was practically certain. Then had followed rapidly the rejection by the miners of the Prime Minister's invitation and the offered resignation of Mr. Hodges. These events and reports of discussions in the miners' ranks and of the narrow majority by which the invitation had been rejected, speedily became known, and wild rumours began to circulate. The effect of the rumours on the attitude of the workers was not easy to gauge; but naturally telephone and telegraphic inquiries began to pour in from all parts of the country, and the union leaders seem at once to have leapt to the conclusion that large numbers of their members, in face of the uncertainty, would refuse to strike.

No one who knows what took place that day at Unity House can be in doubt that, side by side with calculations and surmises such as these, sheer panic played its part. Nerves were all on edge, both in the Triple Alliance and in the Miners' Executive. The deputation which was sent from Unity House to meet the miners and to urge them to reconsider their decision, as soon as it made plain that the cancellation of the strike order was a possibility, found it impossible to discuss the matter dispassionately with the miners, who made no secret of regarding the suggestion as a threat of desertion. Everybody to some extent lost his head. The discussion at Unity House was quite extraordinarily chaotic, and showed obvious signs of panic. The situation was too much for most of the representatives, and the few who were from the first definitely determined to secure the cancellation of the strike had an easy task. The morale of the Triple Alliance had been effectively destroyed by the course of events.

Matters would probably not have fallen out thus had all been going well and smoothly during the earlier stages of the crisis. But, from the first entry of the Triple Alliance upon the scene, there had been friction and dissatisfaction. To begin with, the Miners' Executive was known to be divided over the question whether the National Pool could be secured, and a section of the miners, although they accepted the decision of the majority, were throughout in favour of a compromise settlement. Moreover, the railwaymen's and transport workers' leaders had from the first been most reluctant to call a strike, except in the last resort, and many of them had been all along doubtful, rightly or wrongly, of getting a full response from their members. On both sides there had been a frame of mind not conducive to harmonious joint action. The miners knew that the Alliance leaders would do everything in their power to bring about a compromise, and were inclined to suspect them of being ready to give away too much, and to commit them, if they had a chance, to a form of settlement which they were not willing to accept. Hence, the miners clung jealously to their right to conduct the negotiations in their own way, and were not prepared to admit the right of the other sections to come in as equal parties to them until they were actually committed by strike action. The memory of the Triple Alliance fiasco of the previous year was still fresh, and there were many who refused to believe, even when the strike decision seemed to have been irrevocably taken, that the strike would actually take place. In addition, the long days of waiting and postponed action, the interminable discussions, the long hours spent in the enervating atmosphere of the conference halls, lowered the vitality and reduced the will of the representatives. When the crisis came, it found both the miners and the leaders at Unity House jaded and in a mood in which misunderstanding easily arose and was hard to dispel.

It is a moot point how far the railway and transport leaders were right, either on the 15th April, or during the earlier stages of the crisis, in their estimate of the unwillingness of a substantial proportion of the members to take strike action. Certainly, there would not have been at any time a 100 per cent. response, and certainly the response would have been less on the 15th April than if the strike had taken place at an earlier date. Certainly, too, the executive of the Railway Clerks' Association had definitely failed to persuade the majority of its members to strike, and there were other groups whose response was doubtful. But it seems probable, so far as I have been able to ascertain what was the state of feeling in the country, that the leaders, isolated in London and only indirectly in touch with the opinion of their members, were influenced by the newspapers' anxiety to prove in advance that the strike must fail, and were inclined to underestimate the response that would have been made to the call. This, however, is a point that can be neither proved nor disproved, whereas it is quite certain that most of the leaders, judging no doubt partly by their own feelings, were very doubtful of getting an adequate response, and over-disposed to regard failure as inevitable.

In any case, their decision was taken, and, although all the groups involved coupled their decision to cancel the strike order with a resolution to do all in their power to help the miners in other ways, the Triple Alliance and the other unions concerned practically made their exit from the dispute on the 15th April. The cancelling of the strike inevitably left a bad atmosphere behind; and it was clear that the remainder of the struggle would have practically to be conducted by the miners alone, and conducted in an atmosphere of discouragement and disillusion which would make success far more difficult than it would have been if the Triple Alliance had never entered the field.

'Black Friday' was, in fact, for all practical purposes the end of the Triple Alliance. It was not wound up, and none of the three sections seceded from it. But it has been called upon for no further action, and it is not likely to be called upon again unless occasion arises to reconstruct it in some quite new form. Each section naturally discussed subsequently in its separate conference the events which had led up to the collapse. Both the Transport Workers' Annual Conference and the Railwaymen's Annual Delegate Meeting received, some months after the event, full reports on the events of April, and both bodies endorsed the action taken by their representatives. The miners also discussed the matter fully at the Conference on the 22nd April, and passed the following resolution, which may fittingly close this section:

> 'That this Conference, having fully considered the circumstances surrounding the failure of the other two sections of the Triple Alliance to put into operation their decision to strike in our support on Friday last, and a full report having been given of what transpired at the meeting of M.P.s addressed by Mr. Hodges at the House of Commons, the delegates emphatically protest against the official explanation of the other two sections, attributing their defection to the refusal to the Miners' Executive to meet the coal-owners again at the invitation of the Prime Minister. Over and over again, before and after the Triple Alliance had arrived at their decision to strike, it had been made quite clear that it was impossible for the Miners' Executive to accept a settlement except on the terms of the concession of the National Wages Board and Pool. The real cause of the sudden, unexpected, and unjustifiable withdrawal of the other two sections of the Alliance must be looked for in the character and structure of the Triple Alliance itself.'

I leave this judgment, obviously affected by the nearness of the events to which it referred, to stand without criticism, merely referring the reader, for an explanation of the concluding words, to the discussion of the character and structure of the Alliance in an earlier chapter. If it is desired to apportion blame, the reader is as well equipped as I on the basis of the facts narrated in this section.

Section 7. Abortive Negotiations—The Coal Embargo

When the decision of the Triple Alliance became known, the House of Commons was actually debating the crisis, on the assumption that the strike would take place that evening. The receipt of the news caused the collapse of the debate, and the abandonment for the time of the attempts at mediation which were being made. The Miners' Executive, after discussing the situation among themselves, dispersed immediately to the various districts, for the purpose of reporting to the members, and obtaining a fresh mandate in face of the changed situation. On the excitement, the quick succession of happenings, the expectations almost of revolution, of the days before the 15th April, there followed a period that was uneventful and misleadingly quiet. The Labour movement was endeavouring to readjust itself to the new conditions created by the 'Black Friday' collapse; both the owners and the Government were waiting to see whether, in face of the withdrawal of their allies, the miners would yield, or their resistance suddenly collapse. For some days the only sign of continued activity was the daily interchange of bombardments by the owners and the miners through the medium of press *communiqués*, sent out by the Mining Association on the one hand and by the Publicity Committee of the Miners' Federation on the other. This Committee, in which the miners had the help of a number of prominent Labour writers and propagandists, had been set up on the 9th April, and continued to function after the Triple Alliance collapse.

In these indirect discussions through the medium of the press no approach was made to an agreement. The statements issued by the owners were, indeed, more than once represented as 'new offers', and especially there was discussion over the alleged willingness of the owners to surrender their claim to profits during the period of depression. The miners, on their side, endeavoured to get the owners to make their meaning on this point clear, but without success. In general, each party adhered to its position, the miners demanding a settlement on a national basis, and the owners insisting that they could only agree to district settlements.

Although the Triple Alliance had definitely cancelled its strike order, the Government insisted upon retaining the 'emergency powers' with which it had armed itself at the beginning of the dispute. Further recruiting for the Defence Force was indeed stopped on the 18th April, but both this force and the Army Reserve remained mobilized. The Government's view, stated in the House of Commons on the 19th April, was that it could not safely be asserted that the risk of trouble was over. The dispute, indeed, was destined to drag on still for a long time, but the likelihood of any wide extension of it had completely passed.

On the 21st April the Miners' Executive met again in London in preparation for the National Miners' Conference which had been called for the following day. The reports from the districts were overwhelmingly in favour of standing out for the concession of the National Wages Board and the National Pool. Accordingly the Conference made no modification in the policy previously adopted. It passed the resolution quoted in the last section dealing with the Triple Alliance collapse, and another expressing its confidence both in the secretary and in the Executive. It accepted an offer from the Joint Committee of the Trades Union Congress and the Labour Party to join with the *Daily Herald* in a national appeal for funds to aid the miners in their struggle. And it received and accepted an offer from Mr. Lloyd George to attend a meeting with the owners and the Government for the purpose of seeking a basis for the reopening of negotiations.

On the same day, the 22nd April, the Executives of both the Transport Workers' Federation and the National Union of Railwaymen met in London in order to consider their policy. Various agencies were taking action to bring coal from abroad and to distribute it to the essential services whose stocks were running short. The handling of such imported supplies, and the moving of coal on the railways and at the docks, clearly raised questions of Trade Union principle; for the successful importation and distribution of supplies from abroad would evidently enable the Government to prolong the dispute, and would thus prejudice the position of the miners. Difficult cases had already arisen, and local action was being threatened in a number of districts, where railwaymen and transport workers were refusing to handle coal. In these circumstances, both the Transport Workers' Federation and the N.U.R. decided to place an embargo on the handling of imported coal supplies, and the N.U.R. also instructed the members not to move coal lying in colliery sidings. The National Sailors' and Firemen's Union, however, although it was a part of the Transport Workers' Federation, refused to take part in the embargo. This Union had, from the beginning, opposed the strike policy, and refused to take any action in support of the miners. In addition to declaring a national embargo, the Transport Workers' Federation decided to communicate with the

International Transport Workers' Federation, in order that continental transport workers might refuse to load vessels with coal consigned to British ports.

The meeting, called by the Prime Minister, of owners', miners', and Government representatives took place on the 22nd April. Mr. Lloyd George strongly pressed the owners to submit complete and definite figures, showing their calculation of the wages which they were in a position to pay, and making clear the principles on which they arrived at their figures, and the extent to which they were prepared to forgo their claim to profits during the period of depression. This last point, especially, had not been made at all clear in the statements which the owners had issued. Some newspapers had interpreted the owners as signifying their willingness to forgo all profits, but, as the miners had pointed out, no offer of this sort had been clearly made. After some discussion, the meeting was adjourned until the 25th April, in order that the owners might have time to prepare a full statement, and to submit it to the miners for consideration, in advance of a further joint discussion.

The owners' statement was placed before the Miners' Executive on the 24th April. It contained no definite figures, but took the form of a set of proposals for the future regulation of wages and profits, first on a permanent basis, and secondly during a special temporary period of three months ending with July. The permanent scheme, except for the omission of figures and for some regrouping of the districts suggested, was the same as the owners had originally put forward. The temporary scheme presented several new features. It was now suggested that, within each of the proposed districts taken separately, the wages of each workman, irrespective of grade, should be reduced by a uniform amount per shift, the amount being ascertained on the basis of the financial position of the district. A maximum limit was to be set to the reduction which might be made for each of the three months of the temporary period, and the Government was to be asked to make up by subsidy any deficit which the payment of the minimum wage rates thus established might entail.

On the question of profits, the owners now proposed (*a*) that the owners in the aggregate in any area should not receive any share of the *surplus profit*[1] if their doing so would result in a reduction of the wages fixed for the previous month, and (*b*) that they should go without their *standard profits* to the extent to which the taking of these profits would, without a subsidy from the Government, involve reductions in wages greater than the maximum fixed. It will be seen that this did not amount to an offer on the owners' part to forgo all profits during the temporary period, or even that all owners should forgo surplus profits. The offer was, moreover, strictly confined to a period of three months, and any net loss, though not any claim to profits, was to be carried forward as a charge on the future surplus of the industry, to take precedence over any claim by the miners to the payment of wages above the minimum.

These proposals formed the subject of discussion at the resumed joint conference with the Government and the owners on the 25th April. The owners explained their failure to submit a definite statement as to the wages which they were prepared to pay by saying that, under their revised plan of a flat rate reduction in each area, these would depend on the amount of the maximum reduction agreed upon, which in turn would depend on the amount which the Government was prepared to offer by way of subsidy. The owners thus threw upon the Government the onus of providing a basis for negotiation. It was pointed out that, if the Government was to make a grant, it was indispensable that the owners should produce their detailed estimates of what they were able to pay. Accordingly, on the following day, the owners at last produced figures, and, on the basis of these, the Government, on the 28th April, made an offer as a basis of settlement.

The Government expressed its willingness to 'come to the assistance of the mining industry with a grant of £10,000,000'. It proposed that in May the maximum wage reduction in any district should be 3*s*. a shift, and in June 3*s*. 6*d*. The balance of the £10,000,000 was then to be divided between July and August, two-thirds to July and one-third to August, and used to mitigate further reductions as far as possible. Thereafter, wages were to depend solely on the ability of each district to pay. The offer

[1] For the meaning of the terms 'surplus profit' and 'standard profit', see p. 186.

was made only on condition of the acceptance by both parties of a durable settlement, to last at least a year after the end of the temporary period. It was made clear that, as the Government was still totally opposed to the National Pool, the durable, as well as the temporary, settlement would have to be on a district basis.

While these negotiations were proceeding, the Miners' Conference remained in regular session, awaiting the outcome. The Government proposals, in conjunction with those of the owners, were submitted to delegates on the 28th April, and, after a long discussion, were overwhelmingly rejected. All the districts except one—Northumberland—voted for rejection. The Conference thereupon terminated, and the delegates returned to their districts to carry on the struggle.

In face of the breakdown of negotiations, there was some effort in certain of the districts to bring pressure to bear upon the Miners' Federation to rescind the order issued on the 9th April against any attempt to interfere with the work of the safety men, introduced by the owners, under Government protection, in order to keep the pits from flooding. This proposal, however, did not come before the Conference, and was rejected by the Miners' Executive on the 29th April. Pumping and similar work therefore continued to be carried on without molestation or obstruction, save in one or two isolated cases. Nevertheless, the Government on the 30th April issued a further proclamation, declaring the continued existence of a 'state of emergency' and maintaining its arbitrary powers.

Both parties to the dispute now settled down to a prolonged struggle. Early in May the trouble over the handling of imported coal supplies by railwaymen and transport workers became serious. Railwaymen who refused to move coal, especially in Scotland, were suspended from service, and on the 6th May the suspension of dockers who refused to handle imported supplies led to a general strike on the Clyde, backed by the Scottish Union of Dock Labourers, but not authorized by the Transport Workers' Federation, to which the Scottish Union was affiliated. There were further stoppages during the next few days, both on the railways and at other ports, and a demand arose that the National Union of

Railwaymen should declare a national stoppage. On the 13th May the N.U.R. decided against this course, but stiffened up the terms of the embargo by rescinding the instruction that coal for hospitals and vital public services should be moved without restriction. At a joint meeting held the same day, the Transport Workers' Federation associated itself with the N.U.R. in this stiffening of the embargo. A few days later, the Locomotive Engineers' and Firemen's Union instructed its members to act with the N.U.R. in the matter.

The troubles arising out of the embargo continued throughout May. On the railways a considerable number of men in various parts of the country were suspended for refusing to handle supplies; but the embargo was by no means completely enforced, and, by picking their men and routes carefully, the companies were able to move large quantities of coal both from colliery sidings and from the ports. Among the transport workers, trouble arose in the majority of the ports, and in some cases, as at Bristol, there were general stoppages of short duration. More usually, however, the men went on with other work, merely refusing to handle supplies of coal. In these circumstances, the employers with the aid of the Government enrolled voluntary or 'blackleg' labour, and thus got the coal moved at the cost of friction, sometimes serious, with the regular workers. In some cases, the coal, when it reached its destination, was treated as 'tainted goods', and, as at the Greenwich power-station, strikes took place on account of a refusal to handle the coal or to work with the 'blackleg' labour introduced.

Meanwhile, the attempts of the International Transport Workers' Federation to get coal consigned to Great Britain stopped at its port of origin were meeting with indifferent success. Antwerp was, indeed, held up by a strike of dockers, met, as in Glasgow, by the introduction of voluntary labour. The German workers fairly effectively stopped supplies, but the French dockers seem in most cases to have handled coal for Britain without restriction. The position on the Continent was complicated by the fact that, while the British Transport Workers' Federation was appealing to Continental dockers and seamen to support the embargo, Mr. Havelock Wilson, president of the Sailors' and

Firemen's Union affiliated to the Federation, was instructing his own members to handle supplies and urging the Continental workers to disregard the embargo.

It soon became manifest that the railwaymen and transport workers would have either to go considerably further, or else to recede from the position which they had taken up. Their aim had been, without declaring a strike, to prevent the movement of coal which they regarded as 'tainted'. But this policy was in practice impossible to sustain, for the employers met it by suspending the men on whom fell the onus of refusing to handle the goods in question, and these suspensions naturally led to demands for strike action in order to secure the reinstatement of the men who had been suspended. Moreover, the widespread introduction of 'blackleg' labour at the docks was clearly a menace to the established conditions of the transport workers. In addition, the Government, from the 18th May, made itself definitely responsible for the importation and distribution to vital services of foreign coal, and announced throughout its intention of giving full protection to the 'voluntary workers' who were handling supplies.

In the Clyde area, where the position was most serious, matters were going far from well for the Unions involved. The railwaymen were demanding strike action, and protesting that they could not, by any other means, make the embargo effective. The dockers' strike was not, in face of the 'volunteers', preventing coal from coming in, and the dockers were vigorously calling for national support from the Transport Workers' Federation. On the 25th May, not securing this assistance, they offered to resume work on conditions which included the reinstatement of all strikers and the dismissal of all the volunteers. These conditions were refused, and the dispute dragged on. A further blow was dealt to the embargo policy on the 28th May, when the Locomotive Engineers and Firemen, having received from the Government assurances that imported coal would be used only for vital services and not for general industrial purposes, definitely removed the embargo. The Transport Workers and the N.U.R. tried to maintain it for a few days longer; but on the 31st May they realized that the position was hopeless, and, by joint decision, put an end to the whole policy and removed all the restrictions. The settlement of the Clyde dispute followed on the 6th June, and, in this and other cases, the men who had struck or been suspended were reinstated.

The whole policy of the embargo was indeed hopeless. The chance of a general sympathetic strike of railwaymen and transport workers had definitely passed on ‘ Black Friday ’, but without the possibility of such a strike the embargo could not be enforced. The miners’ leaders throughout recognized this, and neither asked for nor encouraged the action taken, which seems rather to have been an attempt to reinstate the Unions in their own good opinion after the disaster of the 15th April. After the 31st May no more was heard of the participation of transport workers or railwaymen in the dispute, which thereafter was left to the miners alone. The Government continued to import large quantities of coal from abroad, and, for the rest of the dispute period, no restriction was placed on its movement or use. In face of the changed situation, the Army Reserve was demobilized on the 2nd June, but the Defence Force was kept in being, and the ‘ state of emergency ’ was again proclaimed.

Section 8. Attrition

The history of the coal dispute from May to the long-delayed settlement of July is the story of the gradual wearing down of the miners’ resistance. Already in May it seemed almost impossible that this resistance could be much further prolonged. The funds of the Miners’ Associations were exhausted, and the sums raised by the *Daily Herald* and the national Labour bodies, although they were substantial, did not go far among the workers —more than a million in number—directly involved in the dispute. The miners lived, throughout the later phases of the dispute, mainly on credit from shopkeepers and above all from the Co-operative movement. The Miners’ Associations in many of the districts made special arrangements for these credits, supplying the men with credit notes backed by the Associations. The Co-operative Stores and the English and Scottish Co-operative Wholesale Societies supplied very large quantities of goods on credit. But, as the struggle dragged on, their ability, as well as that of the private shopkeepers, to give credit was seriously strained, and towards the end of the dispute the advances which could be secured became more and more restricted. Almost literally, in the end, the miners were starved out.

But, before the end came, there was more than one further attempt to negotiate a settlement. On the 25th May Mr. Lloyd George addressed to both parties a very brief note, merely inviting them, without explanation, to meet in conference on the 27th May. Both sides accepted this invitation, and met Mr. Lloyd George, who outlined fresh Government proposals for settling the dispute. The actual proposals made did not differ greatly in substance from those which had been previously rejected. The Government was still prepared to offer, on conditions, a subsidy of £10,000,000, and the owners' limited offer to forgo a part of their profits for a maximum period of three months stood unchanged. It was now suggested that the Government subsidy should be treated as a fund on which the miners could draw as they thought best. If they agreed to large immediate reductions, the £10,000,000 would last all the longer: if they would only accept smaller reductions, it would be soon exhausted. When it was spent, the wages payable would in any case depend on the financial position of the industry and the terms of the permanent scheme.

The Government still made its offer of any subsidy conditional on arrangements between the miners and the owners for a 'continuing agreement'. But it was now proposed that one of the terms of settlement should be that, if they could not agree among themselves on a permanent scheme, the points in dispute should be referred for final decision to an independent chairman or a board of arbitrators.

The Miners' Executive, on the 28th May, having considered these proposals, decided to refer them to the district associations, which were asked to report their attitude before the 3rd June, for which day a further meeting of the Executive was summoned.

On the 29th May Mr. Lloyd George outlined in the House of Commons the latest proposals of the Government. In the debate which followed, and also in the newspapers, an acrimonious controversy followed. In the course of the negotiations Mr. Lloyd George had stated that, in some circumstances and if either party finally refused to accept a settlement which the Government believed to be reasonable, 'and were, through such a refusal to accept fair terms, holding up the whole of the community, we should, on the other hand, have to exercise all the authority and use all the resources at the disposal of the Government to enforce a settlement'. This and other references were understood by the miners as indicating the Government's intention, if the negotiations broke down, to enforce a settlement by compulsory arbitration backed by Act of Parliament. Mr. Lloyd George, without saying definitely that the Government would not introduce legislation for a compulsory settlement, disclaimed having made the threat, and confined himself in the House of Commons to declaring that any Government assistance must be conditional upon a durable settlement, and that, if the miners and owners could not reach such a settlement among themselves, they must mutually agree to accept the decision of some impartial person or tribunal.

In the midst of this controversy, the district Miners' Associations met to consider the terms proposed by the Government. When the Miners' Executive met again on the 3rd June, it was reported that every district had pronounced against acceptance. Accordingly, on the same day the rejection of the terms was reported to Mr. Lloyd George. A request was made on this day by the Northumberland Miners' Association that a new National Miners' Conference should be held, in order that the delegates, free from instructions, might reconsider the whole situation, and make fresh recommendations to the men, but this application was refused by the Miners' Executive.

On the 4th June Mr. Lloyd George replied to the miners' letter, regretting the rejection of the terms, and stating that, after full consideration, the Government had come to the conclusion that the offer of a subsidy could not be kept open much longer, and that, failing a settlement, it would be definitely withdrawn at the end of a fortnight. By this threat, rather than by direct compulsion, the Government sought to compel the miners to accept a settlement on a district basis.

On the following day this attempt was reinforced by a letter addressed to the Miners' Executive by Mr. Evan Williams,

President of the Mining Association. The coal-owners' president, whose action was confirmed by his association the next day, referred to the threat that the subsidy would be withdrawn, and urged the miners to meet the owners again in order to 'elucidate the position'. The Miners' Executive accepted this invitation, and accordingly on the 7th June the two sides met without Government representatives.

The result of this meeting was a new set of proposals, based on the offer made by the Government. The owners now offered to agree to a 'standard wage' higher than they had offered previously. Their old proposal had been that the standard wage should be the actual wages paid in July 1914, with the addition of any increase made in the actual *standards* [1] since 1914, and of the allowance made to piece-workers on the shortening of the hours of work. The owners now proposed that the new standard should incorporate, in addition to these elements, a minimum percentage of 20 per cent. upon them, to remain in force until June 1922. Thus, where the pre-war shift wage was 6*s*. 6*d*. (the average pre-war figure), and the advance in the standard 9*d*., the minimum wage payable under the owners' new offer would be 7*s*. 3*d*. + 20 per cent. = a total of 8*s*. 8½*d*. per shift. This proposal was conditional on the making of a permanent settlement on a district basis. There was a special provision that, where under the scheme the wage payable to any low-paid day-worker came to less than 'a subsistence wage', the amount would be brought up to a subsistence level by the District Conciliation Board.

It has been pointed out that the Government's offer left it to the miners to determine the amount of the reduction which they would accept for the first month of the temporary scheme, only pointing out that the larger the reduction, the longer would the £10,000,000 subsidy last. The Miners' Executive discussed this point, and decided to fix the maximum reduction for July at 2*s*.

[1] Increases *in* the standard must not be confused with percentage or flat-rate advances *on* the standard. The former are changes made by agreement in the basic wage of each grade, on which percentage additions are calculated. The value of the increases *in* the standard made in the various coal-fields since 1914 ranged from 1*s*. 3*d*. a shift in Cumberland to 3*d*. only in Staffordshire. The average for the whole country was just under 9*d*. per shift.

per shift for adults—being the amount of the reduction which they had offered to accept in April.

They then determined to submit the owners' offer, together with this proposal as to the amount of the reduction, to a full Conference, with a recommendation to the Conference to take upon it a ballot vote of all the men involved. A National Conference was therefore summoned, and met on the 10th June. By a very large majority, it was decided to submit the terms to a ballot-vote. The question then arose whether any recommendation should be made by the Conference. A number of delegates favoured a recommendation to the men to reject the terms, but finally the Conference carried, by 105 votes to 46, the proposal of the Executive that no recommendation at all should be made. Accordingly, at the meetings which followed in the coal-fields, the terms were explaimed, but the miners were left without advice from their leaders as to the way they should vote.

The result, reported on the 17th June, was the decisive rejection of the proposed terms ; 435,614 votes were cast for rejection, and only 180,724 for acceptance. These figures were reported on the same day to the owners and to the Government. The reply was a letter, dated the 18th June, from Mr. Lloyd George to the Miners' Executive. After dwelling upon the gravity of the situation, and the loss which the country was sustaining from the continuance of the dispute, Mr. Lloyd George stated that 'the Government have no option but to make final their decision that their offer of assistance cannot remain open after to-morrow night'. In other words, the offer of a subsidy of £10,000,000 was withdrawn.

In face of the complete deadlock which had now occurred, the Miners' Executive felt itself compelled to make a fresh move. While the coal struggle had been in progress the workers in many other industries had been confronted with demands for the acceptance of substantial reductions in wages, and there were signs in a number of industries in the middle of June that matters were coming to a head. Suggestions were already being made by the building operatives and by other groups that concerted action should be taken by the whole Trade Union movement to set a limit to the reductions that the workers would accept. In these circumstances, the Miners' Executive saw some hope of an issue out of the difficulty through a concerted movement. Accordingly, on the 18th June, it adopted the following resolution:

> 'That we ask various Executive Committees of Unions affected by wage disputes to meet the Executive Committee of the (Miners') Federation with the object of taking national action with the miners to secure their mutual demands.'

Action was taken on the resolution; but within a very few days it became clear that no result was to be expected from it. The other Unions which were negotiating with the various bodies of employers saw nothing to be gained and much to be lost by linking their fortunes with those of the miners, who were now manifestly almost at the end of their resistance. The other sections were, moreover, most anxious to avoid a struggle, and, if they possibly could, to reach settlements by compromise. The Miners' Executive speedily realized that no outside help would be forthcoming.

On the 24th June, therefore, after a full discussion, the Miners' Executive passed the following resolution:

> 'That we ask the Government and the owners for a meeting with a view to negotiating a satisfactory wages settlement which we can recommend our members to accept.'

Negotiations were reopened on the 27th June. The Government expressed its willingness, on the conditions previously laid down, to make a grant in aid of the industry. With remarkable rapidity terms of settlement were arranged, and, on the same day, the Miners' Executive determined to submit these terms to the district associations, with a recommendation in favour of their acceptance. The method of submission to the district associations, instead of the more usual ballot vote of the men, was doubtless adopted because the Executive feared that a ballot would again result in rejection, and had more hope of convincing district conferences of delegates that acceptance was the only alternative to the collapse of the Federation.

The reports of the districts were received by the Executive on the 1st July. Thirteen districts, with a total membership of 832,000, had decided in favour of acceptance; five districts (including Lancashire), with a total membership of 105,000, had decided against. One district, Cleveland, was not affected, as it was not involved in the dispute,[1] and one other, Cumberland, did not report any decision. In face of the reports, the Miners' Executive at once wired to all districts ordering an immediate resumption of work. The great dispute thus ended on the 1st July, and with it ended also the 'state of emergency', which had been regularly proclaimed each month during its continuance. The Lancashire and Cheshire Miners' Federation, indeed, protested against the method adopted to bring the dispute to an end, and held that the terms should have been submitted before acceptance to a Conference, which would have had the power to order a ballot vote. But everywhere work was resumed as far as it was available. The men were exhausted by the long struggle, and only their exhaustion had brought it at last to an end.

Section 9. The Terms of Settlement

The terms on which the coal dispute was settled were, for the miners, terms of defeat. They had failed to secure the National Pool, and without this, as they had pointed out from the first, a national wage system was impossible. The settlement was upon a district basis, and involved the separate determination of wages in each district on the basis of the financial position of the district. Moreover, the proportion of profits to wages and the amount of the new standard wage established in each district were decided on the terms proposed by the owners. The miners did, indeed, secure substantial improvements on the conditions proposed by the owners before the lock-out began; but the settlement was no advance on what could have been secured by bargaining during the early stages of the dispute. Indeed, the terms on which the Government subsidy was granted were less favourable than had been offered at an earlier stage.

[1] The Cleveland Association consists of ironstone miners, who work under a separate agreement.

The terms of settlement were contained in thirteen clauses, and were accompanied by a schedule setting out the districts, thirteen in number, in which in future wage ascertainments were to be separately made.[1] Under the first clause there was to be set up a National Board, consisting of an equal number of representatives from the Mining Association and the Miners' Federation, with an 'Impartial Chairman'. In each district a District Board was to be similarly constituted of representatives from the district associations, also with an impartial chairman in each case. The functions of the National and District Boards were not defined in the agreement, and were left to be worked out in detail later. But it was clear that the National Board thus established had little in common with the National Wages Board for which the miners had contended. They had asked for a Board which would have power, with the National Pool behind it, to make advances or reductions in wages on a uniform national basis. The Board which was actually to be set up could not at most be more than a court of appeal from district decisions, or do more than decide the principles on which wages were to be fixed in the various districts.

The second clause definitely laid down that the basis on which wages were to be adjusted from time to time was the separate ability of each district to pay, ascertained, under Clause 3, by joint audit undertaken by firms of auditors appointed by each party. The principles on which wages were to be adjusted were in substance those originally put forward by the owners. In each district there was to be a standard rate for each grade. This rate, under Clause 7, was to consist of the actual standard or base rates in force in March 1921 (i. e. the pre-war standard with some minor adjustments in most dictricts[2]), *plus* the equivalent of the percentages payable on the standard in July 1914, *plus*, in the case of piece-workers only, the adjustment of percentages made when the hours were reduced from eight to seven. During the currency of the settlement, the lowest rate payable in any district was to be an advance of 20 per cent. on this new standard,

[1] For the full text of the terms, see Appendix D.

[2] See footnote to p. 231.

or a money wage in all rather more than 30 per cent. on the average above the 1914 level. Corresponding to the standard wage (i.e. not including the 20 per cent. minimum advance on the standard wage), there was to be recognized a standard owners' profit, amounting to 17 per cent. of the sum payable as standard wages. The Miners' Federation, it will be remembered, had suggested that the standard profit should be 10 per cent. of a higher standard wage; but the owners' figure was accepted in Clause 4 of the settlement. The surplus revenue of the industry in each district, after allowing for standard wages, other ascertained costs of production,[1] and standard profits, was to be divided in such a way that 83 per cent. of the surplus would be added to wages in the form of percentage advances on the standard. Here, again, the owners' proposal as to the division of the surplus was accepted. If, during any period, the revenue was not enough, after paying costs of production and standard wages, to yield the owners their standard profit, the deficiency was to be carried forward to the next accounting period as a claim prior to any claim for wages over the standard (Clause 4).

If at any time the application of these principles resulted in fixing the total wage of any class of 'low-paid day workers' at less than a 'subsistence wage', the District Board, or failing agreement, the district impartial chairman was to fix a rate which would bring the wage up to subsistence level, the cost of any such allowance being charged as a cost of production against the industry (Clause 5).

For the purposes of this agreement, the coal-fields were to be divided into thirteen districts. This was not quite so drastic a sub-division as the owners had, at an earlier stage, proposed; but it resulted in the cutting up of certain areas which had always been treated as units for purposes of wage variation for many years before the War. The old 'Federated Area',[2] known also as the 'English Coal Conciliation Board Area', was broken into a number of fragments, each of which was in future to be treated as a separate district. The small districts in the south-west of England, which had acted sometimes separately and sometimes together before the War, were also divided permanently. The

[1] See Clause 9 of the Agreement. [2] See p. 9.

new districts, as compared with the pre-war districts, were as follows:

Districts under 1921 Agreement	*Pre-war Conciliation Board Areas*
1. Scotland.	1. Scotland.
2. Northumberland.	2. Northumberland.
3. Durham.	3. Durham.
4. South Wales and Monmouthshire.	4. South Wales and Monmouthshire.
5. Yorkshire, Notts., Derbyshire, Leicestershire, Cannock Chase, and Warwickshire.	5. 'Federated Area' (Lancashire, Cheshire, Yorkshire, Notts., Derbyshire, Leicestershire, Staffordshire, Shropshire, Warwickshire, and North Wales).
6. Lancashire and Cheshire, and North Staffs.	
7. North Wales.	
8. South Staffs., and Shropshire.	
9. Cumberland.	6. Cumberland.
10. Bristol.	(Bristol wages followed Somerset.)
11. Forest of Dean.	7. Forest of Dean.
12. Somerset.	8. Somerset.
13. Kent.	

All the foregoing particulars are those of the main, or 'permanent' agreement. But the settlement made provision[1] also for a 'temporary period' of three months, ending on the 30th September. During this period, Government assistance was to be available in aid of wages; but, whereas the Government had originally offered outright a subsidy of £10,000,000, the settlement provided only for assistance up to a maximum of £10,000,000, and, in fact, only about £7,000,000 was paid out by the Government under it. For the 'temporary period' only, it was agreed that wages should not in any district be reduced by more than certain maximum amounts—2*s*. per shift for workers over 16 years of age during July, 2*s*. 6*d*. during August, and 3*s*. during September, unless the Government subsidy was exhausted.[2] During these months certain special provisions were to apply to the determination of owners' profits. The owners were to claim

[1] In Clause 11 of the Agreement.

[2] For workers under 16 years of age the maximum reductions were 1*s*., 1*s*. 3*d*., and 1*s*. 6*d*.

no share in the 'surplus' when the effect would be to reduce wages below the amounts paid in the previous month. They were also, in districts where the revenue was inadequate to pay standard profits as well as the wages fixed, to forgo under certain conditions their standard profits for July and August. Any deficiency in standard profits was not to be carried forward as under the main agreement; but actual losses were to be carried forward. Where a district could afford to pay a wage higher than the minimum fixed for the month in question any reduction on the wages paid in March 1921 was to be at a flat rate for all grades of workers in the district.

The whole agreement was to run for a year after the end of the temporary period, that is, until the end of September 1922, and was thereafter to be subject to three months' notice on either side. It could not, therefore, be actually terminated until the end of 1922 (Clause 12).

The final clause laid down that every man who had been involved in the stoppage was entitled to return to his previous place of work, as soon as his place was available, and further provided that there should be no victimization of men 'who have been keeping the collieries open', i.e. by undertaking safety work during the dispute.

Section 10. The Aftermath

I propose to deal very briefly with the events which followed the settlement of the 1st July. That settlement, as we have seen, definitely involved for the time being the abandonment by the Miners' Federation of the claim to a national system of wage regulation. It thus removed the main objection which the Federation had felt to the Mining Industry Act of 1920; for the cause of the Federation's refusal to co-operate in working the Act had been the fear that it would be used as the means of a return to a district system of wage negotiation. Under the new conditions, this objection no longer applied, and there were clearly some advantages to be gained by securing the protection of the National and District Boards and Pit Committees which were to have been established under Part II of the Act. Accordingly, on the 19th July, the Miners' Executive recommended the district associations to agree to take part in the working of the Act. Consent was given to this course, and, on the 11th August the Executive notified the Minister of Mines of its willingness to take part in working the Act.

It will be remembered that, in face of the attitude of the miners while the Act was under discussion, a clause was inserted in it providing that Part II, in which the whole of the provisions for Joint Boards and Committees were embodied, should cease to have effect ' if at the expiration of one year it appears to the Board of Trade that the scheme of this part of the Act has been rendered abortive by reason of the failure on the part of those entitled to appoint representatives ', subject only to the passing of a definite resolution in favour of its continuance by both Houses of Parliament.[1] The year of grace was due to expire in August 1921. As the failure of the parties to appoint representatives could not be ascertained until regulations under the Act had been properly framed, and both parties requested to make appointments, Mr. Bridgeman announced, on the 19th August, his intention to issue regulations. These were submitted in draft to the Miners' Federation and to the owners in September; but, whereas the miners were now willing to work the Act, the owners, who had been mainly responsible for its provisions when it was first put forward as an alternative to public ownership and ' joint control ', now refused to have anything to do with it, and urged that the settlement of July provided all the machinery that was needed, and rendered Part II obsolete. In other words, the owners were now hostile to the establishment of Pit Committees, and to any form of State sanction behind the National and District Boards established under the July settlement. On the 20th October the Mining Association intimated its definite refusal to work the Act. The Government, in order to comply with its terms, had nevertheless to issue provisional regulations under Part II. The coal-owners then reiterated their refusal, and, early in 1922, the Board of Trade duly reported to Parliament that, in its opinion, Part II had been rendered abortive by the

[1] For the full text of this clause, and for an account of the provisions of the Act see chap. VII, sect. 2.

owners' refusal. The Labour Party in the House of Commons, and Lord Haldane in the House of Lords, moved the resolutions required to maintain Part II in existence; but, in face of the united opposition of the Government and the employers, these resolutions were defeated, and Part II of the Mining Industry Act passed from the Statute Book. With it disappeared almost the last fruit of the Coal Industry Commission, and the mining industry came again under an unrestricted system of private enterprise. The Mines Department, it is true, remained in being as a sub-department of the Board of Trade, but its powers were very limited, and a determined effort was even made to prevent it from publishing statistics showing the financial position of the mines,[1] with the result that even these were greatly curtailed. The Department itself was threatened with abolition under the Geddes Economy Reports of 1922.

Meanwhile, the miners were working under the settlement of July. No time was lost in establishing the National Board, the rules of which were issued on the 21st July. Mr. Evan Williams, president of the Mining Association, was appointed president of the Board, Mr. Herbert Smith vice-president, and Mr. Frank Hodges and Mr. W. A. Lee, the coal-owners' secretary, joint secretaries. Sir William Plender, the well-known accountant, became 'Impartial Chairman'. The National Board was mainly concerned during the first months in working out the detailed methods of applying the July settlement. Disputes arose as to the interpretation of the agreement, particularly as to the extent to which the owners had undertaken to forgo profits—a matter which had never been made very clear, even in the agreement itself.

At the end of the temporary period, it was evident that, with the withdrawal of the Government subsidy, almost intolerably severe additional wage reductions would fall due under the agreement in certain of the coal-fields. As we have pointed out, under the terms finally arranged the Government had restricted its help to a *maximum* of £10,000,000, and in fact only about £7,000,000 had been spent by the end of September. On the 28th September the miners approached the Government with a request that the

[1] The owners objected to the itemization of costs of production in the figures issued by the Department.

balance of £3,000,000, still remaining out of the sum voted by Parliament, should be used to keep up wages in October to a better level. The miners asked the owners to associate themselves with this application, but the owners would not do this, presumably because they feared that they would be asked to surrender their October profits. On the 19th October the miners met the Government and further pressed the claim upon them, but the Government refused, stating that Parliament had voted the money on the understanding that any sum remaining at the end of September would pass to the Treasury. A further deputation to the Prime Minister on the 9th November was also fruitless.

By the beginning of January 1922, wages in many of the coal-fields had fallen very low indeed. In others, notably South Yorkshire and the Midlands, the position was very much better, as these areas were suffering far less from the slump than the small districts in the west, or than the districts largely concerned with exports or the supply of industries which were themselves abnormally depressed. The following table shows the datal

COAL-MINERS' WAGES—JANUARY 1922—REPRESENTATIVE GRADES [1]
(Figures compiled by the Miners' Federation)

Coal-field	*Wages per shift*		*Coal-field*	*Wages per shift*	
	Skilled coal-getter	*Under-ground labourer*		*Skilled coal-getter*	*Under-ground labourer*
	s. d.	*s. d.*		*s. d.*	*s. d.*
Nottingham	17 3·76	13 7·69	Kent	10 5·0	7 11·0
Derbyshire	16 3·17	11 6·5	Northumberland	9 7·17	5 6·87
South Yorkshire	15 2·57	11 6·5	North Wales	9 5·86	7 4·13
Leicester	14 11·4	10 8·11	Scotland	9 3·72	7 6·77
Cannock Chase	14 11·4	11 2·31	South Wales	9 0·24	6 4·6
East Yorkshire	14 8·28	11 2·31	Somerset	8 11·96	7 9·3
Warwickshire	14 8·28	11 9·21	Cumberland	8 3·45	7 9·6
South Derbyshire	13 7·69	9 5·22	Durham	8 0·93	5 10·63
West Yorkshire	13 7·69	10 10·11	Forest of Dean	7 5·08	5 11·22
Lancashire and Cheshire	12 11·0	9 0·51	Bristol	7 4·45	6 4·74
North Staffordshire	11 1·35	9 7·35			

[1] By the middle of 1922 the fall in wages was very much greater still, and in every coal-field save one, wages were down to the absolute minimum rates payable under the agreement of 1921, i. e. 20 per cent. above the new standards.

rates of pay in the various districts for the two most representative grades—skilled coal-getters and labourers.

This table shows some remarkable reverses in fortune. I cannot find exactly similar figures for the period before the stoppage, but the following table, giving the average wage per shift for all grades in March 1921, shows what was then the relative wage position in the various coal-fields.

COAL-MINERS' WAGES—AVERAGE WAGE PER SHIFT IN MARCH 1921

District	*Wage*	*District*	*Wage*
	s. d.		*s. d.*
Scotland	17 6	Lancs., Cheshire, and North Wales	15 6½
Northumberland	16 11½	Derby, Notts., and Leicester	17 3
Durham	16 9	Staffs., Salop, Worcester and Warwick	15 0
South Wales	18 10	Bristol, Forest of Dean, and Somerset	15 2
Cumberland	17 2		
Yorkshire	16 11		

These figures, it must be noted, represent averages for all grades, and are therefore well below the rates for skilled coal-getters. But it will be seen that the skilled coal-getters' rate in South Wales in January 1922 was less than half the South Wales average rate for all grades, skilled and unskilled, in March 1921. South Wales miners had received the highest wages paid in the country: in January 1922 they were not far from the bottom of the list. Moreover, as many of them were getting only two or three shifts' work a week, as against an average of five before the stoppage, the actual reduction in earnings was very much greater than is shown by the change in rate. Many grades in the coal-fields badly hit by the depression were reduced under the July settlement to what were almost starvation wages. Apart from the unemployed, miners who were in work were compelled in some districts to seek, and to be granted, 'poor relief'. Moreover, many men were long out of work. For some time after the end of the stoppage the number of these approached a quarter of a million, and at the end of January 1922 there remained 117,000 coal-miners wholly unemployed out of a total of 1,131,000 employed in the industry in normal times. These figures take no account of short time, which affected many thousands more.

CONCLUSION

THROUGHOUT this study of labour problems in the British mining industry during the war and post-war period I have stuck very closely to my last. Perhaps too closely; for the method adopted has meant leaving out of account certain political factors, national and international, which had a very important bearing on the course of events. I have, for instance, hardly mentioned the effect of the economic clauses of the Versailles Treaty upon the British coal industry, although it is obvious that the coming into the European market, for re-sale by Allied Governments, of large quantities of German 'reparations coal' was one of the principal causes of the collapse of the British export trade. This omission is, to some extent, remedied by the inclusion in an appendix of a memorandum dealing with the question issued by the Miners' Federation early in 1922.

Again, although it is clear enough that the policy of the British Government in its dealings with the miners from 1919 to 1921 was dictated largely by the general political situation, which, in turn, was partly dependent on the general economic conditions, I have tried, as far as possible, to keep out all references to these broader aspects of the question. I have done this because I have been aiming, not at a definite interpretation of the events, but at a simple narration which will provide material for the interpreter. I have made it my business to state the facts clearly, leaving out, wherever possible, my personal opinion about them, or about the rightness or wrongness of the actions which I have recorded. This means, not that I am without opinions, but that I prefer to let the facts speak for themselves, not only as they speak to me, but with the different voices with which they may speak to others.

Even as I have told the story, the tragedy of it stands out plain enough. The whole history of the mining industry from 1914 to 1922 is one of the tragedies of the War showing as plainly as can be the illusory hopes based on the false prosperity which the War produced, and the cruel aftermath of these hopes—the utter crumbling of the war-time structure in face of the economic

R 2

situation resulting from the War. The war-time accomplishment of the mining industry was admittedly remarkable. With a sorely depleted labour force, and in face of great difficulties in the supply of materials and transport, the output was maintained at an extraordinarily high level. To the miners substantial gains accrued for the time being. The rates of the less skilled grades were brought up to a more reasonable level: the long-desired methods of national negotiation were at last inaugurated. When peace came, the time seemed ripe, to the miners at least, for a change of system which would reorganize the industry and set it on a new basis as a self-governing public service. The Coal Commission encouraged these hopes, and, for a few weeks, the eyes of the whole nation were on the mines. Then slowly the vision faded. The recommendations of the Coal Commission were set aside, and the industry slid down again into a series of wage disputes, culminating in the disastrous struggle which followed the premature removal of Government control. That struggle ended, not merely in the defeat of the miners, but in the collapse of the industry itself and in a degradation of the standard of life in the coal-fields to a level far below that of 1914. It ended with the coal industry in ruins, with the demolition not only of the hopes of 1919, but of the realities of pre-war days.

It is easy to see now that the decline of the past two years, far more than the apparent prosperity of the preceding period, is the real outcome of war, and to trace the decline of the coal industry to its fundamental causes in war exhaustion and economic dislocation perpetuated under the peace. The history of the coal industry reveals, as clearly as anything, the true economic consequences of war, and therein lies the heart of the tragedy. Opinions differ in the apportioning of blame for this or that incident of the calamity, but the calamity as a whole is the fruit of war. A different policy in relation to the industry might have made its effects less terrible: none, under the economic conditions of the post-war period could have prevented it altogether. Every man can make, in the light of the facts, his own estimate of the relative importance of the various causes of the disaster: the fact that it is a war disaster admits of no dispute. The tragedy is felt, day in and day out, in many thousand homes.

APPENDICES

APPENDIX A

OUTPUT, EMPLOYMENT, AND PROFITS IN THE MINING INDUSTRY, 1910–21

Year	*Total output (millions of tons)*	*Workers employed (thousands)*	*Total profits, excluding royalties (£ millions)*
1910	264	1,027 [a]	10 [a]
1911	271	1,045 [a]	9·3 [a]
1912	260	1,068 [a]	15·2 [a]
1913	287	1,110 [a]	22 [a]
1914	265	1,054 [a]	15·5 [a]
1915	253	939 [a]	21·4 [a]
1916	256	984 [a]	37·8 [a]
1917	248	1,006 [a]	27·7 [a]
1918	227	948 [a]	29·5 [c]
1919	229	1,191 [b]	30·4 [c]
1920	229	1,248 [b]	35 [c]
1921	164	1,113 [b]	—

[a] Figures submitted to the Coal Commission by the Mines Department.

[b] Figures given by Mr. Finlay Gibson, in his statistical Tables for the Coal Industry (1922). Mr. Gibson's figures throughout show a rather larger number employed than those submitted to the Coal Commission, e.g., for 1917 Mr. Gibson's figure is 1,021 and for 1914, 1,124.

[c] Estimated by Mr. Finlay Gibson. His figures are £36,400,000 for 1919 and £41,000,000 for 1920. I have deducted £6,000,000 in each year for royalties.

APPENDIX B

BILL SUBMITTED TO THE COAL COMMISSION BY THE MINERS' FEDERATION OF GREAT BRITAIN

The Nationalization of Mines and Minerals Bill, 1919

(Certain important provisions are sidelined)

A Bill to Nationalize the Mines and Minerals of Great Britain and to provide for the National Winning, Distribution, and Sale of Coal and other Minerals.

Whereas it is expedient that mines and minerals should be taken into the possession of the State.

Be it enacted by the King's Most Excellent Majesty, by and with the advice and consent of the Lords Spiritual and Temporal and Commons in this present Parliament assembled, and by the authority of the same, as follows :—

Establishment of Mining Council.

1.—(1) For the purpose of winning, distributing, selling, and searching for coal and other minerals, there shall be established by His Majesty by Warrant under the sign manual, a Mining Council, consisting of a President and 20 members, ten of whom shall be appointed by His Majesty and ten by the Association known as the Miners' Federation of Great Britain.

(2) It shall be lawful for His Majesty, from time to time, to appoint any member of the Privy Council to be President of the Mining Council, under the name of the Minister of Mines, to hold office during His Majesty's pleasure.

(3) The Members of the Mining Council, other than the President, shall be appointed for five years, but shall be eligible for reappointment. Provided that His Majesty or the Association known as the Miners' Federation of Great Britain respectively shall have power to remove any person appointed by them and appoint some other person in his place. On a casual vacancy occurring by reason of the death, resignation, or otherwise of any of such members or otherwise, His Majesty or the Miners' Federation of Great Britain, as the case may be, shall appoint some other person to fill the vacancy, who shall continue in office until the member in whose place he was appointed should have retired, and shall then retire. The members of the Mining Council shall devote the whole of their time to the business of the Mining Council.

Minister of Mines and Parliamentary Secretary.

2.—(1) The Minister of Mines and one of the Secretaries of the Mining Council (to be known as the Parliamentary Secretary and to be appointed by His Majesty) shall at the same time be capable of being elected to and of sitting in the Commons House of Parliament.

(2) The Minister of Mines shall take the oath of allegiance and official oath, and shall be deemed to be included in the First Part of the Schedule to the Promissory Oaths Act, 1868.

(3) There shall be paid out of money provided by Parliament to the Minister of Mines a salary at the rate of £2,000 a year, and to the Parliamentary Secretary a salary at the rate of £1,500 a year.

(4) The Minister of Mines and the Parliamentary Secretary shall be responsible to Parliament for the acts of the Mining Council.

Officers, etc.

3.—(1) The Mining Council shall appoint a Secretary (to be known as the Permanent Secretary), and such assistant secretaries and officers and servants as the Mining Council may, with the sanction of the Treasury, determine.

(2) Subject to the provisions of Section 11 (2) of this Act, there shall be paid to the Permanent Secretary, Assistant Secretaries and other officers and servants such salaries or remuneration as the Treasury shall from time to time determine.

(3) There shall be transferred and attached to the Mining Council such of the persons employed under any Government Department or local authority in or about the execution of the powers and duties transferred by or in pursuance of this Act to the Mining Council as the Mining Council and the Government Department or local authority may with the sanction of the Treasury determine.

(4) Notwithstanding anything in any Act, order, or regulation, any society of workers, all or some of whose members are wholly or partly employed in or about mines, or in any other manner employed by the Minister of Mines, or the Mining Council, or a District Mining Council, or Pit Council, or otherwise under this Act, may be registered or constitute themselves to be a Trade Union, and may do anything individually or in combination which the members of a Trade Union or a Trade Union may lawfully do. Provided further that notwithstanding any Act, order, or regulation to the contrary, it shall be lawful for any person employed under this Act to participate in any civil or political action in like manner as if such person were not employed by His Majesty, or by any authority on his behalf.

Provided, further, that no such person shall suffer dismissal or any deprivation of any kind as a consequence of any political or industrial action, not directly forbidden by the terms of his employment, or as a consequence of participation in a strike or trade dispute.

Constitution of Mining Council.

4.—(1) The Mining Council shall be a Corporation to be known by the name of the Mining Council and by that name shall have perpetual succession, and may acquire and hold land without licence in mortmain.

(2) The Mining Council shall have an official seal, which shall be officially and publicly noticed, and such seal shall be authenticated by the Mining Council or a secretary or one of the assistant secretaries, or some person authorized to act on their behalf.

(3) The Mining Council may sue and be sued without further description under that title.

(4) Every document purporting to be an order, licence, or other instrument issued by the Mining Council, and to be sealed with their seal, authenticated in manner provided by this Act, or to be signed by a secretary or by one of the assistant secretaries, or any person authorized to act, shall be received in evidence and be deemed to be such order, licence, or other instrument without further proof unless the contrary is shown.

(5) Any person having authority in that behalf, either general or special, under the seal of the Mining Council, may on behalf of the Mining Council, give any notice or make any claim, demand, entry, or distress, which the Mining Council in its corporate capacity or otherwise might give or make, and every such notice, claim, demand, entry, and distress shall be deemed to have been given and made by the Mining Council.

(6) Every deed, instrument, bill, cheque, receipt, or other document, made or executed for the purpose of the Mining Council by, to, or with the Mining Council, or any officer of the Mining Council, shall be exempt from any stamp duty imposed by any Act, past or future, except where that duty is declared by the document, or by some memorandum endorsed thereon, to be payable by some person other than the Mining Council, and except so far as any future Act specifically charges the duty.

Transference of mines and minerals to Mining Council.

5. (1) On and after the appointed day, save as in Sub-Section 3 of this Section provided—

(*a*) Every colliery and mine (including all mines, quarries and open workings of ironstone, shale, fireclay and limestone, and every other mine regulated under the Metalliferous Mines Regulation Acts, 1872 and 1875, but not including mines, quarries, or open workings of minerals specified in the First Schedule to this Act), whether in actual work, or discontinued, or exhausted, or abandoned, and every shaft, pit, borehole, level, or inclined plane, whether in course of being made or driven for commencing or opening any such colliery or mine, or otherwise, and all associated properties (including vessels, lighters, railway rolling stock, and all works, including works for the manufacture of bye-products, in the opinion of the Mining Council belonging to any mine undertaking or connected with any colliery or mine, and every house belonging to the owners of any such colliery or mine, which, in the opinion of the Mining Council, is usually occupied by workmen employed at such colliery or mine), (all of which are herein included in the expression 'mine'); and

(*b*) all coal, anthracite, lignite, ironstone, shale, fireclay, limestone, or other mineral, excepting the minerals specified in the First Schedule to this Act, whether at present being worked or not worked, or connected or not connected with any mine, beneath the surface of the ground (all of which are herein included in the expression 'minerals'); and

(*c*) all rights and easements arising out of or necessary to the working of any mine or the winning of any mineral, including all mineral wayleaves, whether air-leaves or water-leaves, or rights to use a shaft, or ventilation or drainage or other royalties, lordships, or rights in connection therewith, whether above or below the ground (all of which are herein included in the expression 'rights')

shall be transferred to, vested in and held by the Mining Council in their corporate capacity in perpetuity, and shall for all purposes be deemed to be royal mines, and the minerals and rights thereof respectively.

(2) The Acts contained in the Second Schedule to this Act are hereby repealed.

(3) Provided that the Mining Council may at any time before the appointed day give notice in writing to the owner of, or person interested in, any mine or minerals or rights, disclaiming, during the period of such disclaimer, all or part of the property in such mine or minerals or rights to the extent specified in the notice, and thereafter such mine or minerals or rights shall, until such time as the Mining Council shall otherwise determine, to the extent specified in such notice, not vest in the Mining Council as provided by Sub-Section (1) of this section. Provided that in such case it shall not be lawful for any person other than the Mining Council, without the permission of the Mining Council, to work such mine or minerals in any way. Provided further that on the termination of such disclaimer by the Mining Council, such mine or minerals or rights shall, to the extent of such notice, as from such date as the notice may prescribe, vest in the Mining Council as if such notice of disclaimer had not been given.

Purchase of mines.

6. The Mining Council shall purchase the mines of Great Britain in them vested by this Act (other than those which are the property of the Crown at the time of the passing of this Act or which have been disclaimed in whole or in part in accordance with Section 5 (3) of this Act) at the price and in the manner provided by this Act. Provided always that the value of any rights as defined by Section 5 (1) (*c*) of this Act shall not be taken into account in computing such price, for all of which no compensation shall be paid.

Mines Commissioners.

7.—(1) For the purpose of assessing the purchase price of mines it shall be lawful for His Majesty, by warrants under the sign manual, to appoint ten Commissioners, to be styled the Mines Purchase Commissioners (herein called the Commissioners) of whom one, appointed by His Majesty, shall be Chairman.

(2) Three of the said Commissioners shall be nominated by the Association known as the Miners' Federation of Great Britain, and three by the Association known as the Mining Association of Great Britain.

(3) At the expiration of twelve months from the passing of this Act, in the event of a majority of the Commissioners failing to agree as to the purchase price of a particular mine or of its associated properties, it shall be lawful for the Chairman himself to fix the purchase price of such mine, which price shall then be deemed to be the price fixed by the Commissioners, but, save as herein expressly provided, the finding of a majority of the Commissioners voting on any question or as to the purchase price of mines shall be final and conclusive and binding on all parties.

(4) It shall be lawful for His Majesty to remove any Commissioner for inability or misbehaviour. Every order of removal shall state the reasons for which it is made, and no such order shall come into operation until it has lain before the Houses of Parliament for not less than thirty days while Parliament is sitting.

(5) The Commissioners may appoint and employ such assessors, accountants, surveyors, valuers, clerks, messengers, and other persons required for the due performance of their duties as the Treasury on the recommendation of the Commissioners may sanction.

(6) There shall be paid to the Commissioners and to each of the persons appointed or employed under this section such salary or remuneration as the Treasury may sanction; and all such salaries and remuneration and the expenses of the Commission incurred in the execution of their duties, to such amount as may be sanctioned by the Treasury, shall be paid out of moneys provided by Parliament.

Valuation of mines.

8.—(1) The Commissioners shall, as soon as may be after the passing of this Act, cause a valuation to be made of all mines other than those disclaimed, whether or not developed or working or abandoned or exhausted, in Great Britain, showing what on August 4th, 1914, and what at the date of the passing of this Act was respectively the total ascertained value of each mine and its associated properties and the rights, as defined by Section 5 (1) (*c*) of this Act, therein, and the total ascertained value of such mine and its associated properties respectively exclusive of such rights; and the owner of every mine and any person receiving any rents, interest, or profit from any mine or possessed of any rights therein or connected therewith, on being required by notice by the Commissioners, shall furnish to the Commissioners a return containing such particulars as the Commissioners may require as to his property, rent, interest, profits, or rights in such mine.

(2) The Commissioners may likewise cause any mine to be inspected, require the production of documents, or do any other thing which may, in their opinion, be necessary to fix the purchase price of the mine or its associated properties.

(3) The Commissioners in making such valuation shall have regard to returns made under any statute imposing duties or taxes or other obligations in respect of mines, or minerals or rights, and to any information given before or to any Commission or Government Department, including the Coal Industry Commission constituted under the Coal Industry Commission Act, 1919.

Ascertainment of purchase price.

9.—(1) The purchase price of mines exclusive of associated properties (other than mines in the possession of the Crown at the time of the passing of this Act shall be computed subject to the provisions of sub-sections (2) and (3) of this section by ascertaining the average annual number of tons of minerals actually raised during the five years preceding August 4th, 1914:

Provided that as regards coal-mines in no case shall the maximum purchase price, exclusive of associated properties, be taken to be more than the following:

	s.	*d.*
When 100,000 tons or less have been raised per annum on the average during such five preceding years, a capital sum equal to one such year's output at	12	0 per ton
When more than 100,000 tons have been raised per annum on the average during such five preceding years, a capital sum equal to one such year's output at	10	0 per ton

(2) The Commissioners in arriving at such computation shall also have regard to the actual gross and net profits which have been made in the mine during such years or thereafter and to the amounts which may have been set aside from time to time for depreciation, renewals, or development, and to the probable duration of the life of the mine, and to the nature and condition of such mine, and to the state of repairs thereof, and to the assets and liabilities of any mine undertaking existing at the time of purchase which are transferable to the Mining Council under section 16 of this Act.

(3) Provided further that where a coal-mine, in the opinion of the Commissioners, has not been fully developed, the amount which would be raised under full development without any increase of capital expenditure shall be taken as the average annual number of tons raised, and the maximum purchase price in such case shall be taken to be a capital sum equal to the product of such number of tons and 12*s.* or 10*s.* per ton respectively, for the purpose of ascertaining the maximum value per ton under sub-section (1) of this section.

Issue of State mines stock.

10.—(1) The purchase price of any mine and such of its associated properties as have been purchased, as ascertained under the provisions of this Act, shall be paid by the Mining Council in mines purchase stock to the persons who, in the opinion of the Mining Council, have established their title to such stock. Provided that an appeal shall lie to the High Court under rules to be framed by the High Court from the decision of the Mining Council as to the title of any such persons, but for no other purpose.

(2) For the purpose of paying such purchase price the Treasury shall, on the request of the Mining Council, by warrant addressed to the Bank of England, direct the creation of a new capital stock (to be called 'Guaranteed State Mines Stock'), and in this Act referred to as 'the stock', yielding interest at the rate on the nominal amounts of capital equal to that payable at the date on which this Act received Royal Assent on what, in the opinion of the Treasury, is the nearest equivalent Government Loan Stock.

(3) Interest shall be payable by equal half yearly or quarterly dividends at such times in each year as may be fixed by the warrant first creating the stock.

(4) The stock shall be redeemed at the rate of one hundred pounds sterling for every one hundred pounds of stock at such times and by such drawings as the Treasury, on the recommendation of the Mining Council may think fit.

(5) The stock may be issued at such times and in such amounts and subject to such conditions as the Treasury may direct, and may be issued as bearer bonds with quarterly or half yearly interest coupons attached.

(6) The stock shall be transferable in the books of the Bank of England in like manner as other stock is transferable under the National Debt Act, 1870.

Powers of Mining Council.

11.—(1) Subject to the provisions of this Act, it shall be lawful for the Mining Council to open and work mines and search for, dig, bore, win and deal with minerals and generally to carry on the industry of mining, distributing, vending, and exporting, together with all other industries carried on in connection therewith. Provided that it shall not be lawful for the Mining Council to lease or sell any mine or minerals or rights to any person, association, or corporation.

(2) The Mining Council may, from time to time, in such manner and on such terms as they think fit—

(*a*) subject to the general consent of the Treasury, appoint or continue in employment or dismiss managers, engineers, agents, clerks, workmen, servants, and other persons; and

(*b*) construct, erect or purchase, lease, or otherwise acquire buildings, plant, machinery, railways, tramways, hulks, ships, and other fixed or movable appliances or works of any description, and sell or otherwise dispose of the same when no longer required; and

(*c*) sell, supply, and deliver fuel, coal and other products, the result of mining operations, either within or without the realm; and

(*d*) enter into and enforce contracts and engagements; and

(*e*) generally do anything that the owner of a mine might lawfully do in the working of the mine, or that is authorised by regulations under this Act or by this Act; and

(*f*) employ local authorities for any purpose they may think necessary to carry out their duties under this Act, on such terms as may be mutually agreed.

(3) In addition to the powers conferred on the Mining Council by the last preceding sub-section, the Mining Council may, in such manner as they think fit, work any railway, tramway, hulk, ship, or other appliance for the purpose of winning, supplying, and delivering coal or other products.

(4) The Mining Council may compulsorily purchase land or acquire such rights over land as they may require for the purpose of this Act, and shall have, with regard to the compulsory purchase of land, all the powers of purchasers acting under the Land Clauses Act, 1845, and the Land Clauses Consolidation (Scotland) Act, 1845, or any other Act giving power to acquire land compulsorily for public purposes, which may hereafter be enacted.

(5) With respect to any such purchase of land under the Land Clauses Acts in Great Britain the following provisions shall have effect (that is to say):—

(*a*) The Land Clauses Acts shall be incorporated with this Act, except the provisions relating to access to the special Act, and in construing those Acts for the purposes of this section 'the special Act' shall be construed to mean this Act, and 'the promoters of the undertaking' shall be construed to mean the Mining Council, and 'land' shall be construed to have the meaning given to it by this Act.

(*b*) The bond required by Section 85 of the Lands Clauses Consolidation Act, 1845, and by Section 84 of the Lands Clauses Consolidation (Scotland) Act, 1845, shall be under the seal of the Mining Council, and shall be sufficient without sureties.

District Mining Councils and Pit Councils.

12.—(1) The Mining Council shall, for the purpose of the carrying on and development of the mining industry, divide Great Britain into districts, and shall in each district constitute a District Mining Council of ten members, half of which shall be appointed by the Miners' Federation of Great Britain.

(2) The Mining Council may delegate to any District Mining Council or Pit Council, such of their powers under this Act as may conveniently be exercised locally, and the District Mining Council shall upon such delegation have and exercise within their district all the powers and duties of the Mining Council as may be delegated to them.

(3) A District Mining Council shall, subject to the approval of the

Mining Council, have power within their area to appoint Pit Councils for each mine or group of mines, composed of ten members, half of whom shall be members of the Miners' Federation of Great Britain, and nominated by the workers of the mine or groups of mines aforesaid, and the District Mining Council may delegate to such Pit Council such of their powers concerning the immediate working or management of a particular mine or group of mines as the District Mining Council may, subject to the approval of the Mining Council, think fit.

(4) The members of District Mining Councils shall be appointed for three years, but shall be eligible for reappointment, and the members of Pit Councils shall be appointed for one year, but shall be eligible for reappointment.

Fuel Consumers' Council and Advisory Conference.

13.—(1) For the purpose of advising the Mining Council it shall be lawful for His Majesty to appoint persons, to represent the interests of consumers, to be known as the Fuel Consumers' Council.

(2) The Mining Council shall have power to convoke at such time as they think fit and under such regulations and conditions as they may prescribe advisory conferences of representatives of District Mining Councils, and the District Mining Councils shall have power in like manner to convoke advisory conferences of Pit Councils within their area.

(3) The expenses of the Fuel Consumers' Council, National and District Mining Conferences shall, subject to the approval of the Treasury, be paid by the Mining Council.

Payment of Mining Council and District Mining Councils and Pit Councils.

14.—There shall be paid to each of the members of the Mining Council, other than the President, such salary as the Treasury may determine, and to the members of the District Mining Councils, and to the Pit Councils, such salaries and emoluments as the Mining Council, with the consent of the Treasury, may determine.

Accounts.

15.—(1) The Mining Council shall cause full and faithful accounts to be kept of all moneys received and expended under this Act, and of all assets and liabilities and of all profits and losses, and shall annually lay such accounts before Parliament.

(2) The Mining Council shall annually cause a balance-sheet of accounts to be made, including a capital account and a profit and loss account for each mine worked under this Act.

(3) Such balance-sheet and statement shall be so prepared as to show fully and faithfully the financial position of each such mine, and the financial result of its operations for the year.

(4) All moneys raised under the authority of this Act shall, as and when raised, and all other moneys received hereunder shall, as and when received, be paid into a separate account called 'The National Mines Account'.

(5) All moneys withdrawn from the National Mines Account constituted under this Act shall be withdrawn only by the order of the

Mining Council or such other person as the Mining Council may from time to time appoint.

(6) All moneys in the National Mines Account, or payable into that account by any person whomsoever, and also all moneys owing by any person under this Act, are hereby declared to be the property of the Crown, and recoverable accordingly as from debtors to the Crown.

Transference of existing assets and liabilities

16.—(1) There shall be transferred to the Mining Council all the existing assets and liabilities of mine undertakings and associated properties, as and when they are transferred to and vested in the Mining Council, other than liabilities for rights including royalty rents, wayleave rents, or any other underground rents or charges, payable or due at the time of the passing of this Act to any person, all of which shall cease to be payable on and after the appointed day.

(2) On the passing of this Act, there shall be ascertained by the Commissioners the amount of all moneys due to or from all mine undertakings, and the findings of the Commissioners as to the amount of such moneys shall be binding and conclusive on all parties.

(3) The net amount of all moneys due to any mine undertaking, after all debts due from any such undertaking have been deducted, as ascertained under Sub-section (2) of this section, shall be paid by the Mining Council to the persons to whom in the opinion of the Commissioners such debts are due, and shall be deemed to be expenses incurred under this Act. Provided that an appeal shall lie to the High Court, under rules to be framed by the High Court, from the decision of the Commissioners as to the title of any such person, but for no other purpose.

Payments out of moneys provided by Parliament.

17.—(1) All sums expended or payable under this Act in carrying out the provisions of this Act for expenses, or for salaries or wages payable under this Act, or in the construction, erection, or acquisition of buildings, plant, machinery, railways, tramways, hulks, ships, or other appliances or works, or otherwise, shall be payable out of moneys provided by Parliament.

(2) Provided that moneys received under this Act in respect of the sale or export or supply of coal or other minerals (including the moneys received from the Government Departments) may be directly expended in or towards carrying out the purposes of this Act.

Payment out of Consolidated Fund.

18.—After full provision has been made for all outgoings, losses, and liabilities for the year (including interest on securities created and issued in respect of moneys raised as aforesaid, and on moneys paid out of the Consolidated Fund), the net surplus profits then remaining shall be applied in establishing a sinking fund and, subject thereto, in establishing a depreciation fund in respect of capital expended.

Regulations.

19.—(1) The Mining Council may, from time to time, make such regulations as they think necessary for any of the following purposes :—

(*a*) The management of mines under this Act;

(*b*) the functions, duties, and powers of the District Mining Councils, Pit Councils, and other bodies or persons acting in the management and working of mines or distribution and sale of fuel under this Act;

(*c*) the form of the accounts to be kept and the balance sheets to be prepared in respect of mines under this Act;

(*d*) the mode in which the sinking funds and other funds connected with mines under this Act shall be held and administered;

(*e*) generally any other purpose for which, in the opinion of the Mining Council, regulations are contemplated or required.

(2) The Mining Council, before making or altering any regulations or conditions of employment, including wages, as affect workmen engaged in the mining industry, shall consult with the association known as the Miners' Federation of Great Britain, and, in the event of such representatives and the Mining Council failing to agree, the matter in dispute may be referred to arbitration on such terms as may be mutually agreed.

(3) Provided that nothing in this section shall be deemed to interfere with the right of any employed person, subject to his contractual obligations, to dispose of his labour as he wills.

Statutory regulations.

20.—(1) Every mine worked under this Act shall be managed and worked subject to the provisions of the Metalliferous Mines Regulations Acts, 1872 and 1875, the Coal Mines Regulation Act, 1908, the Coal Mines Act, 1911, and any other Act regulating the hours, wages, or conditions of labour in mines.

(2) There shall be transferred to and be vested in the Mining Council all the powers and duties of the Secretary of State and of any other Government Department imposed upon them by the Metalliferous Mines Regulations Acts, 1872 and 1875, the Coal Mines Regulation Act, 1908, the Coal Mines Act, 1911, or any other Act regulating or affecting mines or the hours or conditions of labour therein.

Duty of Mining Council to supply coal.

21.—(1) It shall be the duty of the Mining Council to ensure that there is a sufficient supply of fuel at reasonable prices throughout Great Britain, and for this purpose it shall be lawful for the Mining Council, or for any local authority or Government Department acting on their behalf, to establish stores and depots and to employ vehicles and to use all other necessary means for the selling of fuel and to sell fuel within the area of every local authority, and, further, for this purpose it shall be the duty of the railway companies or authorities of Great Britain to provide such facilities for the conveyance of fuel as the Mining Council may deem necessary to enable them to carry out the duties imposed upon them by this section at rates not greater than such railway companies or authorities are now entitled to charge for the conveyance of fuel.

(2) Where the Mining Council delegates to any local authority all

or any of their powers under this section, it shall be lawful for such local authority to exercise all or any of the powers of the Mining Council so delegated to them.

(3) All moneys had and received or expended by a local authority under this section shall be deemed to be had and received or expended on behalf of the Mining Council.

Title and commencement.

22.—This Act may be cited as the Nationalisation of Mines and Minerals Act, 1919, and this Act and the Metalliferous Mines Regulations Acts, 1872 and 1875, and the Coal Mines Regulation Acts, 1887 and 1908, and the Coal Mines Act, 1911, may be cited together as the Mines Acts, 1872–1919, and shall come into operation on the first day of the second month, which shall be the appointed day, after the passing of this Act, and, save in the case of disclaimer, all valuations, purchase, and transference of mines and minerals to the Mining Council, and all other arrangements for the carrying out of this Act shall be concluded on or before the first day of the second year after the coming into operation of this Act.

23.—This Act shall not apply to Ireland.

FIRST SCHEDULE

Minerals excluded from this Act:—

Sandstone.	Slate.	Building Clay.
Granite.	Chalk.	Gravel and Sand.
Cherts.	Flints.	Igneous Rocks.

SECOND SCHEDULE

ENACTMENTS REPEALED

Session and chapter	*Title or short title*	*Extent of repeal*
1 William and Mary, ch. 30.	An Act to repeal the statute made in the fifth year of King Henry IV. against multiplying gold and silver.	The Whole Act
5 William and Mary, ch. 6.	An Act to prevent disputes and controversies concerning Royal Mines.	The Whole Act
55 George III, ch. 134.	An Act for altering the rate at which the Crown may exercise its right of preemption of Ore in which there is lead.	The Whole Act
1 James I of Scotland, ch. 12.	Mines of Gold and Silver pertains to the King.	The Whole Act
12 James VI of Scotland, ch. 31.	Anent the Tenth Part of Mynis.	The Whole Act

APPENDIX C

THE EMERGENCY POWERS ACT, 1920

(See Chapters VIII and IX)

CHAPTER 55

A. D. 1920.

An Act to make exceptional provision for the Protection of the Community in cases of Emergency.[1]

[29th October 1920.]

BE it enacted by the King's most Excellent Majesty, by and with the advice and consent of the Lords Spiritual and Temporal, and Commons, in this present Parliament assembled, and by the authority of the same, as follows:—

Issue of proclamations of emergency.

1.—(1) If at any time it appears to His Majesty that any action has been taken or is immediately threatened by any persons or body of persons of such a nature and on so extensive a scale as to be calculated, by interfering with the supply and distribution of food, water, fuel, or light, or with the means of locomotion, to deprive the community, or any substantial portion of the community, of the essentials of life, His Majesty may, by proclamation (hereinafter referred to as a proclamation of emergency), declare that a state of emergency exists.

No such proclamation shall be in force for more than one month, without prejudice to the issue of another proclamation at or before the end of that period.

(2) Where a proclamation of emergency has been made, the occasion thereof shall forthwith be communicated to Parliament, and, if Parliament is then separated by such adjournment or prorogation as will not expire within five days, a proclamation shall be issued for the meeting of Parliament within five days, and Parliament shall accordingly meet and sit upon the day appointed by that proclamation, and shall continue to sit and act in like manner as if it had stood adjourned or prorogued to the same day.

Emergency regulations.

2.—(1) Where a proclamation of emergency has been made, and so long as the proclamation is in force, it shall be lawful for His Majesty in Council, by Order, to make regulations for securing the essentials of life to the community, and those regulations may confer or impose on a Secretary of State or other Government department, or any other persons in His Majesty's service or acting on His Majesty's behalf, such

[1] Reprinted by permission of the Controller of H.M. Stationery Office.

powers and duties as His Majesty may deem necessary for the preservation of the peace, for securing and regulating the supply and distribution of food, water, fuel, light, and other necessities, for maintaining the means of transit or locomotion, and for any other purposes essential to the public safety and the life of the community, and may make such provisions incidental to the powers aforesaid as may appear to His Majesty to be required for making the exercise of those powers effective:

Provided that nothing in this Act shall be construed to authorise the making of any regulations imposing any form of compulsory military service or industrial conscription:

Provided also that no such regulation shall make it an offence for any person or persons to take part in a strike, or peacefully to persuade any other person or persons to take part in a strike.

(2) Any regulations so made shall be laid before Parliament as soon as may be after they are made, and shall not continue in force after the expiration of seven days from the time when they are so laid unless a resolution is passed by both Houses providing for the continuance thereof.

(3) The regulations may provide for the trial, by courts of summary jurisdiction, of persons guilty of offences against the regulations; so, however, that the maximum penalty which may be inflicted for any offence against any such regulations shall be imprisonment with or without hard labour for a term of three months, or a fine of one hundred pounds, or both such imprisonment and fine, together with the forfeiture of any goods or money in respect of which the offence has been committed: Provided that no such regulations shall alter any existing procedure in criminal cases, or confer any right to punish by fine or imprisonment without trial.

(4) The regulations so made shall have effect as if enacted in this Act, but may be added to, altered, or revoked by resolution of both Houses of Parliament or by regulations made in like manner and subject to the like provisions as the original regulations; and regulations made under this section shall not be deemed to be statutory rules within the meaning of section one of the Rules Publication Act, 1893.

56 & 57 Vict. c. 66.

(5) The expiry or revocation of any regulations so made shall not be deemed to have affected the previous operation thereof, or the validity of any action taken thereunder, or any penalty or punishment incurred in respect of any contravention or failure to comply therewith, or any proceeding or remedy in respect of any such punishment or penalty.

Short title and application.

3.—(1) This Act may be cited as the Emergency Powers Act, 1920.

(2) This Act shall not apply to Ireland.

APPENDIX D

(See Chapter IX)

TERMS OF SETTLEMENT IN COAL-MINING INDUSTRY, JULY 1921

1. A National Board shall be constituted forthwith, consisting in equal numbers of persons chosen by the Mining Association of Great Britain and persons chosen by the Miners' Federation of Great Britain.

There shall also be established District Boards, consisting in equal numbers of persons representing owners and workmen in each district.

The National and District Boards shall draw up their own rules of procedure, which shall include a provision for the appointment of an Independent Chairman for each Board.

2. The wages payable in each district shall be expressed in the form of a percentage upon the basis rates prevailing in the district, and shall be periodically adjusted in accordance with the proceeds of the industry as ascertained in such district.

3. The amount of the percentage to be paid in each district during any period shall be determined by the proceeds of the industry in that district during a previous period, as ascertained by returns to be made by the owners, checked by joint test audit of the owners' books carried out by independent accountants appointed by each side.

4. The sum to be applied in each district to the payment of wages above the standard wages as hereinafter defined shall be a sum equal to 83 per cent. of the surplus of such proceeds remaining after deduction therefrom of the amounts of the following items during the period of ascertainment—

(*a*) the cost of the standard wages ;
(*b*) the costs of production other than wages ;
(*c*) standard profits equivalent to 17 per cent. of the cost of the standard wages ;

and the share of the surplus applicable to wages shall be expressed as a percentage upon the basis rates prevailing in the district.

Provided that if in any period the ascertained proceeds, after deduction of costs other than wages and the cost of the standard wages, prove to have been insufficient to meet the standard profits, the deficiency shall be carried forward as a first charge to be met out of any surplus, ascertained as above, in subsequent periods.

5. If the rates of wages thus determined in any district do not provide a subsistence wage to low paid day wage-workers, such additions in the

form of allowances per shift worked shall be made for that period to the daily wages of these workers as, in the opinion of the District Board, or, in the event of failure to agree by the parties, in the opinion of the Independent Chairman, may be necessary for the purpose. Such allowances shall be treated as items of cost in the district ascertainments.

6. For the purpose of these periodical adjustments the units shall be the districts set out in the Schedule hereto, and shall only be varied by the decision of the District Board or Boards concerned, provided that no variation shall take place prior to 1st February 1922, in the grouping of any district unless it is mutually agreed by the representatives of both sides in the district or districts concerned.

7. The standard wages shall be the district basis rates existing on the 31st of March 1921, plus the district percentages payable in July 1914 (or the equivalents in any district in which there has been a subsequent merging into new standards), plus, in the case of pieceworkers, the percentage additions which were made consequent upon the reduction of hours from eight to seven.

8. In no district shall wages be paid at lower rates than standard wages plus 20 per cent. thereof.

9. The National Board shall forthwith consider what items of cost are to be included for the purposes of paragraph 4 (*b*) above, and in the event of agreement not being arrived at by the 31st July, the matter shall be referred to the Independent Chairman for decision.

10. The wages payable by the owners up to the 31st August inclusive shall be based upon the ascertained results of the month of March, and the wages payable during September shall be based upon the ascertained results of the month of July. The periods of ascertainment thereafter shall be decided by the National Board.

11. During the 'temporary period', as hereinafter defined, the following special arrangements shall apply in modification of the general scheme set out above :—

(*a*) In calculating the proceeds for March the deduction to be made in respect of costs other than wages shall be the average of such costs during January, February, and March.

(*b*) In any district in which reductions in wages continue to be made after the first ascertainment, no part of the surplus proceeds shall be assigned to profits if and in so far as this would have the effect of reducing the wages below the level in the preceding month.

When in any district there is a break in the continuity of reductions in wages upon the periodical ascertainments, at that point and thereafter the general scheme shall apply fully in regard to owners' surplus profits.

(*c*) The proviso to paragraph 4 regarding the carrying forward of deficiencies in standard profits shall not apply, but any net losses shall be so carried forward.

(*d*) The Government will give a grant not exceeding £10,000,000 in subvention of wages.

(*e*) The subvention shall be available for making such increases to the wages otherwise payable in any district as may be necessary to prevent the reductions below the March rates of wages being greater than the following amounts :—

During July, 2*s*. a shift for persons of 16 years of age and upwards, and 1*s*. a shift for persons under 16.

During August, 2*s*. 6*d*. and 1*s*. 3*d*. respectively.

During September, 3*s*. and 1*s*. 6*d*. respectively,

provided that the balance of the subvention is sufficient for this purpose.

(*f*) If any district in which in any month the proceeds available for wages, calculated in accordance with the terms of this settlement, are sufficient to admit of a rate of wages equal to or higher than the rate payable under the maximum reduction for that month, the wages payable by the owners shall be calculated not in terms of basis plus percentage, but on the same basis as during March, less flat rate reductions uniform throughout the district for persons of 16 years of age and upwards, and persons under 16 years of age respectively.

(*g*) In any district in which the wages calculated in accordance with the terms of this settlement are less than the wages payable under the maximum reductions aforesaid, the difference shall be met by the owners in that district during September to the extent of the aggregate net profits realized by them on the district ascertainment for July, and during October to the extent of the aggregate net profits realised by them on the district ascertainments for July and August.

(*h*) The expression 'temporary period' means the period from the date of the resumption of work to the 30th September 1921.

12. The period of duration of this agreement shall be from the date of resumption of work until the 30th September 1922, and thereafter until terminated by three months' notice on either side.

13. It is agreed as a principle that every man shall be entitled to return to his place when that place is available for him, and that men temporarily occupying places during the stoppage shall give way to men working in those places before the stoppage.

It is agreed that, on the other hand, there shall be no victimization of men who have been keeping the collieries open, not in the sense that they are to remain at the jobs they filled during the stoppage, but that they shall not be prevented from going back to their own jobs or from working subsequently at the colliery.

For and on behalf of each member of the Central Committee of the Mining Association of Great Britain and for the Mining Association,

EVAN WILLIAMS, President.
THOMAS R. RATCLIFFE-ELLIS, Secretary.

For and on behalf of each member of the Executive Committee of the Miners' Federation of Great Britain and for the Miners' Federation,

HERBERT SMITH, Acting President.
JAMES ROBSON, Treasurer.
FRANK HODGES, Secretary.

For and on behalf of His Majesty's Government,

WILLIAM C. BRIDGEMAN, Secretary for Mines.
E. A. GOWERS, Under-Secretary for Mines.

Mines Department, July 1st, 1921.

SCHEDULE REFERRED TO

Scotland.
Northumberland.
Durham.
South Wales and Monmouth.
Yorkshire, Nottinghamshire, Derbyshire, Leicestershire, Cannock Chase, and Warwickshire.
Lancashire, North Staffordshire, and Cheshire.
North Wales.
South Staffordshire and Salop.
Cumberland.
Bristol.
Forest of Dean.
Somerset.
Kent.

APPENDIX E

(See Conclusion, p. 243)

MEMORANDUM UPON THE EFFECT OF THE REPARATION AGREEMENT UPON THE EXPORT OF BRITISH COAL

Prepared by the British Miners' Federation

The latest comparative figures of export coal from the United Kingdom reveal a growing disparity between the coal exported in 1913 and in 1921.

The export of British coal to Russia during the eleven months ended November 30th, 1913, was 5,598,000 tons, and in the eleven months ended November 1921, 126,400 tons, or a net reduction of five and a half million tons in eleven months.

Exports to Germany for the eleven months ended 30th November 1913, amounted to 8,300,000 tons, as against 659,000 tons in the eleven months ended November 1921, a reduction of nearly 8,000,000 tons of coal.

The amount of coal exported to France from this country during the eleven months ended the 30th November 1913, was 11,676,000 tons, and in the eleven months ending November 1921, 5,161,000 tons of coal, or a net reduction of over 6,000,000 tons of coal.

It will be seen, therefore, that the total loss of coal exports to Russia, Germany, and France, as compared with the pre-war period amounts to a figure of 19½ million tons of coal.

The effect of this loss in export trade upon the exporting districts in the country is damaging to a degree.. Not only has it rendered large numbers of men unemployed—about 50,000 mine-workers are out of work in South Wales alone—but the cutting of prices in an attempt to recover the continental market, and particularly the French market, has had an equally disastrous effect on the wages of the workmen who are employed, most of whom do not work more than four shifts per week.

The effect of the Spa Coal Agreement has been to damage materially the prospects of trade recovery in the exporting districts of this country. Under the Agreement, Germany is compelled to export to the Allied countries 22,000,000 tons of coal per annum. This coal finds its way into Belgium, France, and Italy, and in consequence of the character of the Treaty no cash transactions take place between the receiving countries and the German Government. The respective Governments, however, in selling the coal to consumers in their countries, charge them the current prices in their country. But if they are unable to dispose of it at home, they re-export it to other countries and obtain the world price. Therefore, the net effect of this process is that coal is being sold so cheaply in the countries referred to, that British coal has to be sold at a price below cost in order to find any kind of market at all, and only the better classes of British coal are able to secure a market, in view of the large quantities of coal coming into these countries under the Reparation Clauses.

The German Government is given credit for the coal so exported as a set off against the reparation payable by her, but the price at which it is credited to her is the actual price at which similar classes of coal are sold in Germany, plus the freightages to the frontier. When these prices are expressed in the rate of exchange of the receiving countries, they are considerably below any price at which British exporters can sell their coal as a paying proposition. In our judgement, it is folly for this country to pursue a reparation policy which has such a disastrous effect on our own countrymen. It has been argued that if the German mine-workers would only insist upon getting a wage commensurate with the increased cost of living in Germany, the price of German coal would necessarily be higher. The plain fact is that the German mine-worker at present works a shorter working day than his English co-workers (the working day of the former being seven hours bank to bank), and from time to time he has endeavoured to secure such advances in wages as correspond with the declining mark and consequent increase in the cost of living. On two occasions this year has he made such application, but he has never been able to secure the full claims which he set forth. From time to time he has actually threatened to strike in order to secure a living wage, but he has been met by the statement that a strike of any magnitude would result in the military occupation of the Ruhr Valley, which would, of course, have the effect of retarding the regular delivery of reparation coal to France.

The export of a large quantity of coal from Germany is, we are credibly informed, having disadvantageous effects upon their own home industries, which are being seriously crippled in consequence of the shortage in the supply of coal and the inferior quality that has to be used. This causes some amount of stagnation in industry, and this stagnation in turn prevents Germany from importing the usual quantities of coal from Great Britain, which, as has already been indicated, amounted to more than 8¼ millions in the eleven months ending 30th November 1913.

It is clear from the above that the only solution to the present difficulties affecting the export trade in coal from this country is the drastic revision of the Treaty, although it should be said that all the miners who are members of the International Miners' Federation, including German miners, are of opinion that any losses in coal caused by the devastation in the French coal-mines should be made good (and it will undoubtedly be made good) from coal produced in the German mines, and that coal payments should continue until French production reaches its pre-war quantities. The present price of British export coal is such as to have definitely excluded America from the European market, but the effect of the Spa Agreement is to compel British exporters to sell their coal in Europe at a price which is entirely uneconomical and which cannot and does not yield either a living wage for the men engaged in the export districts or the profit for the owners in those districts necessary for the continuous expansion of the industry. This state of affairs, in addition to the small amount of time worked in consequence of restricted markets, has placed the mining industry in Britain's export districts in a position of penury.

A NOTE ON BOOKS AND SOURCES

THE best general book on the mining industry as a whole, dealing with business organization, resources, and output, and legislation as well as labour conditions, is *The British Coal Trade*, by H. S. Jevons, published in 1915. For wages questions, see *Wages in the Coal Industry*, by J. W. F. Rowe (1923).

For the history of mining Trade Unionism, see S. and B. Webb, *History of Trade Unionism*; Sidney Webb, *The Story of the Durham Miners*; John Wilson, *History of the Durham Miners' Association* (*1870–1904*); E. Wellbourne, *Miners of Northumberland and Durham*; H. Fynes, *Miners of Durham and Northumberland* (*1873*); and, for the period up to 1830, J. L. and Barbara Hammond's *The Skilled Labourer*.

For the war period, the only sources, apart from the Reports of the Coal-mining Organization Committee, and the useful summaries given in the *Labour Year Books* of 1916 and 1919, are newspaper files and the proceedings of the Miners' Federation and the various district Miners' Associations. There are a few pamphlets, but they are unimportant.

The Coal Commission produced a literature of its own. The two volumes of Reports and Evidence (Cmd. 359 and 360 of 1919) and the volume of Statistical Appendices (Cmd. 361 of 1919) are invaluable for reference. The best summary is contained in two pamphlets, *Facts from the Coal Commission* and *Further Facts from the Coal Commission*, both by R. Page Arnot, published jointly by the Miners' Federation and the Labour Research Department. Mr. Frank Hodges's book, *Nationalization of the Mines*, and his pamphlet, *Workers' Control in the Coal-mining Industry*, expound the aims of the Miners' Federation in the nationalization struggle. Other important pamphlets are *The Nationalization of the Coal Industry*, by R. H. Tawney, and *The Problem of Nationalization*, by Lord Haldane. See also G. D. H. Cole's *Chaos and Order in Industry* for an account of the nationalization struggle.

For various plans of workers' control in the coal industry see *The Miners' Next Step*, issued by the Unofficial Reform Committee of the South Wales Miners' Federation in 1912; *Towards a Miners' Guild*, issued by the National Guilds League in 1916; *National Guilds and the Coal Commission*, by G. D. H. Cole (National Guilds League, 1919), *A Plan for the Democratic Control of the Mining Industry* (South Wales Socialist Society, 1919), as well as the works mentioned above.

For the 1920 strike, see the pamphlet, *Facts about the Coal Dispute*, issued by the Triple Alliance and the Labour Research Department.

For the 1921 dispute, see *The Miners' Struggle with the Mine-owners*, by John Thomas. Some information may also be gleaned from *The*

Mining Crisis, by W. Livesey, which is, however, misleading in many respects.

Labour in Transition, by W. A. Orton, is a competent account of Labour events from 1914 to 1921, both in the mines and in other industries. A useful account of the period from the Armistice to the end of 1922 is also given in *The Workers' Register of Labour and Capital, 1923*, prepared by the Labour Research Department. Mr. Finlay A. Gibson's *The Coal-mining Industry of the United Kingdom* is a useful collection of tables dealing with output, wages, prices, &c., up to 1921. See also Sir R. A. S. Redmayne's *The British Coal-Mining Industry during the War*, uniform with the present volume.

There is a useful collection of documents and newspaper cuttings dealing with Mining Trade Unionism in the Labour Research Department (162, Buckingham Palace Road, London, S.W.1).

INDEX

OUTLINE OF PLAN

FOR THE

ECONOMIC AND SOCIAL HISTORY OF THE WORLD WAR

I

EDITORS AND EDITORIAL BOARDS

(Further arrangements to be announced later.)

GREAT BRITAIN

AUSTRIA-HUNGARY

THE BALTIC COUNTRIES

BELGIUM

Professor H. Pirenne, Editor.

FRANCE

Professor Charles Gide, *Chairman.*
M. Arthur Fontaine.
Professor Henri Hauser.
Professor Charles Rist.
Professor James T. Shotwell, *ex officio.*

GERMANY

Dr. Carl Melchior, *Chairman.*
Professor Dr. Albrecht Mendelssohn Bartholdy.
(Executive Secretary).
Ex-Chancellor Gustav Bauer.
Dr. Hermann Bücher.
Dr. Carl Duisberg.
Professor Dr. Max Sering.
Professor James T. Shotwell, *ex officio.*

ITALY

Professor Luigi Einaudi, *Chairman.*
Professor Pasquale Jannaccone.
Professor Umberto Ricci.
Professor James T. Shotwell, *ex officio.*

THE NETHERLANDS

Professor H. B. Greven, Editor.

RUMANIA

Mr. David Mitrany, Editor.

RUSSIA

Editor, First Series.
Sir Paul Vinogradoff, F.B.A.

YUGO SLAVIA

Professor Velimar Bajkitch, Editor.

LIST OF MONOGRAPHS

This list includes only those published and in course of preparation, and may be changed from time to time. The monographs fall into two main classes, those which may be said to constitute full numbers in the series, volumes of from 300 to 500 pages; and partial numbers or special studies of approximately 100 pages or less, which may ultimately be incorporated in a full volume along with others dealing with cognate subjects. Titles have been grouped to indicate the proposed volume arrangement, but this grouping cannot be regarded as final in the larger and more complicated series. It is the intention, however, to keep to the total number of volumes indicated. Separate announcements will be made concerning volumes dealing with countries outside Europe.

Monographs already published are indicated by an asterisk, partial numbers by a double asterisk.

British Series

*Bibliographical Survey, by Miss M. E. Bulkley.

*Manual of Archive Administration, by Mr. Hilary Jenkinson.

British Archives in Peace and War, by Dr. Hubert Hall.

War Government of Great Britain and Ireland (with special reference to its economic aspects), by Professor W. G. S. Adams, C.B.

*War Government of the British Dominions, by Professor A. B. Keith, D.C.L.

*Prices and Wages in the United Kingdom, 1914–1920, by Professor A. L. Bowley.

British War Budgets and Financial Policy, by Mr. F. W. Hirst and Mr. J. E. Allen.

Taxation and War-Time Incomes, by Sir Josiah C. Stamp, K.B.E.
- Taxation during the War.
- War-Time Profits and their Distribution.

The War and Insurance.
- A Series of Studies: Life Insurance, by Mr. S. G. Warner; Fire Insurance, by Mr. A. E. Sich and Mr. S. Preston; Shipping Insurance, by Sir Norman Hill; Friendly Societies and Health Insurance, by Sir Alfred Watson; Unemployment Insurance, by Sir William Beveridge; with an additional section on the National Savings Movement, by Sir William Schooling.

Experiments in State Control at the War Office and the Ministry of Food, by Mr. E. M. H. Lloyd.

British Food Control, by Sir William Beveridge, K.C.B., and Sir Edward C. K. Gonner, K.B.E.

*Food Production in War, by Sir Thomas Middleton, K.B.E.
Effect of the War upon British Textile Industries :
The Wool Trade during the War, by Mr. E. F. Hitchcock.
**The Cotton Control Board, by Mr. H. D. Henderson.
English Sea Fisheries during the War, by Sir W. A. Herdman, K.B.E.
*Allied Shipping Control ; an experiment in International Administration, by Sir Arthur Salter, K.C.B.
General History of British Shipping during the War, by Mr. C. Ernest Fayle.
*The British Coal Industry during the War, by Sir Richard Redmayne, K.C.B.
The British Iron and Steel Industry during the War, by Mr. W. T. Layton, C.H., C.B.E.
British Labour Unions and the War, by Mr. G. D. H. Cole :
**Trade Unionism and Munitions.
**Labour in the Coal Mining Industry.
*Workshop Organization.
*Labour Supply and Regulation, by Mr. Humbert Wolfe, C.B.E.
Effect of the War upon Public Health :
Public Health Conditions in England during the War, by Dr. A. W. J. Macfadden, C.B.
Health of the Returned Soldier, by Dr. E. Cunyngham Brown, C.B.E.
Industries of the Clyde Valley during the War, by Professor W. R. Scott and Mr. J. Cunnison.
Scottish Agriculture and Fisheries (with a supplementary chapter on the Jute industry).
A series of studies of War-Time Economics, by Mr. H. M. Conacher, Mr. Joseph Duncan, Mr. D. T. Jones, and Dr. J. P. Day, with Introduction by Professor W. R. Scott.
Effects of the War upon the Economic and Industrial Development of Ireland, by Professor Charles H. Oldham.
Wales in the World War, by Thomas Jones, LL.D.
Manchester : A Study of Local War-time Conditions, by Professor H. W. C. Davis.
Guides to the Study of War-Time Economics :
Dictionary of Official War-Time Organizations, by Dr. N. B. Dearle.
Economic Chronicle of the War, by Dr. N. B. Dearle.
Cost of War to Great Britain (to be arranged).

Austrian and Hungarian Series

Austria-Hungary :

Bibliography of Austrian Economic Literature during the War, by Professor Dr. Othmar Spann.
Austro-Hungarian Finance during the War, by Dr. Alexander Popovics.

Military Economic History, a series of studies directed by Professor Dr. von Wieser, Generals Krauss and Hoen, and Colonel Glaise-Horstenau.

Conscription, &c., by Colonel Klose; Munitions and Supply, by Colonel Pflug; Transportation under Military Control, by Colonel Ratzenhofer; Military Economic Administration, by Dr. Hornik. Others to follow.

Economic Use of Occupied Territories: Serbia, Montenegro, Albania, by General Kerchnawe.

'Mittel-Europa': the Preparation of a New Joint Economy, by Dr. Gratz and Dr. Schüller.

Exhaustion and Disorganization of the Habsburg Monarchy, by Professor Dr. Friedrich von Wieser, with a section on the Disruption of the Austro-Hungarian Economic Union, by Dr. Richard Schüller.

Empire of Austria:

War Government in Austria, by Professor Dr. Joseph Redlich.

Industrial Control in Austria during the War, a series of studies directed by Dr. Richard Riedl.

Food Control and Agriculture in Austria during the War, a series of studies directed by Dr. H. Löwenfeld-Russ.

Labour in Austria during the War, a series of studies directed by Mr. Ferdinand Hanusch.

Austrian Railways during the War (Civil Control), by Ing. Bruno Ritter von Enderes.

Coal Supply in Austria during the War, by Ing. Emil Homann-Herimberg.

Kingdom of Hungary:

Economic War History of Hungary: A General Survey, by Dr. Gustav Gratz.

Effects of the War upon the Hungarian Government and People, by Count Albert Apponyi.

Hungarian Industry during the War, by Baron Joseph Szterényi.

History of Hungarian Commerce during the War, by Dr. Alexander Matlckovits.

History of Hungarian Finance during the War, by Dr. Johann von Teleszky.

Hungarian Agriculture during the War, by Dr. Emil von Mutschenbacher, and Food Control in Hungary during the War, by Professor Johann Bud.

Social Conditions in Hungary during the War, by Dr. Desider Pap.

Public Health and the War in Austria-Hungary:

General Survey of Public Health in Austria-Hungary, by Professor Dr. Clemens von Pirquet.

The Effect of the War upon Public Health in Austria and Hungary. A series of studies by Drs. Helly, Kirchenberger, Steiner, Raschofsky, Kassowitz, Breitner, von Bókay, Schacherl, Hockauf, Finger, Kyrle, Elias, Economo, Müller-Deham, Nobel, Wagner, Edelmann, and Mayerhofer, edited with Introduction by Professor Dr. Clemens von Pirquet.

Belgian Series

Belgium and the World War, by Professor H. Pirenne.

Deportation of Belgian Workmen and the Forced Labour of the Civilian Population during the German Occupation of Belgium, by M. Fernand Passelecq.

Food Supply of Belgium during the German Occupation, by Dr. Albert Henry.

German Legislation with Reference to the Occupation of Belgium, by Drs. J. Pirenne and M. Vauthier.

Unemployment in Belgium during the German Occupation, by Professor Ernest Mahaim.

Destruction of Belgian Industry by the Germans, by Count Charles de Kerchove.

Economic Policies of the Belgian Government during the War, by Professor F. J. van Langenhove.

Czecho-Slovak Series

*Financial Policy of Czecho-Slovakia during the first year of its History, by Dr. A. Rašín.

(A further volume to be arranged.)

Dutch Series

**War Finances in the Netherlands up to 1918, by Dr. M. J. van der Flier.

Economic and Social Effects of the War upon the Netherlands. A series of studies by Messrs. Posthuma, Vissering, Holstyn, Zaalberg, Methorst, Alting, and others. Volume to be arranged.

French Series

Bibliographical Guide to the Literature concerning France for the Economic History of the War, by Dr. Camille Bloch.

Effects of the War upon Government:

- Effect of the War upon the Civil Government of France, by Professor Pierre Renouvin.
- A Guide to Official War-Time Organizations, by M. Armand Boutillier du Retail.
- Problem of Regionalism, by Professor Henri Hauser.
- The Organisation of the Republic for Peace, by M. Henri Chardon.

Studies in War-Time Statistics :
Effect of the War upon Population and upon Incomes, by M. Michel Huber.
Prices and Wages during the War, by M. Lucien March.
Supply and Control of Food in War-Time :
Rationing and Food Control, by MM. Adolphe Pichon and P. Pinot.
Agriculture during the War, by M. Michel Augé-Laribé.
The History of French Industry during the War, by M. Arthur Fontaine.
Effects of the War upon Textile Industries, by Professor Albert Aftalion.
Effects of the War upon Metallurgy and Engineering, by M. Robert Pinot, and Effects of the War upon Chemical Industries, by M. Eugène Mauclère.
Effects of the War upon Fuel and Motive Power :
Coal Industry and Mineral Fuels, by M. Henri de Peyerimhoff.
Hydro-electric Power, by Professor Raoul Blanchard.
Forestry and the Timber Industry during the War, by General Georges-Chevalier; and War-Time Aeronautic Industries, by Colonel Paul Dhé.
Organization of War Industries, by M. Albert Thomas.
Labour Conditions during the War, by MM. William Oualid and M. C. Picquenard.
Studies in War-Time Labour Problems (2 volumes) :
Unemployment during the War, by M. A. Créhange.
Syndicalism during the War, by M. Roger Picard.
Foreign and Colonial Workmen in France, by M. B. Nogaro.
Women in Industry under War Conditions, by M. Marcel Frois.
Effects of the War in the Occupied Territories :
The Organization of Labour in the Invaded Territories, by M. Pierre Boulin.
Food Supply in the Invaded Territory, by MM. Paul Collinet and Paul Stahl.
Damage Inflicted by the War, by M. Edmond Michel.
Refugees and Prisoners of War :
The Refugees and the Interned Civilians, by Professor Pierre Caron.
Prisoners of War, by M. Georges Cahen-Salvador.
Effects of the War upon Transportation :
French Railroads during the War, by M. Marcel Peschaud.
Internal Waterways, Freight Traffic, by M. Georges Pocard de Kerviler.
Effects of the War upon French Shipping :
Merchant Shipping during the War, by M. Henri Cangardel.
French Ports during the War, by M. Georges Hersent.
Effects of the War upon French Commerce, by Professor Charles Rist.
The Blockade, by MM. Denys-Cochin and Jean Goût.

French Commercial Policy during War, by M. Etienne Clémentel.
Effects of the War upon French Finances :
War-Time Finances, by M. Henri Truchy.
War-Time Banking, by M. Albert Aupetit.
Studies in Social History :
Co-operative Societies and the Struggle against High Prices, by Professor Charles Gide.
Effects of the War upon the Problem of Housing, by M. Henri Sellier.
Effects of the War upon Public Health :
Public Health and Hygiene, by Dr. Léon Bernard.
The Wounded Soldiers, by MM. Cassin and Ville-Chabrolle.
Economic History of French Cities during the War (2 volumes):
Lyons, by M. Edouard Herriot.
Rouen, by M. J. Levainville.
Bordeaux, by M. Paul Courteault.
Bourges, by M. C. J. Gignoux.
Paris, by M. Henri Sellier.
Tours, by Professor M. L'héritier.
Effects of the War upon Colonies and Possessions :
The Colonies in War-Time, by M. Arthur Girault.
Effects of the War upon Northern Africa, by M. Augustin Bernard.
Effects of the War upon Alsace-Lorraine, by M. Georges Delahache.
The Cost of the War to France:
War Costs : Direct Expenses, by Professor Gaston Jeze.
The Costs of the War to France, by Professor Charles Gide.

German Series

The plan for the completed German Series is given below indicating those volumes that have been already arranged.)

Bibliography of German Literature for the Economic History of the War, by Professor A. Mendelssohn Bartholdy and Dr. E. Rosenbaum.
Effect of the War upon Government and Constitution of Germany (Imperial and State), by Professor A. Mendelssohn Bartholdy; with supplementary chapters on The Aqministration of Occupied Territories, by Ex-Minister Dr. von Köhler, Dr. von Kries, and Freiherr von Gayl.
Social (Mental and Moral) Effects of the War. A series of special studies : Morals, by Professor Otto Baumgarten and Ex-minister Dr. David; Religion, by Professor Dr. Erich Foerster and Professor Dr. Arnold Rademacher; Education, by Dr. Wilhelm Flitner; Law, by Professor Dr. Moritz Leipmann.
Effect of the War upon Population, by Professor Dr. Meerwarth.
General Economic Effects upon Production, by Professor Dr. Max Sering.
The Problem of Food Supply, by Professor Dr. A. Skalweit.

Mobilization and Demobilization of Industries for War Purposes, by State-Secretary Professor Göppert.

Raw Materials. 'The Hindenburg Program', by State-Secretary Dr. Koeth.

The Economic Exploitation of Occupied Territories: in Belgium and Northern France, Professor Dr. Jahn; in Rumania and the Ukraine, Professor Dr. Mann; in Poland and the Baltic countries, by Freiherr von Gayl and Dr. von Kries.

Economic Co-operation with the Allies of Germany, by Geheimrat Frisch.

Industrial Conditions at the Close of the War; New Industrial Organizations, by Geheimrat Dr. Hermann Bücher.

German Trade Unions and the War, by Ex-Chancellor Bauer, A. Erkelenz, M. d. R., Ex-Premier Stegerwald and Herr P. Umbreit.

Labour in the Munition Industries; Women in Industry.

The New Legal Position of Labour, by Professor Dr. Sinzheimer.

Effect of the War upon Agriculture:

Agricultural Production, by Staatsminister Dr. Warmbold.

Agrarian History, Landholding, &c., by Professor Max Sering.

Effect of the War upon Shipping, by Dr. E. Rosenbaum.

Effect of the War upon German Commerce; Internal and External, by Professor Kurt Wiedenfeld.

Effect of the War upon German Finances:

State Finances, Loans and Taxation, by Professor Walter Lotz.

Money and Banking, by Professor H. Schumacher.

Italian Series

Bibliographical Survey of the Economic and Social Problems of the War, by Professor Vincenzo Porri, with an introduction on the collection and use of the documents of the War, by Comm. Eugenio Casanova.

The Economic Legislation of the War, by Professor Alberto De' Stefani.

Agricultural Production in Italy 1914–19, by Professor Umberto Ricci.

The Agricultural Classes in Italy during the War, by Professor Arrigo Serpieri.

Food Supply and Rationing, by Professor Riccardo Bachi; and Food Supply of the Italian Army, by Professor Gaetano Zingali.

War-Time Finances, by Professor Luigi Einaudi.

Cost of the War to Italy, by Professor Luigi Einaudi.

Currency Inflation in Italy and its Effects on Prices, Incomes, and Foreign Exchanges, by Professor Pasquale Jannaccone.

Vital Statistics and Public Health in Italy during and after the War, by Professor Giorgio Mortara.

The Italian People during and after the War: A Social Survey, by Professor Gioacchino Volpe.

Social and Economic Life in Piedmont as affected by the War, by Professor Giuseppe Prato.

Portuguese Series

Economic and Social History of Portugal as affected by the War, by Professor George Young.

Rumanian Series

The Rural Revolution in Rumania and South-eastern Europe, by D. Mitrany.

The Effect of the Enemy Occupation of Rumania, by Dr. G. Antipa.

The Effect of the War upon Public Health in Rumania, by Professor J. Cantacuezino.

First Russian Series

(To the Bolshevik Revolution)

Effects of the War upon Government and National Finances in Russia :

- Effects of the War upon the Central Government, by Professor Paul P. Gronsky.
- State Finances during the War, by Mr. Alexander M. Michelson.
- Russian State Credit during the War, by Mr. Paul N. Apostol.

Effects of the War upon Currency and Banking in Russia :

- Currency in Russia during the War, by Professor Michael V. Bernadsky.
- Private Banks in Russia during the War, by Mr. E. M. Epstein.
- German Capital in Russia and the War, by Mr. Basil B. Eliashevitch.

Municipalities and Zemstvos during the War :

- Effect of the War upon Russian Municipalities, and the All-Russian Union of Towns, by Mr. N. I. Astroff.
- The Zemstvos, by Prince Vladimir A. Obolensky ; The All-Russian Union of the Zemstvos and the Zemgor, by Mr. Sergius P. Turin.
- The War and the Psychology of the Zemstvos Workers, by Mr. Isaak V. Shklovsky.

Effects of the War upon the Co-operative Movement in Russia :

- Effect of the War upon Agricultural Co-operation and Co-operative Credit, by Professor A. N. Anziferoff.
- Co-operatives and Consumers in Russia during the War, by Professor V. T. Totomianz.

The Russian Army in the World War : a study in social history, by General Nicholas N. Golovine.

Rural Economy in Russia and the War, by Professor A. N. Anziferoff, Professor Alexander Bilimovitch, and Mr. M. O. Batcheff.

Effect of the War upon Land Holding and Settlement in Russia, by Professor Alexander D. Bilimovitch and Professor V. A. Kossinsky.

Problem of Food Supply in Russia during the War, by Professor Peter B. Struve.

State Control of Industry in Russia during the War, by Mr. Simon O. Zagorsky.

Effects of the War upon Russian Industries :
Coal Mining, by Mr. Boris N. Sokoloff.
Petroleum, by Mr. Alexander M. Michelson.
Metal Manufacturing Industries, by General Hermonius.
Chemical Industry, by Mr. Mark A. Landau.
Effects of the War upon Labour and Industrial Conditions :
Flax and Wool Industry, by Mr. Sergius N. Tretiakoff.
Textile (Cotton) Industry, by Mr. Theodorovitch G. Karpoff.
Wages in War-Time, by Miss Anna G. Eisenstadt.
Workmen's Family Budgets, by Mr. Stanislas S. Kohn.
Changes in the Conditions and Composition of the Working Classes, by Mr. W. T. Braithwaite.
Effects of the War upon Trade and Commerce :
Internal Russian Trade during the War, by Mr. Paul A. Bouryshkine.
Russia in the Economic War, by Professor Boris E. Nolde.
Effects of the War upon Transportation in Russia, by Mr. Michael B. Braikevitch ; and the Social History of the Ukraine during the War, by Mr. Nicholas M. Mogilamsky.
Effects of the War upon Education and Public Health in Russia, by Professor L. A. Taracievitch.
Elementary and Secondary Schools during the War, by Professor D. M. Odinez.
Universities and Academic Institutions during the War, by Professor P. J. Novgorodzoff.
Vital Statistics of Russia during the War, by Professor A. A. Tschuproff.
Russia in the World War ; a historical synthesis, by Sir Paul Vinogradoff.

Scandinavian Series

Economic Effects of the War upon Sweden, by Professor Eli Heckscher.
Economic Effects of the War upon Norway, by Professor W. Keilhau.
Economic Effects of the War upon Denmark, by Dr. Einar Cohn, with a section on Iceland by Mr. Thorstein Thorsteinsson.

Yugo-Slav Series

Economic Situation of Serbia at the Outbreak and during the First Year of the War, by Professor Velimir Bajkitch.
Economic and Social Effects of the War upon Yugo-Slavia (volume to be arranged).